# ATHENS AND JERUSALEM

## The Role of Philosophy in Theology

by
*Jack A. Bonsor*

PAULIST PRESS
New York and Mahwah, N.J.

Copyright © 1993 by Jack A. Bonsor

Library of Congress Cataloging-in-Publication Data

Bonsor, Jack Arthur, 1944–
    Athens and Jerusalem: the role of philosophy in theology/by Jack A. Bonsor.
      p.  cm.
    Includes bibliographical references.
    ISBN 0-8091-3398-9 (pbk.)
    1. Philosophical theology.   I. Title.
  BT40.B58   1993
  230'.01—dc20
                                  93-14771
                                      CIP

Published by Paulist Press
997 Macarthur Blvd.
Mahwah, N.J. 07430

Printed and bound in the United States of America

# CONTENTS

To Tom and Roger
Dear Friends Sorely Missed

# ACKNOWLEDGMENTS

This work arose out of my work with beginning and graduate students of philosophy and theology. I wish to thank the students of St. Joseph's and St. Patrick's Seminaries for teaching me so much. Let me also express my gratitude to Archbishop John R. Quinn for assigning me to this work and for his constant support.

I also wish to express my gratitude to those who helped me in the preparation of this text: Frederick Cwiekowski, James Fredericks, Robert Giguere, Frank Norris, Sis Watts and Cecil White.

Jack A. Bonsor
St. Patrick's Seminary
Menlo Park, Cal.
1992

# PART I
# BEGINNINGS

# PHILOSOPHERS AND THEOLOGIANS

| YEAR | PHILOSOPHER | THEOLOGIAN | |
|---|---|---|---|
| **ANCIENT** | | | |
| 550 B.C. | THALES | | |
| 400 | SOCRATES | | |
| | PLATO | | |
| | ARISTOTLE | | |
| | | | |
| -A.D. 30 | **[LIFE, DEATH AND RISING OF JESUS]** | | |
| | | | |
| 164 | MIDDLE PLATONISM | JUSTIN MARTYR | |
| | | (APOLOGISTS) | |
| 240 | PLOTINUS (NEOPLATONISM) | ORIGEN | PATRISTIC |
| 400 | | AUGUSTINE | "FATHERS" |
| 500 | BOETHIUS | | |
| | | | |
| **MEDIEVAL** | | | |
| 1060 | | ANSELM | SCHOLASTICS |
| 1250 | | BONAVENTURE | |
| | | THOMAS AQUINAS | |
| | | | |
| **MODERN** | | | |
| 1660 | DESCARTES | | |
| | SPINOZA/LEIBNIZ | | RATIONALISTS |
| 1770 | HUME | | |
| | ROUSSEAU | | ENLIGHTENMENT |
| 1781 | KANT | | |
| | HEGEL | SCHLEIERMACHER | |
| 1870 | MARX | (VATICAN I) | |
| | NIETZSCHE (EXISTENTIALISM) | | |
| | MILL (EMPIRICISM) | NEO-THOMISM | |
| | (POSITIVISM) | LEO XIII | |
| 1900 | JAMES (PRAGMATISM) | | |
| 1920 | HEIDEGGER (POST-MODERN) | BARTH | |
| | | BULTMANN | |
| 1950 | | RAHNER | |
| | | KÜNG | |
| | | LONERGAN | |
| 1962 | | (VATICAN II) | |
| | | PANNENBERG | |
| | | | |
| **POST-MODERN** | | | |
| | HABERMAS | HERMENEUTICAL | |
| | DERRIDA | LIBERATION/BOFF | |
| | GADAMER | | |

# CHAPTER 1

# INTRODUCTION

## I. METHOD AND OUTLINE

"What has Athens to do with Jerusalem?"[1] The question was asked by Tertullian, a third-century theologian. What do the philosophers of Athens have to do with God's revelation in Jesus?

Today the same question is frequently put, if less poetically, by students of theology. Theology departments routinely require some philosophical background of prospective students. Theological texts abound with references to philosophers. Novice theologians find themselves amidst the mysteries of Plato, Aristotle, Descartes, Kant, Hegel and company. Not surprisingly they wonder about their fate. What have these thinkers to do with Jesus and the church?

Tertullian's response to his own question indicates the intrinsic and complex relationship between philosophy and theology. For, while Tertullian firmly negates a role for philosophers in theology, his own theological reflections draw upon philosophical resources. He calls Plato "the caterer to all these heretics" but turns to the Stoics and Aristotle in his treatise on the soul.[2] In this, Tertullian exemplifies the inevitable fact that philosophy is intrinsic to both the practice of theology and the consequent content of Christian doctrine.

My aim in this book is to help beginning students of theology understand the intrinsic relationship between philosophy and theology in the Catholic tradition. My method is to offer examples from the history and practice of theology. We will consider the magisterium's teaching on philosophy, see the effect of philosophy on the formulation of doctrine, study the influence of philosophy on a number of great theologians past and present, confront some of the difficult questions presented to faith today, and see how philosophy offers contemporary theologians ways to address these questions.

Each chapter invites the reader to consider the philosophical character of a theological topic. The choice of topics is thematic rather than historical. This is not a history of philosophy and theology. My aim is to engage the reader in the practice of theology—to ask questions, consider responses and, in the process, see how philosophy is intrinsic to this practice.

3

This approach is determined by my experience as both a student and teacher of philosophy and theology. Frequently classes in these areas offer a series of historical answers to questions no one in the room has asked. I think this is pedagogically deadening. We engage a topic, or grasp an answer, only when the question is our own. Plato's dialogues are a classic philosophical example of this method. Socrates questions his interlocutors until they see that what they thought was certain cannot be so. Only in this confusion, *aporia,* can true questioning and learning occur. Similarly, the great theologian St. Thomas Aquinas organized his *Summa Theologiae* around disputed questions. Aquinas' approach is an example of "the exalted pedagogical methods set up in the XIIth century universities: 'active methods,' mindful to keep open, even under the dead-weight of school work, the curiosity of both the student and the master."[3]

Like St. Thomas, our questioning occurs within the context of faith. As a Catholic theologian I am not calling into question the truth of revelation or of church teaching. Rather, I invite the reader to think with the tradition, to understand these truths more deeply and so be able to express them more clearly to our contemporaries. This work is neither a catechism nor an introduction to Catholic belief. My presumption is that the reader is both familiar with and accepts scripture and church doctrine. On that foundation we pursue St. Anselm's classic definition of theology as *fides quaerens intellectum,* faith seeking understanding.

This method manifests faith, a confidence that Christian truth cannot be overturned, but only strengthened, by investigation. If science, history or philosophical argument present us with data which seemingly challenge the faith (for example, science vs. Genesis), we reject neither that data nor the faith. We neither call our faith into question nor flee reasonable data in fundamentalism or fideism. Rather, we draw on our tradition, other theologians, on philosophy and our own minds to seek that one truth manifest in both revelation and creation. Our faith knows it has nothing to fear from the facts. Pope John Paul II gave voice to this element of the Catholic tradition in 1987 when he observed that:

> Religious faith itself calls for intellectual inquiry; and the confidence that there can be no contradiction between faith and reason is a distinctive feature of the Catholic humanistic tradition as it has existed in the past and as it exists in our own day.[4]

The preceding paragraphs reflect a premise of Catholic theology: knowledge of nature and history cannot contradict revealed truth. Chapter 2 considers this premise more carefully. But it is important to indicate from the outset that this premise is the locus where theology and philosophy meet. It makes philosophy an intrinsic element in Catholic theology. Philosophy literally means the love of wisdom; theology is the science of God. Both disciplines, then, involve the human quest for knowledge. "Wisdom" and "God" indicate that these two fields of study seek ultimate knowledge, i.e., the meaning and purpose of human existence. This commonality has led to a conversation between philosophy and theology which spans the course of Christian history.

The metaphor of conversation mentioned above indicates the perspective underlying this book. Every work about philosophy, theology and doctrine involves a point of view. The interpretation of great teachers and their ideas is itself philosophy and theology. This work is no exception. I propose that the relationship between philosophy and theology be understood through the metaphor of conversation. This metaphor is suggested by the contemporary philosopher Hans-Georg Gadamer. Gadamer's thought will be treated explicitly in the text. For now I wish to alert the reader to the basic hypothesis guiding my interpretation.

God's revelation in Christ occurred at a specific moment and in a specific place within human history. Jesus was a human being, a Jew living in first-century Palestine. His message and fate are comprehensible only within that context.

When Jesus' followers proclaim the gospel in other places, in other languages, in other cultures, in other times, the message must be translated. Translation is a complicated task. It requires a competence in two cultures, in two languages. Frequently what is to be translated (words, categories, ideas, customs, etc.) has no identical corollary in the new context. The process of translating involves adaptation.

One can conceive of translation as a conversation. Imagine that you express an opinion about something quite important—a religious belief, a political conviction, or the like. Sometimes people respond with a statement or question that indicates they have not understood or that they disagree with you. Conversation ensues. The goal of the conversation is mutual understanding. This requires not only clear explication on your part but listening. How does this person understand my statements? Is she using the same words with slightly different meanings? Does she have convictions, presuppositions that are different from mine? In real conversation participants listen and adapt. New perspectives emerge. While total agreement may not be achieved, both partners to the conversation change.

Conversation is not dictation. Persons who are certain they know the truth, like some teachers, sometimes state their position and anticipate (require) agreement. Students may have had classes where they were required simply to repeat their teacher's lectures. But this approach to education respects neither the students nor the subject matter. A good teacher honors both by conversing with his or her students. The questions, experiences and insights which students bring to the subject matter is respected and attended to. New perspectives emerge and a good teacher learns from her or his students.

The story of Christian theology is similarly a kind of continuing conversation between believers and the various contexts within which Christianity has existed. The early church, following the example of St. Paul, did not require that Gentile converts become Jews like Jesus. Rather, the faith entered into conversation with Gentile cultures and, thereby, both Christianity and the Gentile world were transformed.

The philosophical environment of the early church was dominated by forms of Platonism. These philosophical perspectives provided a rich source for Christian reflection, a source that continues to enlighten revealed truth. Chapter 3 indicates how the early appropriation of the faith within Greco-Roman culture determined both the form of Christian theology and the content of many Christian doctrines. Chapter 4 continues this theme by indicating how Neoplatonism was an essential element of St. Augustine's eucharistic theology. Again, this is of more than historical interest. The reader will find in Augustine's thought rich resources for a contemporary eucharistic theology.

In the second millennium St. Thomas Aquinas emerged as the dominant theologian within the Catholic tradition. Part II, consisting of five chapters, is dedicated to his thought. Chapter 5 asks the reader to struggle with St. Thomas' theory of knowledge. Epistemology, theory of knowledge, is a central issue in modern philosophy. Studying Aquinas' epistemology offers us access to his thought and gives us a foundation for understanding how contemporary Catholic philosophers and theologians have placed Thomas in conversation with the modern debate about knowledge.

Chapter 6 considers the role of St. Thomas in modern Catholic thought. There are competing interpretations of Aquinas among Catholic thinkers, interpretations which reflect differing approaches to contemporary philosophy and church governance. This chapter seeks to offer the reader some insight into the intellectual foundations of the sometimes heated debates that characterize the theological scene today.

Chapters 7 and 8 ask the reader to think with St. Thomas about a philosophical question which is fundamental to his own thought and all subsequent theology—the meaning of being. The chapters treat the topics of creation and Christology. To grasp St. Thomas' position on these topics one must be able to think his distinction between essence and existence; one must think about being with him.

Chapter 9 presents Karl Rahner's interpretation of St. Thomas. Rahner is probably the most significant Catholic theologian of this century. He established the philosophical grounds for his theology through an interpretation of Aquinas, an interpretation which manifests the influence of many modern thinkers. In this, Rahner's thought exemplifies what I have called the conversation between philosophy and faith. His interpretation of Aquinas also serves as a bridge to contemporary theology.

While much of Catholic theology is in conversation with St. Thomas, it must also deal with questions that have emerged since the Middle Ages. One of the most challenging aspects of contemporary thought to Christian orthodoxy is our awareness of history. I have suggested in these brief, introductory remarks that Christianity is profoundly affected by the cultures and historical periods in which Christians live and think. This assertion is an example of historical consciousness. Historical consciousness is a fundamental characteristic of the contemporary, intellectual life of the west.

Part III treats historical consciousness. Chapter 10 considers both the nature of historical consciousness and the historical-critical method which flows from it. The historical-critical method has offered contemporary scripture scholars and historians of doctrine important tools for understanding the origins and development of the faith. But it has also raised serious questions about scripture and doctrine, problems that have demanded a good deal of theological attention in recent years. Chapters 10 and 11 take up two doctrines which are being rethought in view of historical consciousness—the resurrection of Jesus and the church's teaching about its origin in Jesus. Chapter 12 concludes Part III by considering the philosophical foundations of human historicity in the thought of Martin Heidegger and Gadamer.

In Part IV we will look at the relationship between some philosophers and theologians. Specifically, chapter 13 shows how the Protestant theologian Wolfhart Pannenberg uses Hegel's thought. Chapter 14 indicates the importance of Karl Marx to liberation theology, using Leonardo Boff as an example. The last chapter returns to the teaching of the church on the role of philosophy in theology.

## II. HOW TO USE THIS BOOK

The material which follows presumes that the reader has some familiarity with the philosophers discussed. One might use it while taking classes in philosophy to see how the thinkers studied influence theological reflection. The reader can consult the annotated bibliographies, offered at the end of each chapter, which suggest works by and about the thinkers treated. Complete bibliographic information on works cited is found at the end of this volume.

This work can serve as an introduction to some important figures in the history of theology. But it cannot substitute for primary sources. If one is to

truly understand theologians, one must study their work. Each chapter's bib-
liography suggests primary sources pertinent to its topic. Chapters 4 and 5
presume the reader has consulted specified texts.

The order of chapters roughly traces the history of philosophical influences on theological reflection. The thinkers and topics considered are, of
course, selective. This work is certainly not a complete account of the rich
interplay between philosophy and theology in the Catholic tradition. It is
suggestive rather than exhaustive; it is introductory and, one hopes, offers an
impetus for further investigation.

While each section builds on what precedes, I have tried to compose
the chapters so they can be read on their own. My goal is to make the book
useful to students regardless of what period, thinker or philosophical topic
they might be studying.

Finally, this introduction indicates the hermeneutical hypothesis which
underlies my understanding of the relationship between philosophy and theology. Readers are invited to take issue with my position. Critical reading is
an excellent introduction to the practice of theology. The issues, problems
and questions considered in what follows are topics any serious student of
contemporary philosophy and theology must address. If my efforts stimulate
the reader to think about these important questions, even to refute me, then
this work has succeeded.

## NOTES

1. Tertullian, *Prescription of Heretics*, 7.9.
2. Tertullian, *On the Soul*, 5.2, 23.5.
3. M.D. Chenu, *Toward Understanding Saint Thomas* (Chicago: Henry Regnery, 1964), p. 96.
4. John Paul II, "Catholic Higher Education," *Origins* 17 (October 1, 1987):269.

# CHAPTER 2

# FAITH AND PHILOSOPHY
# THE DOCTRINE OF VATICAN I

The First Vatican Council (1869–1870) is most commonly identified with the dogma of papal infallibility. The council also promulgated the dogmatic constitution *Dei filius*. *Dei filius* addresses the relationship between faith and reason, between revealed and natural knowledge. The dogmatic constitution's teaching offers an excellent introduction to the relationship between philosophy and theology within the Catholic tradition.

It is important to appreciate the historical context that gave rise to *Dei filius*. Modern science and rationalism presented fundamental challenges to Christian doctrine and to the very possibility of religious belief. The church responds in *Dei filius*. But this response is not merely of historical interest. The intellectual climate of modern, western society remains in many ways hostile to religion. Not a few of our contemporaries wonder whether Christian faith and intellectual honesty are compatible. What is the relationship between faith and reason?

## I. FAITH AND REASON

Theology is faith seeking understanding. Catholic theologians have carried out their task on the sure foundation that scripture and church doctrine express God's revealed truth. The human intellect can probe revelation, enriching the church's understanding of and life in the truth. These basic convictions about revelation and human reason have long grounded the relationship between philosophy and theology in Catholic thought.

The rise of rationalism as a dominant intellectual force in western history presented a critical challenge to this Catholic understanding of theology. Rationalism, as with so many other "isms," encompasses a wide spectrum of viewpoints, from the technical thought of philosophers and scientists to general presuppositions held by more common folk. Philosophically the term can be applied to a variety of thinkers—to Descartes, to Hume and the empiricists, to Enlightenment thinkers, to Kant and post-Kantian idealists. In general, rationalism is characterized by the conviction that human reason alone offers access to reality, certainty and truth.

Philosophically one can identify the beginnings of modern rationalism with the French philosopher René Descartes (d. 1650). Descartes' passion for certitude was rooted in the mathematical model of knowledge and the scientific methodology of doubt. The purpose of method is to achieve rational certitude through a systematic exclusion of extraneous factors. One seeks to know, asks a specific question, by first setting aside personal, societal and cultural biases. Through reason alone (autonomous reason), unencumbered by other interests, one observes and tests. One does not conclude, but doubts, until reason requires assent.

The scientist seeks to understand reality inductively, letting the facts (in a sense) speak for themselves. A scientist seeks to exclude from an experiment any prejudice or preconception that might influence observation. The scientist does not accept the traditional way of looking at things, but insists that our understanding must be based on reason and observation. Assertions of truth must be demonstrable in the facts (empirical data) and demonstration (experiment) must be repeatable by anyone. Whether the observer is a Catholic or Communist, American or Russian, ought not be of significance. Until such standards are achieved we doubt and we cannot say we know.

Descartes' philosophy begins with doubt, doubt about everything. It seeks an apodictically certain starting point, and a rational progression from that point, in order to establish a field of certain knowledge. His apodictically certain starting was, of course, his famous dictum, *cogito ergo sum*, "I think, therefore I am." The very fact that I am doubting confirms that I exist. Descartes sought to establish a basis for all knowledge on the indubitable fact that "I am."

Descartes thus attempted to apply a methodology which had proved successful in mathematics and science to the question of human knowledge in general. He sought the certitude of mathematics and science for all knowledge. Much of western thought has been guided by this project. What do I know? How do I know that I know? How can I be certain? What do I do when I know? These kinds of questions came to dominate western philosophy after Descartes.

The Catholic Church exists within the wider culture and is always affected by its intellectual environment. The church makes a truth claim. It offers a vision of God and creation, and a consequent code of moral behavior. The church bases these claims on divine revelation and faith. But, for rationalism, notions like revelation and faith can make no claim within the arena of reasonable discourse. The church seemingly has been excluded from the west's intellectual life.

A good deal of the rationalist tradition is hostile to any form of religious belief. Some think reason alone, free and unhindered, offers access to reality, truth and certainty. Claims based on faith are not only unreasonable, they inhibit reason. The very possibility of a supernatural revelation is excluded, as is the possibility of miraculous events which violate the reasonable laws of nature. Christian doctrine is perceived by these rationalists as an oppressive holdover from a previous, more primitive age. Beliefs held in faith, and taught by an authoritative tradition, are not simply unreasonable, they are the enemies of the rational life. The Catholic Church, and all religions, are viewed as purveyors of superstition and enemies of human progress.

Not all the rationalist tradition takes such a negative view of religious belief. But what characterizes rationalism is a firm and clear division between reason and faith. Faith cannot be used within the context of a reasonable argument. Reason alone brings certain knowledge of the world in which we live. The beliefs of religion deal with some other, disconnected realm or with the personal. Such a position stands in contradiction to what Catholic theology had always been, a conversation between the truths of revelation and the truths attained by reason. Much of church doctrine found its roots in this conversation. The church had always been in conversation with the intellectual life of its environment. Rationalism excluded the Christian faith from the west's intellectual dialogue. Seemingly the faith had nothing to say to or learn from modern thought.

Rationalism not only challenged the faith from without, but also had an effect on thinkers within the church as they reflected on the relationship between faith and reason. How do we know God offers a Self-revelation in Jesus? Is it reasonable to believe, or is Christian faith simply an act of the will independent of intellectual considerations? These are questions the church was forced to consider.

The reaction within the church to the challenge of rationalism is complex and it continues. We consider here the teaching of the First Vatican Council on the topic, a teaching which asserts the relationship between faith and reason in Catholic belief. The teaching of the council shows why philosophy is always an explicitly integral element of Catholic theology.

The reactions of Catholic theologians to the challenge of rationalism were varied. Nineteenth-century Catholic theology was characterized by different attempts to relate reason and faith. We need not consider the details of the frequently controversial attempts by theologians to explain the relationship between faith and reason. It is enough to observe that there are two extremes excluded by the teachings of Vatican I.

One extreme, sometimes called semi-rationalism, tends to downplay the elements of revelation and faith when considering the nature of Christian truth. The nineteenth-century theologian Anton Gunther, for example, argued that one could attain knowledge of the triune nature of God from a reflection on human self-consciousness. Some taught that reason could bring one to the truth of Christian revelation and of the Catholic Church, without the gift of faith, without the help of the Holy Spirit.

At the other extreme is fideism. This point of view accepts the rationalist separation of faith and reason, relegating Christian truth totally to the realm of faith. One believes by the gift of faith. There are no reasonable grounds for belief. The realms of faith and reason are essentially disconnected.

The challenge of rationalism is the context for the First Vatican Council's dogmatic constitution *Dei filius*. *Dei filius* consists of four chapters and eighteen canons, dealing with a variety of topics beyond our interest. Our concern is its teaching on the question of faith and reason.

*Dei filius* rejects the separation of faith and reason which rationalism posits. One God both creates and reveals. God freely created an ordered universe which human reason can know. God also ordered humanity to a supernatural end, revealing divine mysteries beyond the capacity of human understanding. While in principle we can distinguish the natural, created order from the supernatural, these two are intrinsically related in the world as we know it.

This relationship between the natural and supernatural is the basic principle which underlies Vatican I's teaching on faith and reason. It will be treated in more detail below. Two theologically important consequences flow from this fundamental principle.

First, the act of faith is reasonable. One cannot prove from reason alone that God's revelation is present in scripture and church doctrine. Faith in God's revelation is a divine gift of the Spirit. But the act of faith remains a reasonable act. Reason can attain the existence of God, and divine providence has provided us with signs that point to revelation. Theologians have called the reasonable indicators of revelation signs of credibility or, more recently, warrants for belief. Thus, reason can lead one to revelation, to that point where one is reasonably open to the Spirit's gift of faith.

Second, the fathers of Vatican I point out that the continuity between the natural and supernatural orders is of primary importance for the practice of theology. Reason and faith cannot contradict one another for they deal with the same reality. In fact, reason, informed by faith, can be of great use in grasping and studying the divine mysteries of revelation. Of course, human understanding can never completely grasp the object of faith, which is God's very self. But reason can deepen our understanding of God's revelation. More, revelation can guide human efforts to reasonably understand the world in which we live.

The basic conviction that reason and faith together offer humanity access to the truth of our world grounds the place of philosophy in Catholic theology. Philosophy is that effort of human reason to understand the nature of reality and the meaning of human existence. Philosophers seek the truth.

They seek to know. Philosophy is the effort of critical reason to fathom the mystery of existence and the nature of the real. *Dei filius* teaches that this human enterprise can offer us access to the one truth that is completed in God's revelation.

Reason and faith probe one truth. They are partners in humanity's search to know our meaning and goal. To believe in God's revelation is a reasonable human act. To reasonably investigate the mysteries of revelation is an enriching and important task. The work of philosophers from the various periods and cultures of history can shed light on the mysteries of Judeo-Christian revelation. In turn, the truths of revelation can serve as a guide and corrective to humanity's search for wisdom. Reason and faith, revelation and philosophy, are each essential elements in theology's task, in faith's search for understanding.

## II. NATURE AND GRACE

Vatican I's teaching on faith and reason is rooted in the Catholic understanding of the relationship between the natural and the supernatural, between human nature and grace. This relationship grounds the place of philosophy in Catholic theology. More, the critical question of how nature and grace relate is a consistent issue within all theology, a constant factor underlying various theological perspectives. It is a question that demands the attention of any serious student of theology.

God offers every human being the possibility of eternal participation in the divine life, in the beatific vision. The beatific vision is our sharing in God's Self-knowledge and love, in the divine Self-vision which constitutes God's very being. To go to heaven is to go to God, to enter fully into the divine life. Our lives are our response, our yes or no to God's Self-offer. Our end is heaven or hell.

Human freedom for eternal union with God is grounded in God's Self-offer. God must first offer the divine life to us if we are to have a choice for or against. This gift of Self, this uncreated grace, is granted by God's free choice to share the divine life with human creatures.

It is possible to conceive of human existence, of rational creatures, not ordered to a divinized destiny. Human existence could be purely natural. Human life and destiny could remain in the realm of creation. In such a conception God would create, order, reward and punish in a created realm "outside" the divine being. Human existence and fate would remain within the realm of nature, of creation.

But we know by revelation that our world is graced. God has raised human creatures to a supernatural state of existence, to a destiny within the uncreated being of divine existence. By God's free gift of Self, humanity has an unmerited supernatural destiny. Human existence is divinized, raised above the natural (created) realm. Note the meaning of "supernatural." Theologically this term refers to humanity's destiny in God. It is important not to confuse this theological use with common parlance where supernatural refers to ghosts and other strange phenomena.

The distinction between nature and grace flows from these considerations. The relationship between reason and faith parallels the human condition of graced nature. Reason refers to humanity's natural capacity to know. Faith refers to the revelation of our supernatural destiny.

How one understands the relationship between nature and grace is pivotal. We will consider two issues. First, the traditional Protestant conception, that grace contradicts nature, will be contrasted with the traditional Catholic understanding, that grace elevates human nature. Second, I will indicate the significance of a debate which occurred earlier in this century, among Catholic theologians, as to whether one can distinguish the orders of grace and nature as neatly as our use of these terms might suggest. In considering these questions the implications for the relationship between reason and faith will be noted.

First, Christians have conceived of the relationship between human nature and God's Self-gift in two basic ways: grace contradicts and overcomes nature, or faith elevates nature. Vatican I, and the Catholic tradition, generally opt for the latter.

Both options find warrants in the tradition. The first, that grace contradicts nature, reflects St. Paul's theology of the cross. In 1 Corinthians 1, for example, Paul writes that he preaches only Christ crucified. The message of Christ's cross is the contradiction of human wisdom. "Where is the master of worldly wisdom? Has not God turned the wisdom of this world into folly?" Paul suggests that God's Self-revelation in the cross of Christ does not reflect what human reason anticipates or understands by the word "God." Rather, the cross contradicts human reason and wisdom. Grace contradicts nature. There is a discontinuity between faith and reason.

This tradition is historically reflected in the Protestant Reformation and finds resonance in the critical questions dividing the Catholic and Protestant churches. It would be hard to overestimate the importance of this issue which underlies key Protestant teachings on the relationship of faith and works, the place of the sacraments in salvation, the veneration of the saints, and so on. Protestant teachings on all these questions have their roots in an understanding of the relationship between nature and grace. Grace contradicts nature. Human efforts and works fail. Faith alone can save.

This view of nature and grace led Luther and the Protestant Reformation to reject the philosophical approach that characterized the scholastic theology of the Middle Ages. According to the reformers the use of philosophy by Catholic theologians reflects the efforts of sinful humanity to reach God. It is works, humanity's futile effort to save itself. Salvation is God's gracious gift. What we know of God we know from revelation alone, and all revelation is found in the Bible (*Sola scriptura!*). Suffice it to observe that in classic Protestant thought grace contradicts nature. Philosophy is a work of human nature and can tell us nothing about God's gift of grace in Christ.

In contrast, Catholic theology presupposes a continuity between nature and grace. The foundation of this continuity is found, above all, in the doctrine of the incarnation.

Jesus is God incarnate, the unity in one individual of humanity and divinity. If the incarnation of God really occurred in Jesus, then God must have so created human nature that it would have the potential for such a unity. In other words, human nature must have the capacity for unity with the divine, even though only God can make this perfect unity happen. (The tradition calls this an obediential potency, a passive capacity that can only reach its fulfillment by divine initiative.) If this be the case, as is revealed in Jesus, then human nature must be ordered to the divine. There must be a fundamental continuity between nature and grace. Grace must be nature's final and greatest possibility, though one achievable only by God's free gift.

This perspective of continuity determines the relationship of reason to faith in Vatican I's teaching. Reason alone cannot attain the truths of revelation. God's divine Self-gift raises human nature beyond anything it, of itself, could achieve. Humanity has a supernatural end. But this supernatural end does not contradict human nature. Rather, by God's creative design, grace elevates nature.

The efforts of human reason, thus, find their completion in God's revelation and grace. Grace elevates nature and draws reason beyond its natural limits. Revelation informs us of the final goal and meaning of human existence, enlightening reason's efforts to understand. Reason and revelation, grace and nature, are intrinsically related. They form a unity established in creation and fulfilled in Christ.

This perspective is the ground for Vatican I's teaching and the assumption for the practice of theology within the Catholic Church. All human efforts to know, all true advances in human knowledge are consistent with and complementary to revealed truth. The efforts of scientists, artists and philosophers to probe the world in which we live enrich our understanding of God, creation and revelation. In turn, revelation can guide and correct the efforts of human reason.

Second, granting this perspective among Catholic theologians, at mid-century a significant controversy occurred within Catholic theology about the relationship between nature and grace. The distinction presumes the possibility, mentioned above, that God could have created a purely natural human being, ungraced nature. This way of thinking reflects the influence of Aristotle on Catholic thought. Aristotle conceived of nature as a closed, self-contained unity. If one imagines creation in this way, grace becomes a kind of extrinsic reality laid across what is an otherwise complete unit. Humanity's divine end is something extrinsic, added on to an already complete nature. This is how many Catholic theologians thought about the relationship between nature and grace after Thomas Aquinas introduced Aristotle into theology.

The controversy at mid-century occurred when Henri de Lubac argued that the fathers and St. Thomas Aquinas had no such conception as pure nature. Rather, they conceived of humanity as the image of God, made for unity with the divine. Grace is an intrinsic element of human existence for those who have accepted God's gift.

Only one element of this controversy need concern us. If one accepts Aristotle's view of nature, then reason can be distinguished from grace. Reason refers to rational patterns of the natural order. Grace has no effect on reason's capacity to know the rational order. In contrast, an anthropology which understands grace as more intrinsic to nature will not be so optimistic about our capacity to distinguish between the two. Reasonable argumentation becomes a more complex matter. This difference has significant implications. For example, it determines how one understands Vatican I's teaching that the act of faith is reasonable.

## III. THE NATURE OF REASON AND THE ACT OF FAITH

While *Dei filius* asserts the reasonable nature of the act of faith, and suggests reasons for belief, it does not specify the nature of reason itself. What constitutes reason? This section argues that the nature of reason is not a fixed set of accepted principles. Rather, what constitutes a reasonable argument differs depending on the matter being considered and the context (historical-cultural) of consideration. More, if one conceives of grace as intrinsic to human existence, then reason and faith cannot be neatly separated. These observations again indicate the central place of philosophy in theological reflection.

The nature of reason is not arbitrary. The world we live in presents us with data and recurrent patterns which attentive and intelligent people recognize. Principles found in both classical and modern logic are agreed to and generally applied. But reason cannot be reduced to mere observation or formal logic. The matter is more complex.

What constitutes a reasonable argument or demonstration? The first, and rather obvious point is that the nature of a reasonable argument is profoundly affected by the matter at issue. If, for example, I seek to explain my answer to a problem in geometry, I must demonstrate how my answer flows from the set of axioms and rules for proceeding that define this mathematical discipline. Within geometry there is an established framework of relationships which constitute the field. A reasonable argument must reflect the consistency of that field.

But what of other reasonable positions one might hold with equal, or perhaps more conviction? For example, I know my wife loves me. I know Bach is a great composer. I know human beings should be free. We shall not enter into these examples in detail. The point is that the examples of knowledge listed here can be reasonably defended. If one considers how such a reasonable demonstration might proceed it becomes clear that different kinds of reasons will be offered. I know my wife loves me, not by a deduction from universal principles, nor by an objective gathering of empirical data. This knowledge is an intuitive induction from the confluence of my life experiences with her. It is reasonable to assert her love.

What constitutes a reasonable argument depends, at least in part, on the matter at issue. This is an important consideration in understanding the relationship between faith and reason. *Dei filius* asserts that it is reasonable to assent in faith to God's revelation in Christ and to church teaching. How theologians carry out this teaching of the council is affected by how they understand the nature of revelation, the objects of belief and the relationship between nature and grace.

Yet the matter is still more complex. What constitutes a reasonable argument is also affected by the intellectual context within which the argument is formulated. Arguments are formulated differently within different philosophical contexts. A convincing argument within Plato's thought will not be persuasive to Descartes. The deductive arguments of classical thought do not persuade within the inductive demands of modern science.

In the medieval intellectual world of St. Thomas, arguments from authority, for example that a position was held by Aristotle or Augustine, were not only persuasive but necessary (though arguments from authority were not the most important). In a rationalist context, as we have seen, arguments from authority are not only useless but suspect. Thus, the philosophical context of church life affects theological arguments for the reasonable character of the faith.

Today theological demonstrations of the reasonableness of faith must take seriously what the wider intellectual community considers reasonable. A relatively new element, essential to any reasonable argument for the faith, is historical consciousness.

We have noted above how different historical-cultural contexts count different forms of argument as persuasive. A new and unique element of the modern worldview is the recognition of this fact. How people view the world

has always been profoundly influenced by their culture and historical context. Recognition of this, which emerged in the eighteenth and nineteenth
centuries, is called historical consciousness. The modern appreciation of the
historical nature of human knowledge has serious implications for theology,
as we shall repeatedly note. The point I wish to suggest here is how historical
consciousness affects the teaching of *Dei filius* that the act of faith is reasonable. In our day any attempt to demonstrate the reasonable nature of the faith
must involve an appreciation of the historical difference between ourselves
and the worlds within which scripture and doctrine were formulated.

We can clarify the issue by considering the foundational Christian doctrine that Jesus was raised from the dead and is Lord. In scripture and
Christian history the belief that Jesus has risen is the foundation of faith.
Everyone agrees that Jesus lived. What makes one a Christian is the belief
that this same Jesus rose from death.

At the end of the last century some theologians sought to work out *Dei
filius'* teaching on the reasonable nature of the act of faith by arguing that the
apostolic proclamation about Jesus' appearances, and the scriptural testimony
about the empty tomb, constitute convincing evidence for the resurrection of
Jesus. The resurrection was thus demonstrable through a reasonable consideration of the evidence. On this foundation it is certainly reasonable to place
one's faith in Christ.

But can such an argument be reasonably persuasive today? Historical
consciousness, and the resulting historical-critical method, exclude such an
argument as reasonable. We must consider this more closely.

The recognition of historical consciousness was a factor in the rise of
the modern, historical-critical method. Under the influence of rationalism,
scientifically oriented thinkers began to study ancient texts with a critical
eye. Texts from ancient cultures, like scripture and the formulations of many
church doctrines, frequently assert events that seem mythic. These kinds of
events do not occur in our world. The visitation of angels, bodies ascending
into the clouds, and people rising from the dead are not things which happen
today. These stories seem to reflect pre-scientific, pre-modern, and mythical
worldviews.

According to the principle of analogy, formulated by Ernst Troeltsch,
critical historians do not accept such ancient narratives as historical. That is,
historians exclude from the critical study of history a literal understanding of
such miraculous narratives. The principle of analogy holds that scholars can
only admit as historical events which occur in the world we know. Thus, an
ancient text that asserts Caesar was murdered can be accepted as historical
because such an event occurs in the world as we know it. But a text that says
the prophet Mohammed was taken up into the heavens is not taken literally
since bodies do not float up into the clouds.

Similarly, the critical method precludes a historical demonstration of Jesus' resurrection. People do not rise from the dead in the world as we know it. Thus, the historical critical method excludes, by its very nature (a priori), the resurrection as a historical event.

It is important to appreciate what is asserted here. The reality of Christ's resurrection is not necessarily being denied. Rather the point is that one cannot get to the resurrection by historical reasoning alone. In brief, this argument for the reasonableness of the act of faith will no longer work.

This is not to say that *Dei filius* was mistaken. The argument that reason could get us to sure knowledge of the resurrection is not the position of the council, but an attempt to work out the council's teaching about the reasonable nature of the act of faith. Theologians today must (and do) offer other reasonable grounds for faith. This theological endeavor is called fundamental theology.

We began this section by observing that what constitutes reason is affected by the matter at hand. The resurrection of Jesus asserts his transition from everyday historical existence to Lordship. He sits at the right hand of the Father. He is with us, he will return. One ought hardly be surprised that such assertions cannot be proved by merely examining the evidence of our everyday experience. Belief in the resurrection has to do with life beyond this world, beyond death, with the proclamation that there is more.

Yet the teaching of *Dei filius* remains. Our belief is not a fideism. It is reasonable. Karl Rahner's consideration of the resurrection, treated again in chapter 9, offers an example of how a modern theologian works out the reasonableness of faith. Rahner's position also reflects a stance on the relationship between nature and grace. In the world God created grace is intrinsic to human existence. The warrants Rahner offers for believing in Christ's resurrection are intrinsically related to the experience of grace.

Rahner argues that the proclamation of Christ's rising addresses humanity's universal hope that life has some meaning, that who we become during our lifetime has some validity. Life is not absurd, it is not death into the void. Rahner holds that all human beings hope for such meaning because God has offered everyone a share in the divine life—grace. Hope is rooted in the experience of grace, whether people are aware of it or not.

One can believe in the proclamation of Jesus' resurrection because one already knows something about resurrection from hope. The warrant for belief in Christ's rising, the reasonableness of faith, does not come prior to the act of hope but only within it. When one hopes one finds the meaning of Christ's rising. The proclamation of the resurrection interprets our hope.

The reasonableness of faith, for Rahner, is not like a geometric deduction or a scientific induction. It is not addressed to pure nature, to ungraced reason. It is more like the reasonableness of the conviction that my wife loves me. In the experience of hope and faith there is a validation. The confluence of my experiences within the life of belief in the risen Christ makes it reasonable for me to believe. I find validation in the faith (hope) itself.

One cannot prove to the unbeliever that Christ rose. That would be the kind of semi-rationalism rejected by *Dei filius*. Nor can one believe blindly and irrationally. That would be fideism. Within the act of faith itself one finds reasonable warrants. Nature is completed by grace. Faith fulfills nature and in that fulfillment faith finds its reasonable ground.

Rahner's explication of Christ's resurrection is but one approach within contemporary Catholic theology. The question of Christ's resurrection (its meaning, how we understand it, the grounds for belief in it, etc.) is a widely discussed topic within Christology and fundamental theology. We will return to this topic and observe the philosophical categories which ground various interpretations.

## IV. CONCLUSION

This chapter has considered some basic principles which undergird the place of philosophy in Catholic theology. These abstract principles, set forth by the First Vatican Council, reflect the long history of theological practice. The conversation between philosophy and revealed truth goes back to the very beginning of Christian history. A variety of theological questions have also been introduced to which we will return.

Having been thus introduced to the theological conversation, we shall now turn to its origins. The practice of theology emerged from the appropriation of the faith within the Greco-Roman world of the church's first centuries. This appropriation of the faith not only determined how we do theology, it also gave rise to many of the doctrines that remain central to Christian faith. Considering these early centuries offers us an example of the profound influence of philosophy on theology and doctrine.

## BIBLIOGRAPHY

Frederick Copleston's *A History of Philosophy* is an excellent overview of western thought. He treats rationalism in Volume IV. Descartes' *Meditations on the First Philosophy* is a good introduction to his thought and to the methodology of doubt. *Dei filius* can be found in *The Church Teaches* pp. 25–52. Gerald McCool's *Catholic Theology in the Nineteenth Century* contains an excellent account of the various theological approaches to faith and reason which served as the background for *Dei filius*. For a brief overview of the complex debate about the relationship between nature and grace, see Joseph Komonchak's essay "Theology and Culture at Mid-

Century: The Example of Henri de Lubac" in *Theological Studies* 51 (Dec. 1990):579–602. Chapter 1 of Francis Schüssler Fiorenza's *Foundational Theology* treats the role of Jesus' resurrection in fundamental theology during this century. Rahner's interpretation of Christ's resurrection is found in *Foundations of Christian Faith*, pp. 264–285.

# CHAPTER 3

---

# THE HELLENISTIC RECEPTION
# OF CHRISTIAN FAITH

The Christian faith makes a claim to universal truth. Jesus is God's full and final revelation for all humanity, for people of every time and place.

There is a tension implicit in this fundamental Christian claim. As all human beings, Jesus lived in a particular time and place. He was a first century, Palestinian Jew. His teaching and fate reflect his historical context. If he is God's revelation, must Christians accept Jesus' historical perspective? Must we become first century, Palestinian Jews?

As the letters of St. Paul indicate, the New Testament church struggled with this question. The Pauline answer, that Gentile converts need not become Jews, finally carried the day. But the relationship between Jesus' historical particularity and universal claim remains problematic. How does this individual reveal God to all the times and cultures which constitute human history?

The history of Christianity can be described as a kind of conversation between the story of Jesus, told in scripture and tradition, and the many historical contexts within which that story has been appropriated. The universal claim of the faith occurs in this conversation as believers in various contexts make Christ their own. As in any conversation, both partners change. Christianity has transformed the cultures in which it has thrived. In turn, the various historical and cultural contexts of faith have transformed our perception of the Christ. The many images of Jesus in Christian art well exemplify these transformations.

The history of theology is the story of attempts to understand the faith within the different intellectual contexts of the church's past and present. This is why the study of theology demands a knowledge of the history of philosophy. Whether believers are aware of it or not, the philosophical presuppositions of time and place profoundly affect how Christians understand their faith. In this chapter we will consider how one of the earliest appropriations of the faith has affected both the practice of theology and the form of Christian doctrine.

The first Christians were, like Jesus, Palestinian Jews. They were members of the Jewish religion who believed Jesus to be risen Lord and Messiah. Within the first hundred years of Christian history, the church changed into a predominantly Gentile community. While there remained a Jewish community within the church, the vast majority of Christians were Gentile.

It would be hard to overestimate the importance of this change for the history of the church. Gentile Christians were generally unfamiliar with the Jewish scriptures and with the religious customs and categories that formed Jesus' world. The Christ story had to be appropriated, understood and lived, in ways that made sense to Gentile converts. What follows indicates some of the philosophical and theological elements of this appropriation.

We begin with a brief description of the Jewish understanding of God and of revelation which is manifest in Jesus' teaching. I then indicate how the Platonic notion of divinity differs from that of the Jews. These two traditions, the Hellenist and Jewish, were fused during the first centuries of Christian history. The chapter concludes with some brief observations about the doctrines of God and Christ that emerged from this conversation.

## I. THE GOD OF JESUS

The God of Jesus is revealed in Jewish history. To know God is to know the story. It is to know God's promise, God's fidelity to that promise, and the people's response. This is a story of freedom. It is a story of human freedom to live according to God's will and of divine freedom to punish, relent and renew the promise.

The God of the Old Testament is not primarily the object of human speculation or abstract knowledge. God is the God of the promise, the God who acts in history. Consider a few key moments in the story. God offers a covenant, an agreement, through Moses. "I will be your God, you will be my people." The terms of the covenant are clear. The people are to worship God alone and to keep the divinely revealed law. In turn, God gives land and security to the people (Ex 19:5–6). But the relationship between God and Israel is not static. It has a history.

Following the practice of the nations around them, the people want a king. God grants their wish first with Saul, then David (1 Sam). God's promise of fidelity to the people becomes a promise to the house of David (2 Sam 7:11–16).

Consider the prophets Amos, Hosea, and Jeremiah. The people are unfaithful to the covenant. They fail to follow the law and are threatened with divine punishment. Punishment comes to the northern kingdom through conquest by Assyria. Later punishment comes to Jerusalem and Judah through conquest by Babylon. The temple is destroyed and the people are taken into exile.

But God is faithful. Consider Isaiah 40–55. The land has been lost but God will redeem the promise. There will be a return. More, God will use the suffering of the people in exile as a sign to all nations. Consider Ezekiel 37. There will be a resurrection of Israel, a return of the nation to life.

In the history of the Jews, God sends prophets to speak the divine will. The prophets interpret the events of their time in terms of God's will and promise. The threat of being conquered is divine judgment. The promise of rebirth is God's fidelity.

In brief, the history of the Jews is a history of the free relationship between God and the people. God is faithful, but frequently in new and unanticipated ways.

As God continues to act in different situations Israel's understanding of the divine promise develops. The divine fidelity is first toward the people as a whole. It is the promise of the land. By the time of Jesus the understanding of God's fidelity has expanded. God's fidelity cannot be fulfilled within history. History is always the story of sin and failure. God's fidelity will be fulfilled at the end of history. God will establish a divine kingdom, the reign of God. The dead will be raised and judged. For the just, death and suffering will be done away with. God will bring the just into an eternal kingdom of joy and peace.

Here is the core of Jesus' message. "Repent for the kingdom is at hand." He preached this message and, as prophets before him, was killed. God is faithful but, again, in a new and unexpected way. The anticipated general resurrection of the kingdom did not occur. Rather, Jesus rose from the dead as guarantor of the promise.

These remarks hardly do justice to the story of God's chosen people. Only one point is at issue. The God of Jesus Christ is a God who acts in history. God is faithful and trustworthy. Jesus trusted his Father even to the cross. One proclaims God's fidelity by telling the story. God has been faithful and can be trusted to remain so in the future. The promise of the kingdom is the promise of God's final fidelity.

The God who has been faithful is also free. God has responded in ever-new ways to the events of human history. The exact manner of divine fidelity is not known in advance. The initial promise of the land has become, in Christ, a promise of the eternal kingdom beyond history. We are not secure because we comprehend God or know the divine plan in advance. Rather, we are secure because we trust in God's fidelity.

An example of the unanticipated form of God's fidelity can be seen in the earliest days of the church. The first Christians thought that Christ's resurrection meant the imminent end of the world. They thought Jesus would soon return to establish the kingdom. St. Paul's earliest writings clearly indicate his conviction that the end would come during his natural lifetime (1

Thess 4:15). Yet Christ did not return. The later writings of the New Testament show the church's adaptation to Christ's unexpected delay. In John's gospel, for example, Jesus' message about the nearness of the kingdom has given way to the salvific nature of the person of Christ. The pastoral letters (1 and 2 Timothy and Titus) treat questions of ecclesial organization which do not arise in a community anticipating the imminent end of time. God has made the final offer of salvation in Jesus, but not in the manner anticipated by the first believers. Our security in the faith does not rest on what we know. It rests on our trust that God will be faithful.

When the Christian faith entered the Gentile world it entered an environment with a very different view of reality. The Gentile world that existed beyond Palestine had been profoundly influenced by Greek thought and is thus commonly called Hellenistic. The God of Jesus, the God of history, had to become comprehensible to people schooled in the thought of Plato and other philosophers. The fusion of these two traditions, the Jewish and the Greek, determined the nature of theology and the form of important Christian doctrines. We can now turn our attention to this Hellenistic appropriation of the faith.

## II. HELLENISM AND THEOLOGY

The spread of the Christian faith within the Hellenistic environment of the Roman Empire occurred with amazing rapidity. The appropriation of the faith within this new context gave rise to theology as it has been practiced in the church to our day.

The Hellenistic world had its own wisdom, the wisdom of the great thinkers of ancient Greece—Socrates, Plato, Aristotle, and others. For the Christian faith to get a hearing it could not present itself as the contradiction of this ancient tradition. Jesus was, after all, a recent figure in history. The giants of Greek thought were figures of antiquity, fathers of an ancient wisdom. One could hardly expect people to jettison this ancient wisdom in favor of a recent Jewish rabbi.

The first Christian theologians, called the apologists, writers of the second and early third centuries, frequently chose a different strategy. They presented Jesus not as the contradiction of Greek wisdom, but as its fulfillment. The apologists Justin Martyr (c. 100–c. 165) and Clement of Alexandria (c. 150–c. 215), for example, admitted that Christians had no monopoly on wisdom. They taught that the truth sought and explicated by Socrates and Plato found its fullest expression in Christ. The One whom Plato taught to be the source of everything was the Father of Jesus the Christ.

The synthesis attempted by the apologists, between the wisdom of the Greeks and Christian revelation, defines the theological task. Its presupposition undergirds the history of Catholic thought. The truth is one. The God of creation and revelation is the same. The goal of reason, to know the source and ground of reality, is attained in revelation. Faith completes reason; reason enlightens faith. The natural and supernatural constitute one reality. Reason and revelation are partners in the quest for truth.

The conversation initiated by the apologists, between Hellenism and Christian faith, was essential if Christianity were to be credible in the Gentile world of the Roman Empire. The apologists were themselves Hellenists who believed in Jesus. Their efforts to express the Christian faith in new categories cannot be understood as if they stood outside both the Jewish and Greek worlds (horizons) attempting some clever combination. Rather, the appropriation of Christianity within the Hellenistic world was the work of believers attempting to formulate their faith in such a way as to show it was coherent, intelligent, believable.

In any conversation participants change. Consider a disagreement between friends about a common memory, the meaning of a movie or a book, the correctness of a political position. Friends not only express their own views; they listen. In such an exchange the views of the participants change. New possibilities for understanding occur.

In the conversation between the initial (Palestinian-Jewish) Christian formulation and its new Hellenistic environment, both partners changed. Neither lost its soul. Something new emerged.

A brief example of this conversation, and its consequences for Christian belief, might be helpful. Consider the Christian belief in the resurrection of the body. Jesus and his Jewish followers believed in and proclaimed the resurrection of the body at the coming of the kingdom. In contrast, the Greeks thought of death as a release from physical existence. Life after death is a return of the soul to higher, spiritual realms. Physical existence means distance from the One. Death is release from the physical, movement back toward the source and unity of being.

Within the Hellenistic context Christian belief in the resurrection was difficult, to say the least. Recall in Acts 17 how the citizens of Athens gave Paul a hearing until he mentioned the resurrection of the body. They then sneered and cut him off. Chapter 15 of Paul's first letter to the Corinthians was written to correct members of the church at Corinth who denied the resurrection of the body.

The tension between these contrasting views is clear in early theology. The church continued to proclaim the resurrection in the liturgy, in the gospels and in its creeds. But understanding of the resurrection was frequently absorbed into the Hellenistic category of an immortal soul. St. Ambrose (c. 339–397) understood the resurrection to be the transference of the soul's immortality to the body. Origen (c. 185–c. 254) thought physical resurrection to be an allegory for the more simple–minded, an allegory for the soul's immortality.[1]

To this day the immortality of the soul remains, for many Christians, the chief way to understand life after death. The reader might consider her or his own religious education. Was death not understood as the separation of soul from body? The body drags us down. Its natural tendencies pull us away from the spiritual, from God. Death is release for the spiritual. The doctrine of physical resurrection is neglected. If this is not what you were taught, it probably is what your parents learned.

The point at issue is that the appropriation of the faith within the Hellenistic world had a profound and lasting effect on the Christian belief. We shall now consider how the doctrines of God and Christ also reflect the Hellenistic appropriation of the faith.

## III. THE CHRISTIAN DOCTRINE OF GOD

### A. The Divine in Hellenist Thought: Plato

We saw above how Jesus' understanding of God came out of Jewish history. God is a free actor in and the master of history. God is revealed to be faithful within history, responding to human freedom and events, fulfilling the divine promise in ever–new situations. God's fidelity is manifest in raising Jesus from the dead. Here is the promise of final fidelity to all humanity, the promise of the kingdom proclaimed by the Christ.

The Hellenistic notion of God was quite different. While the Jews found stability amid historical flux in the fidelity of God, the Greeks found stability in an unchanging reality which underlies the world of appearance and change. Change and history deal only with the appearance of things. Truth, *aletheia* (uncovering), is attained through reason. It is the uncovering of things, the unconcealing of all which veils the genuine being of beings. Appearances conceal. Only reason has access to the being of beings, to the unchanging, to the essence, to the unity which underlies the appearances of change and history.

Let us briefly consider some elements of Plato's epistemology and of the ontology which undergirds it. Plato presumes that we know the real. For Plato knowledge is absolute and infallible. Therefore, knowledge cannot be a matter of mere sense perception because the world of sense objects is transitory and relative. The object of knowledge must be stable, capable of being grasped and defined. It must be the universal.

In contrast to most contemporary views (philosophical and common sense), Plato sees the universal and abstract as the real. The abstract idea is the permanent reality which underlies the world of appearance. When we know we attain the universal which the sensed object reflects. For example, I know the object seen when I grasp tree. "Tree" is a universal, a concept which renders this object intelligible. The universals, forms, are the reality which cause physical things to be what they are.

The causality at issue here is exemplary, as a design in the mind of a builder is the cause (example, model) of the object built. This kind of causality must be distinguished from efficient causality, i.e., the builder actually at work. The efficient cause in creation, that which relates form to object, is the Demiurge treated by Plato in the *Timaeus*.[2]

To do justice to Plato's position one must avoid thinking of the forms as "things" which exist somewhere. This is a caricature Aristotle makes of Plato's position. Rather, the form is the intelligibility of the known. One can think, for example, "tree" without seeing a specific tree, or imagining a tree. The word has meaning apart from its occurring as an object. For Plato, intelligibility is the real.

In middle-Platonism, i.e., Platonic thought in the period when Christianity first entered the Hellenist world, the forms were understood as ideas in God's mind. Created objects reflect these forms in the sense that created objects conform to God's design of them. While this notion of ideas in the mind of God is not Plato's, it is the point of view generally accepted within Christian theology.

One critical question which led the Greeks to philosophy is: how is it possible to know concrete things in terms of a universal when all we experience in the world are concrete, particular objects? Whence the universal? Plato's answer is that knowledge is memory. In the *Phaedo* Plato suggests that the human soul preexisted and, in some sense, knew the forms before bodily existence. Sensation of an object "reminds" one of what is already possessed.

The very multiplicity of beings described here (physical objects, souls, forms) offends against the Greek quest for stability and unity. Thus Plato posits, as the ground for all that exist, one simple principle—the Good. The Good is likened to the sun. It is not one more object we see, but that which grants visibility (intelligibility) to all that is. The Good is the source of intelligibility and, for Plato, intelligibility is the most real. As the source of all being and multiplicity the Good must itself be One, simple, lacking in any division. The One transcends all that is. Plato speaks of the forms and the Demiurge as that by which we are related to the Good. But the One transcends all human predication since to predicate is to divide. The Good is indivisible and remains mystery.

## B. The God of Jesus and Plato's One

That there are differences between the Jewish and Hellenistic notions of God ought, by now, to be clear. Yet the apologists, and their theological successors, presumed the God of Jesus and the God of Plato to be the same. The synthesis of these two conceptions of divinity gave rise to the Christian doctrine of God. This synthesis is both a brilliant achievement and a source of continuing intellectual tension. Let us consider a few of its elements.

While we formulate our topic as a Hellenistic appropriation of the Jewish religious tradition, early Christian theologians did not think of their task in this manner. They were Hellenists who believed in Christ. They read the scripture from that perspective. The synthesis of the two traditions occurred in the way these theologians interpreted the scriptures. They read the scriptures from a Greek perspective, understanding what they read in terms of their own worldview.

Different people, in different times and places, understand texts differently because they come to texts from different perspectives. Consider our own situation as an example. If we read the scripture and its language of freedom and justice we do so as twentieth-century Americans. While we recognize that our notions of justice and freedom are different from the notions of the original authors of scripture, we apply God's demand for justice in our own lives in a manner that reflects our present understanding. In other words, our lived response to the scripture's demand for justice is profoundly affected by our contemporary, American understanding of the term.

This is the nature of human understanding and has always been so. As moderns we recognize that one's historical context affects the interpretation of scripture. This awareness is commonly called historical consciousness.

Early Christian theologians read the scriptures from within their Hellenistic context and found in scripture a Platonic God. For example, both Tertullian (c. 160–c. 225) and St. Augustine (354–430) were convinced that the Mosaic and Platonic traditions must have been in contact with each other. How else could one explain the similarities between the two? Justin Martyr argued that Plato must have taken his notion of creation, his teaching on the Demiurge in the *Timaeus,* from Moses.[3]

Modern scholars reject any historic connection between Plato and Moses. Greek thought had an influence on Judaism after the conquests of Alexander the Great. This influence is manifest chiefly in the Wisdom literature. But the texts attributed to Moses were written before this period. The Platonic elements attributed to scripture were supplied by the interpreters. They read the texts from a Platonic perspective.

One presumption of Greek thought was that God and matter are coeternal. The world and its history have no beginning or end. While Plato held the

One to be the ground of reality and its intelligibility, he did not understand this in a temporal sense. That is, Plato did not conceive of the relationship between the world and the divine as having a beginning. A linear notion of history came into western thought through Judeo-Christian revelation.

Christian monotheism, and the divine supremacy, could not admit anything coeternal with God. To guard the divine supremacy, and protect against any hint of pantheism, Christian thinkers argued that nothing is coeternal with God. God creates all that exists *ex nihilo*, out of nothing. God exists without and "prior" to creating. Creation is free, separate from God, not part of the divine, not necessary to God.

The doctrine of creation *ex nihilo*, central to the Christian understanding of God, is a classic example of how the Hellenistic appropriation of Christianity resulted in something new. Scripture's account of creation does not assert the doctrine of creation *ex nihilo*. The scriptures do not treat such speculative questions. Genesis simply tells the story of God calling into existence and ordering all that is.

Nor did Plato, or other Greek philosophers, hold such a view of creation. The doctrine could only develop when Judeo-Christian monotheism, and the Genesis account, came into conversation with the categories and questions of Greek thought. The doctrine results from the ensuing conversation.

The doctrine of creation has profound implications for the Hellenistic conception of God. It introduces an act of will into the divine being, i.e., God's free choice to create. The simplicity and immutability of God are thus compromised in a manner that remains problematic for the Greek mind. But divine will and freedom are essential to the doctrine of creation *ex nihilo* and to the history of God's relationship with humanity. The freedom of God to act, to alter the divine relationship with creation (e.g., in the incarnation and resurrection), is essential to Christian belief. The history of revelation and the doctrine of providence require it.

The problem of logical consistency in asserting an immutable, simple and freely acting God is an example of the kind of question that could only occur in the conversation between Hellenistic thought and Christian revelation. This conversation gave rise to the doctrine of creation *ex nihilo* which protected monotheism and divine providence. While this doctrine clearly reflects the philosophical mind of the Greeks, it manifests more of the scriptural notion of God than the Platonic.

But the doctrine of creation *ex nihilo* also raises serious philosophical and theological questions, especially if one understands the teaching in too imaginative a way. If we think of God existing "before" creation, and giving being to everything in the created world, then did God know of and will evil? And if not, how is evil possible? And if God knows everything, and wills all into being, then God must have also known and willed human destiny. Human freedom thus becomes problematic and double predestination (some destined to glory, others to hell) seems to follow.

These questions remain significant challenges to the Christian conception of God to our day. They are not merely of historical interest. For many of our contemporaries, the reality of evil and the defense of human freedom are powerful reasons for denying the existence of God.

## IV. THE INCARNATE LOGOS AND THE TRINITY

Christianity's central claim is that Jesus of Nazareth is the full and final revelation of God for all humanity. We return to a question raised earlier. How can a historic individual have universal significance?

Within the original, Palestinian-Jewish context of Jesus' own environment his universal significance was understood in terms of the second coming. Jesus had preached an end of time when the Son of Man will come in the clouds. The dead will rise for judgment and God's kingdom will be established for the just.

In his resurrection Christ became that heavenly figure who will return to establish the kingdom of God. Jesus' message about the kingdom was confirmed in his rising. Resurrection happens at the end of time. The earliest Christians were convinced that Jesus would soon return to establish the kingdom. One of their earliest prayers was "Come Lord Jesus."

Jesus thus had universal significance since he was the one who would bring the end of history and the eternal kingdom of God. He was understood in terms of this function. The title Son of Man, the one who brings the kingdom, was of great importance to the early understanding of Jesus Christ.

In the Hellenistic world, into which Christianity soon spread, the categories of resurrection and of an end to history were strange. The title Son of Man had no eschatological meaning outside of Judaism. While Christian scripture, creeds and worship continued to proclaim Christ in eschatological categories, Gentile Christians developed ways of understanding Jesus that made sense within the Hellenistic world.

A key bridge between the Jewish and Hellenistic interpretations of Jesus was provided in the prologue to the gospel of John. "In the beginning was the Word (Logos), and the Word was with God, and the Word was God. ...Through Him all things were made....The Word became flesh" (John 1:1, 3a, 14a).

The Logos of John's gospel provided a common ground for conversation between early Christianity and the Hellenistic world. The doctrines of God and Christ that emerged in the early centuries of the church reflect this conversation.

## A. Logos

Logos could provide a bridge for understanding Jesus because it had rich meaning in both Jewish and Greek thought. In Genesis, which John 1 clearly evokes, God creates by the power of the divine word. "God *said*, 'Let there be light,' and there was light" (Gen 1:3). God's word comes to the people through the prophets and in the law. God's word is spoken by the prophet. "The word of the Lord came to me thus" (Jer 1:4). In the Word is manifest the eternal wisdom of God, a wisdom frequently personified. "Wisdom sings her own praises.... 'From the mouth of the Most High I came forth'" (Sir 24:1a, 3a).

The Word of God was thus a rich notion within the Jewish tradition. For early Jewish Christians, Jesus was God's full and final word, the eschatological prophet, God's wisdom. In Jesus is revealed God's eternal and mysterious plan for universal human salvation, a mystery hidden within God from all eternity (1 Cor 2:7).

The expression of Jesus' universal significance as Logos was also deeply evocative within the Greek tradition. "Logos" had rich and varied meanings within Greek philosophy and within the popular forms of Platonism which characterized the Hellenistic world within which Christianity spread. Heraclitus had used Logos to indicate the order of reality, that universal coherence which stands under the world of appearance and flux. The Stoics understood Logos as the divine mind which guides and controls all things. Philo, a Jewish thinker who attempted a synthesis between Greek and Jewish thought, understood Logos as God's plan for the universe and the instrument of creation.

The unique element in Christian thought, unknown and incomprehensible within either Hellenism or Judaism, is John's assertion that the Word became flesh. Universal meaning occurs in a historical figure.

Within a very brief time, viewing Jesus as the incarnate Logos became the universal and nearly exclusive way to understand him. Church doctrines about Jesus, and about God, emerge from reflection on the incarnation of the Logos, a reflection which took place within the world of middle and Neoplatonism.

## B. Logos and Christian Doctrine

Judaism and early Christianity told the story of God's relationship with humanity from creation to sin, from promise to re-creation in Christ. When this story was told in the Hellenistic world it became a cosmic drama performed within a middle Platonic and, later, Neoplatonic universe.

Sin had destroyed the unity of creation. Humanity had fallen from unity with God. Only the creator could re-create, could save. The Logos descends that humanity might ascend. Consider the gospel of John. Jesus is light come into the world's darkness (1:4–5; 9:5), life amid death (11:25–26). Recall Jesus' words to Nicodemus. Humanity must be reborn in the Spirit. "No one has gone up to heaven except the One who came down from there—the Son of Man. Just as Moses lifted up the serpent in the desert, so must the Son of Man be lifted up, that all who believe may have eternal life in him. Yes, God so loved the world that he gave his only Son that whoever believes in him may not die but may have eternal life" (3:13–16).

These sections of John's gospel express what Jesus does, how he saves. He descends from the Father that believers might ascend with him to God. This description of Christ's work seems to fit into the Platonic cosmology popular in the church's first centuries. All reality emanates from the One, to the forms and down to the world of physical things. The Logos descends from the One into the flesh so that humanity might ascend back to the One.

But the Greek mind could not rest with a mere telling of what Jesus did. The mind seeks to know the underlying intelligibility of things. What something does leads to the question about what it is. The mind does not rest with a description of function, which remains on the level of change and appearance. The intellect strives to know the being of a thing, its "whatness" (*quidity*), its essence.

Thus the description of what Jesus does in the work of salvation leads to the question about what Jesus is. In the Hellenistic world the description of Jesus' work as savior gave rise to the ontological question about what Jesus is. Functional Christology leads to an ontological Christology. If Jesus is the Logos incarnate, in flesh, what is the nature of the Logos? Is the Logos God or creature?

This is a significant question for both Jewish monotheism and the Hellenistic conception of God. Both insist on the oneness of God. John says the Word was divine. Yet the incarnate Logos is not the Father. What, then, is the Logos?

That Jesus came from the Father is clear from the scriptural testimony. Theologians like Origen understood scripture within the context of middle Platonism, i.e., to mean that the Logos emanates from the One, as all reality comes from the One. The Logos is the first such emanation from the One and, thus, less than the One.

Arius (c. 250–c. 336) put the question with stark simplicity. How many Gods are there? One. Is the Logos the Father? No. Therefore, the Logos is not God.

Others, like Athanasius (c. 296–373), responded that if the Logos incarnate in Jesus is not divine, and only God can save, then we are not saved by Jesus. The functional and ontological questions are the same. The essence of Christian faith is at issue.

This crisis in theology, and the doctrines of God and Christ which flow from it, rise out of the conversation between Christian faith and Hellenistic philosophy. The church's resolution of this crisis, spanning the conciliar doctrines from Nicea (325) to Constantinople II (553), reflects this continuing conversation. The consequent doctrines of the Trinity and Christ constitute a new understanding, a modification of both Jewish and Hellenist perspectives.

Nicea answered Arius by asserting that the Logos is *homoousios* (the same substance) with the Father. The word *homoousios* reflects Arius' ontological question. The term is taken from Greek philosophy and taught by the church with an authority nearly equal with the scripture. Thus the Hellenistic appropriation of the faith begins to set the boundaries of orthodoxy.

The Council of Chalcedon (451) later settled christological controversies with a similar use of philosophical terms. Jesus is two natures, fully divine and fully human, unmixed, united in one hypostasis, one prosopon. We will return to the dogma of Chalcedon, and its philosophical categories, in later chapters. Suffice it to indicate here that the philosophical environment of the church's first centuries profoundly influenced both the development and form of doctrine.

## V. CONCLUSION

The appropriation of the faith by Hellenist Gentiles well exemplifies the essential relationship between philosophy and theology in the Catholic tradition. Both the practice of theology and the form of doctrine have their roots in the conversation described above. A serious student of theology must enter into this conversation and struggle with its frequently difficult categories, ideas and vocabulary.

The doctrines of these early centuries remain essential to the Christian faith. In later chapters we will return to the topics of God, creation and Christology. We will see how these ancient doctrines of the church continue to disclose God's truth as they find new expression through appropriation within the ever changing philosophical contexts of church history. In other words, the conversation continues.

Finally, this chapter has mentioned in passing but a few of the theological giants from the patristic period. Ambrose, Origen, Tertullian, Athanasius and many other patristic writers are an enduring source for the church's theological reflection. The next chapter treats St. Augustine, the most significant theologian of the western church from these early centuries. Specifically, chapter 4 shows how Neoplatonic philosophy is an intrinsic element in his theology of the eucharist. Augustine's eucharistic theology not only exemplifies the influence of philosophy on theology. It also has much to teach us about the mystery of Christ and his church.

## BIBLIOGRAPHY

See Plato's *Phaedo* and *Timaeus*. For secondary material on Plato, see the first volume of Copleston's *A History of Philosophy*, especially chapters 19, 43 and 44. There are a number of good, introductory accounts of the development of early doctrines. See, for example, pages 283–294 and 439–460 of Richard McBrien's *Catholicism*. J.N.D. Kelly's *Early Christian Doctrines* and the first volume of Jaroslav Pelikan's *The Christian Tradition* provide more detailed accounts. My interpretation of the development of doctrine is deeply indebted to Wolfhart Pannenberg, especially his essay "The Appropriation of the Philosophical Concept of God as a Dogmatic Problem of Early Christian Theology," in *Basic Questions in Theology* II.

## NOTES

1. Origen, *Against Celsus,* 5.18–19, 23; Ambrose, *On the Passing Away of His Brother Satyrus,* 2.50–52, 65.
2. The fathers of the church frequently associated the demiurge with the Logos. Philo, a Jewish philosopher at Alexandria, had prepared the way for Christian thinkers here by interpreting the Jewish Wisdom tradition in Platonic categories.
3. Justin Martyr, *First Apology*, 59–60.

# CHAPTER 4

# NEOPLATONISM, AUGUSTINE AND THE BODY OF CHRIST

## I. INTRODUCTORY REMARKS

Of the great patristic figures, St. Augustine (AD. 354–430) has been the most influential within the theological tradition of the western church. His thought well exemplifies the intrinsic place of philosophy within theology. Reading Plotinus, and other thinkers whom we now call Neoplatonists, was an essential step in his conversion to Christianity. The rich theology Augustine left the church reflects this philosophical perspective. The study of Augustine draws one into the world of Neoplatonism, and familiarity with this philosophical perspective is essential if one is to understand him.

This chapter indicates the intrinsic place of Neoplatonism in Augustine's theology by considering his teaching on the eucharist, the mystery of the body of Christ. These reflections also show that Augustine still has much to teach us. I suggest that the reader study some of Augustine's sermons before reading the chapter. Specifically, see his sermons for Easter and the Ascension (Sers. 225, 231, 243, 261, 263, and 264) and his homilies on chapter 6 of John's gospel (*Homilies on the Gospel of John,* Tracts 26 and 27).

Augustine's theology of the eucharist, his understanding of the mystery of the Lord's body, involves the entire mystery of salvation. God's act of salvation in Jesus is a cosmic drama acted out within a Neoplatonic universe.

According to Augustine, human existence is a quest for happiness, a quest fulfilled in the God who exists beyond the world in which we struggle. The God for whom we long is the spiritual source of the created world but, as spirit and source, transcends and is hidden. God, like Plato's Good, exists in unapproachable light, beyond our world yet beckoning us.

The world is the creation of God's Word and manifests the divine. In Augustine's Neoplatonic view, all creation can serve as a sign of its creator. Creation can awaken the human spirit to the higher reality, drawing us into the ultimate mystery, God's very Self. Humanity should focus on the higher and the inner things.

Yet, because of sin, we are incapable of this true perception of the created world. Rather than contemplate creation as a means of ascent to God we stop at creation itself, seeking to find happiness in the finite and the transitory. This is the reason for human unhappiness and our need for redemption. Left to ourselves we cannot ascend because sin has rendered us unable to perceive the Word manifest in creation.

The Word descended, becoming flesh, to enable us to overcome sin. Jesus came to draw us to God, to take us beyond the earthly to the heavenly. He came to give humankind the capacity to see the reality that is the source and meaning of creation. This capacity comes from faith in the ascended Christ, from faith which grants true vision.

According to Augustine we touch the Word by faith. Faith (the *intellectus spiritualis*) is a union with the Word who took flesh and ascended. By faith we are enabled to contemplate the divine, for by union with Christ believers are drawn beyond the earthly to our heavenly home.

The incarnation (descent) and ascension, by which Christ draws us to heaven, constitute the mystery of the Lord's body celebrated in the eucharist. Augustine sets forth this mystery in his Easter and Ascension sermons.

## II. AUGUSTINE'S EASTER AND ASCENSION SERMONS

Augustine observes that we seek happiness in money and earthly things, not realizing that there is no happiness found there. Until the coming of Christ we were "dull of heart," not realizing the futility of these efforts for happiness (Ser. 231.5).

Christ descended to share our lot on earth. He found only suffering and death. But God raised him from death. Augustine tells his church to "keep your eyes fixed on the resurrection." We find no happiness here but the Lord has been raised up and "He has invited you to His own table, abundant in all good things, the table of heaven, the table of angels where He Himself is the bread." Happiness in this life is possible only in communion with Him who ascended (Ser. 231.5). In the ascended Christ we find that heavenly reality for which we pine.

> He has ascended. Who? He who descended. He came down from heaven to heal you; He ascended to heaven to lift you up. You will fall if you attempt to raise yourself; you will remain there if He has raised you up (Ser. 261.1).

Christ's ascension reveals His divinity and the true meaning of life. It calls us to look beyond the earthly to the ultimate reality, God. The eternal Word took flesh and ascended to God with that flesh. Thus he draws humanity beyond earth to heaven. "In order that people might eat the bread of angels, the Lord of angels became man" (Ser. 225.2).

Faith is belief in the ascended Christ, a communion by which the believer enters heaven. After his resurrection, Augustine points out, the apostles wanted Jesus to stay among them "as a Teacher, as a Comforter, as a Consoler and a Protector, in a word, as a man such as they themselves were." But so seeing him in the flesh did not permit them to see him as the Word. The apostles, like ourselves, sought to cling to the earthly, but Christ withdrew from them so that they might know him as the Heavenly One and, thus, be united with humanity's true goal—God (Ser. 264.2).

Augustine makes the same point when preaching on the story of Mary Magdalene at the tomb (Jn 20). Christ tells her not to touch him. "Why?" Augustine asks. He reminds his people of the story of the woman with a hemorrhage (Mt 9:21; Lk. 8:45–46). In the midst of a crowd pressing upon Him Jesus asks "Who touched me?" Of course, in the press of that crowd many were physically touching Jesus' body. But that is not the touch which heals and saves. By faith the woman had seen who he was; she perceived the Word. Seeing beyond the flesh by faith she had touched that Word and was healed (Ser. 243.2).

Touch means faith. To perceive Christ as the incarnate Word is to touch the ultimate reality beyond his flesh. This can be done only by faith in the ascended Christ. Thus Christ tells Mary not to touch him, i.e., not to touch his flesh which she sees. Rather, touch the Word by faith in the ascended Christ. Do not remain with the earthly but perceive the heavenly and have communion with the ascended One (Ser. 243.1 and .2). "He has ascended into heaven without departing from us, so we, too, are already there with Him...we are not separate from Him" for Christ tells those who wish to ascend "be my members" (Ser. 263.2).

> He has so attached us to Himself as His members that He is one and the same with us....He ascended with a body and with us who are destined to ascend, not by reason of our own virtue, but on account of our oneness with Him. For there are two in one flesh; this is the great mystery in Christ and in the Church (Ser. 263.3).

Here is the mystery of the Lord's body. The Word has returned to heaven with his body, the church. To believe is to touch, to have communion with the Word, to ascend with him. Mary at the tomb is a symbol of the church, and Christ's words are a reminder not to cling to the things of earth but to the heavenly. Persons of an earthly mentality see only the man. Believers have communion with the heavenly Christ as members of his body (Ser. 243.2).

For Augustine "body of Christ" refers to this entire mystery, the Word's incarnation and ascension with the church. He understands the union between Christ and his members as the work of the Holy Spirit. The church is a body. A body is made up of matter and soul. The soul unites and gives life to the body. So Christ and his members are united by their participation in the same Spirit. The Holy Spirit gives life to Christ's body and outside that body (the church) there is no Spirit, no life (Tract 27.6).

### III. AUGUSTINE'S NOTION OF "SACRAMENT"

Before turning to Augustine's eucharistic theology it is necessary to treat his understanding of sacrament. *Sacramentum* for Augustine refers not only to church rituals, to the liturgical signs. This term embraces the entire mystery presented in sign.

To appreciate Augustine's sacramental thought we must attend to his Neoplatonic view of the world. In this view all creation stems from the Word and, in some degree, reflects its creator. There is a hierarchy within creation and each level reflects God to the degree and in the manner appropriate to its nature. Because humanity is spiritual, created in the divine image, it is possible for us to "see" the Word manifest in creation. We can discover the deeper, invisible truth which is the source of the created world.

This perspective grounds Augustine's understanding of sacrament. The visible, sensible world signifies the invisible and spiritual. All reality is, in this sense, sacramental.

Thus, for Augustine, the visible can draw our spirits toward the spiritual. In his letter to Januarius (#55) Augustine observes that by the symbolic and allegorical the soul "is borne to corporeal representations and from them to spiritual ones, which are symbolized by those figures, it gains strength by that transition." In the Neoplatonic conception all creation suggests, signsforth, something higher and mysterious. This is how human psychology operates. Thus sacraments suggest, enflame and reveal. They afford the believer a glimpse of the divine reality signified, drawing us into the mystery. When material things (lower creation)

> are adapted to the dispensation of the sacraments, they become a
> sort of eloquence of redemptive doctrine, fit to win the affections
> of its disciples from the visible to invisible, from corporal to
> spiritual, from temporal to eternal.[1]

But, as seen earlier, humankind is trapped by sin in the earthly and can fail to see the divine reality manifest in creation. So it is with the sacraments which manifest the mystery of Christ. Their truth must be perceived with the eyes of faith, the *intellectus spiritualis*. Thus, Augustine cites Colossians. 3:1–3:

> If you have risen with Christ...seek the things that are above, where Christ is seated at the right hand of God. Mind the things that are above, not the things that are on earth (Ser. 321.3).

Recall Augustine's comments on Christ's injunction to Mary not to touch him in the earthly flesh, but to touch him by faith in the heavenly. This perspective is critical to Augustine's preaching on the eucharist.

Faith perceives a resemblance between the sign and the reality signified. This resemblance is not mere convention or the arbitrary decision of faith. The resemblance reflects the capacity of physical creation to manifest and draw humanity toward the spiritual. In Letter 98 Augustine observes:

> If the sacred rites had no resemblance to the things which they represent, they would not be sacred rites; they generally take their names from the mysteries they represent. As, then, in a certain manner the sacrament of the Body of Christ is the Body of Christ, and the sacrament of the blood of Christ is the blood of Christ.

So, too, the sacrament of faith, baptism, is the faith. Paul did not say "'We symbolize burial,' but says plainly: 'We are buried with Him.' Therefore, he calls the sacrament, which is the sign of so great effect, by the same name as the effect" (Letter 98). Augustine calls the resemblance between sign and signified "similitude."

Similitude reflects Augustine's Neoplatonism. Elements of physical creation manifest their origin in the higher, the spiritual. The capacity to see the spiritual thus manifest is the *intellectus spiritualis* and is a gift of faith. The function of the spoken word at the sacramental celebration (what the later tradition calls the form of the sacrament) is to proclaim the sign's meaning for the believer's understanding. For example, Augustine says of baptism,

> ...take away the word, and what is the water but water? The word is added to the element, and it becomes a sacrament, as it were, a visible word...when has water this so great a power to touch the body and wash the heart, but by the word doing it, not because it is spoken, but because it is believed.[2]

The word makes the sign's similitude explicit that the believer might encounter the mystery of Christ in the sign.

The suggestive character of "word" in the tradition allows Augustine to move from the church's sacramental rites to the sacramental nature of the entire mystery of salvation in Christ. Word refers not only to what is spoken at the church's rituals, but also to the word of faith and the Word made visible in the incarnation. Jesus is the Word, the sacrament par excellence. Augustine's writings and homilies reflect an interplay of these three meanings which again reflects his Neoplatonic perspective.

All creation manifests God's Word. When contemplated with the eyes of faith creation can draw the believer toward God. All is thus sacramental. In history the Word has been manifest in special signs that humanity might know God and have life. The manna and water from the rock are two examples (Ex 16, 17). Augustine says that Moses and Aaron ate the manna and did not die because they understood it spiritually (Tract 26:11). Finally, the eternal Word became flesh so that he might give life to those who have communion with him in faith.

This entire reality, from creation to Christ's ascension, is the mystery of Christian faith. It is the mystery of Christ and his body which is celebrated in the rites of the church. Augustine does not use the word "sacrament" in the later, more technical manner to refer to seven specific rites. "Sacrament" and "mystery" are used interchangeably. Christ is the Word eternally present to the Father, manifest in creation, prefigured in the Old Testament, incarnate and ascended with his members. This is Christ in the totality of his mystery, summing up the entire human relationship with God—a mystery culminating in our incorporation into the body of Christ. It is the mystery, the sacrament celebrated at the Lord's supper.

## IV. AUGUSTINE ON THE EUCHARIST

Augustine's theology of the eucharist reflects his understanding of the mystery of the Lord's body explicated above. Humanity hungers for God and is satisfied only in this food and drink taken for immortality. In the full and perfect fellowship of the saints there is perfect unity and peace. To this end the Lord gave us his body and blood in things, bread and wine, made one out of many parts, grain and grape (Tract 26:17).

In speaking to the newly baptized Augustine likens their initiation into the body of Christ to the making of bread. Like separate grains of wheat,

[Y]ou began to be ground into flour through fasting and exorcisms; afterwards, when you came to the font, you were sprinkled, and kneaded into one mass; then, the fire of the Holy Ghost having been enkindled, you were baked into bread—the bread of the Lord....You are there on the table; you are there in the chal-

ice. You are this body with us, for, collectively, we are this body
(Ser. 6).

Applying his theology of the word, Augustine says "that the bread
which you see on the altar, consecrated by the word of God, is the Body of
Christ...what the chalice holds, consecrated by the word of God, is the blood
of Christ." He reminds us of St. Paul's words, "...the bread is one; we
though many, are one body," for as the many grains of wheat have become
one bread, so by the fire of the Holy Spirit at Pentecost, "you became bread,
that is, the Body of Christ. Hence, in a certain manner, unity is signified.
You are members." Where is the head? In heaven so "Lift up your hearts!"
(Ser. 227)

In this sacrament the entire mystery of salvation is manifest.
Humanity, unable to find God and trapped in death, is raised up by Christ
and given his life. As food nourishes the body, so the Word nourishes the
soul, "by participation of the Son, through the unity of His body and blood,
which eating and drinking signify. We then, live by Him, eating Him, that is
receiving Him as that eternal life which of ourselves we do not have" (Tract
26:19).

Here Augustine's notion of similitude is at work. The reality is the
communion of members in Christ. In that communion believers are nour-
ished by the Word, drawn into heaven to the banquet of angels. Recall
Augustine's imagery when he spoke of the church's ascension with Christ:

In order that we might eat the bread of angels, the Lord of angels
became man (Ser. 225.1).
He has invited you to His own table, abounding in all good
things, the table of heaven, the table of angels where He Himself
is the bread (Ser. 231.5).

In view of humanity's tendency to cling to what is earthly, failing to
see the spiritual truth, Augustine warns his church that life comes from the
sacrament by eating inwardly (by faith) not simply by physically consuming
the bread and wine (Tract 26:12). Here is the meaning of the "Lift up your
hearts." Those who belong to the body by faith are ascended. They have the
faith, the *intellectus spiritualis* by which they see their eucharistic communion as a sign of heavenly communion. Without this vision there is no true
communion, but only a sign.

Augustine underscores this latter point in his homily on John 6:59–71
(Tract 27). Jesus proclaimed the need to eat his flesh and drink his blood if
one is to share in his life. Augustine begins by reminding his church that
these are mystical words in which Christ is admonishing them that they must

be in his body, as his members. To eat is to be in communion with Christ, to be part of his body.

Some of Jesus' followers heard these words and were scandalized. This was because they heard Jesus in an earthly manner, thinking he meant to divide his earthly flesh for them to eat. To contradict this earthly understanding Jesus asks, "What, then, if you were to see the Son of Man ascend to where he was before?" Augustine's point is the same as in the story of Mary at the tomb. True faith does not cling to the earthly but sees beyond to the ascended Christ.

Christ wants us to understand his words and see that life does not come from earthly flesh. To this end Jesus says, "It is the Spirit that gives life; the flesh is useless." Those without faith, failing to see the true meaning of Jesus' words, were horrified by his call to eat his flesh. But for those to whom the Spirit has granted faith, the ability to grasp the truth of Jesus' words, communion in the flesh is communion with the risen Lord—unity in the body of Christ.

To eat Christ's flesh and drink his blood means communion with him. We dwell in him as his members. As the human body has life by the soul, so the Body of Christ has unity and life by the Holy Spirit. The Spirit makes Christ and his members one organism. Those without the Spirit, outside the body, cling to the earthly and understand Jesus' words in an earthly manner. But believers understand. Communion in the body is an eating and drinking of the incarnate Word, a spiritual reality manifest (by similitude) in the eucharistic meal.

## V. SOME CONCLUDING REFLECTIONS

The point of this chapter is to show how Augustine's Neoplatonic worldview leads him to a rich eucharistic theology. Participation in the eucharist is participation in the entire mystery of Christ. Our celebration of the body of Christ is the celebration of our own mystery, of our unity in the risen Lord.

Readers familiar with Catholic theology might wonder about Augustine's position regarding the real presence. Does he hold the church's doctrine of transubstantiation?

The question is anachronistic. That is, it takes an issue from later theological disputes and asks it of Augustine's theology. Augustine never asked the question in this way. He did not focus on what happens to the elements of bread and wine. More, his Neoplatonic perspective never suggested the question of substance.

Augustine's lack of a clear answer to this later question has vexed western theologians since the Reformation. The nature of Christ's presence in the eucharist was an issue leading to the division of the church in the sixteenth century. Both Catholics and reformers claimed Augustine because there are elements in his thought which seem to favor both sides of this later dispute (1000 years later!).

Augustine has a good deal to teach us on this topic. The west's eucharistic controversies came to center on the elements (the bread and wine) and their relationship to the body of Christ. Are the consecrated bread and wine actually the body and blood of Christ? When we receive communion do we take the flesh and blood of Christ? How do we explain the change in the elements (transubstantiation, consubstantiation, transsignification, transfinalization)?

While important, these questions about the nature of the elements can distort the wider mystery of what occurs in the eucharistic celebration. Augustine's theology of eucharist places that wider reality before us. The risen body of Christ is not a resuscitated human body gone to heaven. Augustine reminds us that with Easter and Pentecost the "body" refers not simply to Jesus' earthly, physical body, but to the risen Christ—Head and members, living and dead. When we celebrate the eucharist we do not render an absent Christ present. Rather, the eucharist is the sacrament of the risen Lord who is always with us and to whose body we are already united.

Augustine's eucharistic homilies are of more than historical interest. They are a rich source for a renewed theology of the eucharist. While we may not live in his Neoplatonic universe, that perspective suggested to Augustine an understanding of the Lord's body which can enrich our own eucharistic thought and piety.

## BIBLIOGRAPHY

Quotations from Augustine's sermons in the preceding text are taken from *The Fathers of the Church,* volumes 11 and 38. Tracts 26 and 27 can be found in volume 79 of *The Fathers of the Church.* Augustine's *On Christian Doctrine* is a good introduction. For an account of Neoplatonism, and Augustine's philosophy, see Copleston's *A History of Philosophy,* Volume I, chapter 55 and Volume II, chapters 4–6. Peter Brown's *Augustine of Hippo* is an excellent biography.

## NOTES

1. See Augustine's Letter 55.
2. *Homilies on the Gospel of St. John*, Tract 80.3.

# PART II
# ST. THOMAS AQUINAS

The thought of St. Thomas Aquinas (1225—1274) has had a profound influence on Catholic philosophy and theology through most of the second millennium. Even in the theological tumult of the past fifty years, Thomas remains a key conversation partner. The practice of theology within the Catholic tradition requires familiarity with him.

The next five chapters consider the thought of St. Thomas as it appears within the contemporary philosophical and theological conversation. My goal is to introduce the reader to this contemporary conversation. That goal determines the topics treated.

Epistemological questions have dominated modern philosophy since Descartes. These concerns have affected the course and content of thought within the church. Catholic thinkers have introduced St. Thomas' description of human knowing into the modern, epistemological debate. This revival of Thomas follows two competing strategies. Some present Aquinas as an alternative to the modern project, while others place his thought in conversation with modern thinkers. In turn, these competing approaches to Thomas reflect wider ecclesial concerns and perspectives. Our consideration of Aquinas introduces us to this conversation and, one hopes, into the rich possibilities his thought offers.

Chapter 5 treats St. Thomas' description of knowledge. The reader is asked to study specified sections of the *Summa theologiae*. The chapter is commentary on these sections. The topics considered introduce some of the most important elements of St. Thomas' thought. Chapter 6 presents the historical context of the Thomistic revival. The chapter suggests that vying interpretations of St. Thomas reflect very different convictions about the relationship between the church and the modern world.

Chapters 7 and 8 ask the reader to think with St. Thomas about being.

This thinking is one of Aquinas' most profound contributions to western thought, a thinking essential to his understanding of God, creation and Christology. Lastly, chapter 9 considers Karl Rahner's interpretation of Aquinas, an interpretation that has profoundly influenced both Catholic and Protestant theology. Rahner's transcendental Thomism exemplifies how Aquinas can be placed in conversation with modern thought.

# CHAPTER 5

# AQUINAS' ACCOUNT OF
# HUMAN KNOWING

Writing introductory material about great thinkers is, at best, a questionable enterprise. If one wants to understand a philosopher or theologian one must study primary material, i.e., the works of that thinker. This book can serve as a companion to the study of primary sources. It is certainly no substitute for this most rewarding, if sometimes difficult task.

In this first chapter on St. Thomas Aquinas the reader is asked to read specified sections of the *Summa theologiae*. What follows is a brief commentary on these selections. The comments below are few and selective. The sections of the *Summa* considered contain a wealth of material not touched upon. The purpose of the chapter is to familiarize the reader with some basic elements of Aquinas' philosophy and, thereby, to begin thinking with him.

The structure of St. Thomas Aquinas' *Summa* is determined by the academic traditions of his time. Theological questions were disputed and debated. The *Summa* reflects these debates. It is divided into questions or topics. In turn, these questions are subdivided into a number of articles. Each article asks a specific question. For example, the first question in the *Summa* treats "The Nature and Extent of Sacred Doctrine." The first article of this question asks, "Whether, besides Philosophy, Any Further Doctrine is Required?"

Having asked a question, Thomas first presents "Objections." The Objections are answers to the question which differ from the answer Aquinas will propose in the body of the article.

Following the objections Thomas presents his own position. He begins by citing an authority ("On the contrary..."). Here one finds quotations from scripture, church teaching, Aristotle, Augustine, and so on. Aquinas then argues for his answer to the question ("I answer that..."). After Thomas has presented his position he concludes the article with specific answers to the objections with which the article began ("Reply Obj. 1...").

While very important material frequently occurs in the objections and replies, it might be easiest to read the question under consideration (the heading under the article number) and then go directly to "I answer that."

The sections commented on below treat St. Thomas' description of human knowing:

*Summa theologiae* Part I, q. 79, arts. 2, 3, 4, and 9;

q. 84;

q. 85, arts. 1–5.

I suggest you read from the *Summa* before looking at these comments. Let St. Thomas speak for himself.

QUESTION 79:

Art. 2—Potency and act are critical here, as in much of St. Thomas. Potentiality refers to a capacity for something. Act refers to the state of attainment. To be human is to be a potential lover. To love a close friend is act.

Aquinas holds that human beings are a potency for knowledge of everything. When we know a specific thing that potency comes partially to act. The reference to the Divine Intellect is to pure act. God has no potentiality for God knows everything, i.e. God is pure act.

In Thomas' answer he makes reference to being, intellect, God, angels, and humanity. This might seem an odd combination of terms, but it reflects Aquinas' understanding of the relationship between knowledge and the hierarchy of being. We must pause here a moment with this difficult notion.

We cannot understand God but, to grasp Thomas' point, let me suggest a thought experiment. Pay attention to your present state of consciousness. You are thinking of something and are aware of yourself in that thought. I can suggest a series of ideas or images which you bring to mind (e.g., your mother, car, school, shoes, and so on). At each suggestion you are conscious of that object, or memory, or image. You are yourself (self-conscious) in that thought. In a sense, you exist as self-conscious in your attending to the image suggested.

From this thought exercise we can extrapolate to Aquinas' notion of God. God is one simple act of Self-consciousness in which all being (everything) is known. The divine Being is one simple *act* of self-awareness in which all beings are known. There is no potency in God for there is no more than what God is. God possesses all being(s) in one divine act of existence— pure Being or absolute Being.

God is the "top" of the hierarchy of being. We humans are quite a way down. We are not as far down as rocks, which lack life and self-consciousness, but we are a long way from God. One can think about everything that exists in terms of how close to God it is. Rocks are unconscious matter. Plants live and have a form of consciousness in that, for example, they turn to the sun. Dogs live and have a rather high form of animal consciousness. Then there are we humans, and above us angels. This hierarchy of consciousness is a hierarchy of being. God knows all being in one simple act of Self-consciousness. Each time we know something we attain more being, i.e., we possess (know) more of what is.

As spirits in a body we come to know more by knowing particular objects, i.e., I know this tree, then another tree, and so on. Angels are important in Thomas' epistemology because they stand as a kind of "half-way house" between humanity and God. Angels, as pure spirits (they have no bodies despite all the pictures you've seen) do not come to knowledge by knowing particular physical objects. Rather, by the infusion of a universal idea, they know it completely, in all its instances. For example, by infused knowledge of the universal "tree" they know all trees. Thus, their knowledge fulfills the potency to know tree (act) in a way beyond human competence.

In this article Thomas points to this difference between angelic knowledge, which stands closer to the divine intellect, and human. The human intellect is a clean tablet upon which all reality can be written, i.e., we are potential to know all. That potential comes to act by knowing specific beings. In sensation we encounter beings to be known. In this way our understanding is passive, i.e., it receives (in sensation) what it has the potential to know (act). The next article indicates that the mind is also active in achieving knowledge.

Art. 3—This article deals with the critical difference between the epistemologies of Plato and Aristotle (with Aquinas following the latter whom he calls "the philosopher"). For Plato *the real* are the forms. Ideas are the ultimate reality, the sensed objects of the physical world are imitations. In contrast, for Aristotle and Aquinas the objects of experience are the real. *All human knowledge* begins with the physical world, even our knowledge of Being and first principles.

Aquinas states that the form of the sensed object is not known directly. God and angels know the universal, forms, directly. Humanity does not know in this fashion. Rather, we encounter individual things, "informed" matter. Perhaps in contemporary English the phrases "matter in some form" or "matter in the shape of..." say it better.

But knowing is not simply looking, as if my mind grasped the universal, the idea, the form directly (Plato). In Aquinas' epistemology the mind is active. It must go to work on sensation. Only in the activities of abstraction (formation of a concept, e.g., tree) and judgment does the human mind come to know.

Thus, knowing is not simply passive. The intellect moves from potency to act by its own activity, its dynamism to know. This point is critical to much of contemporary Thomism.

Art. 4—Two points are of interest here. Aquinas cites Aristotle to call that power in the soul which makes things knowable, "light." It is the active intellect which sheds light on the sensed object, moving from simple sensation to knowledge.

Second, Aquinas argues that this power in the soul requires the divine Intellect. God creates a rationally ordered world. That is, creation reflects and operates according to the design of its creator (exemplary causality). God also creates embodied spirits (humanity) with the capacity to come to know the rest of creation, i.e., to repeat the divine act of understanding. Humanity is created in the image of God.

Art. 9—Here we see what a down-to-earth thinker Thomas is. The point of this article is that *all* human knowledge is based in the experience of the concrete, sensible world. "Higher" knowledge (of God, the spiritual and first principles) is rooted in the "lower" functions of reason, i.e., encounters with the concrete, physical world.

The foundation of this insight is Aquinas' notion of human nature as embodied spirit. Body and spirit (soul) are not two "things" coming together. There is no human spirit apart from its encounter with the material world. The soul is the form of the body. It is potentiality for knowledge and love. But that potentiality can only come to being (act) through encounter with what is other, i.e., physical objects to know and people to love. Our highest achievements are always grounded in our interaction with the physical world. Thus, the human spirit is not trapped in flesh, in the physical, seeking for release to its higher, spiritual home, as in Plato. The human soul belongs in the body and needs the body to be.

In terms of modern philosophy, note how Aquinas' position is located somewhere between empiricism and rationalism. Rational functions, including first principles, are rooted in sense experience but reason is not reducible to sensation.

QUESTION 84:

Art. 1—The problem at issue in this article goes back to the origins of western thought. Knowing involves the combination of a particular physical object with a universal concept. For example, this object (particular) is a tree (universal). Specific things are always changing, yet knowledge involves universal and unchanging concepts. For example, I may look out to an object and call it tree. Later in the day I might call it lumber, and a week later I call it house. This constant change undermines the possibility of certain knowledge, of permanence, of truth.

Plato's response was to make the reference of knowledge not material objects but the eternal forms which they reflect. Aquinas rejects this thesis on a number of grounds, the most important of which is that it makes physical science impossible.

Aquinas thinks that Plato made his mistake by thinking that the form (the object of knowledge) must exist in the knower and known in the same manner. In us (knowers) forms are universal, immaterial and unchanging. So the objects known must in some sense possess (or be possessed by) similar forms. [Note that in this scheme the object of knowledge is the form, the idea, rather than the particular thing. This position is philosophical idealism. Aquinas, in contrast to Plato, is a realist. The real is the concrete object, not the idea through which we know it.]

Aquinas responds with one of his most famous dictums: "The received is in the receiver according to the mode of the receiver." My knowledge of that object involves my possession of a universal idea, "tree." But I ought not conclude that the concept tree occurs in the object in the same way as it occurs in my mind. Rather, I possess the form of the object in the manner proper to human knower (embodied spirit), not in the manner of the tree.

Perhaps the distinction can be clarified by saying that the object I see is matter in the shape of a tree. The word "shape" does not suggest that there is a concept or idea "out there" in the object. My mind grasps the shape through an idea. Shapes exist in human knowers as concepts. In contrast, objects are simply matter in some shape, matter in some form.

Art. 2—There are two significant points at work in this article. First, the hierarchy of being appears again. We saw above that God exists at the top of this hierarchy. God is pure act, pure intelligence. At the bottom is prime matter.

Prime matter does not exist as such. By definition it cannot. Prime matter is un-in-formed matter (matter without shape). I challenge you to imagine it. Whatever you imagine is matter in some form. Prime matter is a limit concept for Aquinas. He sees reality as a hierarchy from God to angels to humans to animals to plants to rocks. Note that this hierarchy is a hierarchy of consciousness and a hierarchy in capacity to know. The higher the level of existence the more conscious and the less material. Further, the higher the level, the more to know, the more intelligibility. When one reaches God there is all being in one act of intelligibility.

In this scheme, therefore, the more material, the less intelligible. Matter itself, without form, is unintelligible. What we know, the intelligible, is the form or shape of a thing. Intelligibility is, therefore, immaterial. This is the second point which flows from the first. While as embodied spirits we know through the physical world, knowledge itself is not material. We need sensation and imagination to know but knowledge does not occur on that level. To know something is an act of intelligibility.

Let us try another thought experiment to make this point. I say the word "tree" or "car." You may think of a specific car or you may imagine a car (picture one in your mind). But the word has meaning even without that picture. I can say "vehicle" and you know the meaning of the word without any image. We have come to know the meaning of these words by seeing cars and trees, or by imagining. But the words have meaning free of seeing or image. That meaning is intelligibility, the substance, what we know.

[While we cannot pursue it here, this point is critical to St. Thomas' theology of eucharist. His use of the term "transubstantiation" relies on it. Transubstantiation refers to the change of bread and wine into the body and blood of Christ. What changes in the bread and wine cannot be seen or imagined. The substance of the bread and wine, what they are for the intellect, changes. The accidents, what bread and wine are for the senses (and imagination), remain the same.]

Arts. 3 and 4—Aquinas here sets his own position against that of Plato both epistemologically (3) and metaphysically (4). For Plato, the forms exist apart from matter. Knowledge is memory of an inner intelligibility. The human soul is a substance separate from matter. In contrast, for Aristotle and Aquinas, forms exist in matter (matter in some form). All knowledge comes from sensation. The human soul is the form of the body.

Art. 5—Here we see the influence of Augustine in Aquinas' thought. Augustine had been influenced by Neoplatonism, which placed Plato's forms (ideas) in the mind of God. Christian thinkers found this a congenial notion and Aquinas exploits it here. Things (creatures) are what they are because they reflect the divine design (exemplary causality). In this sense things reflect eternal forms. Human beings come to a share in this knowledge by knowing particular, material objects (again, contrast the human way of knowing with that of God and angels). God's very Being is a simple act of consciousness in which all beings are known. Our knowledge, intellectual light, is a small share in the eternal, divine light.

Art. 6—Here we come to Thomas' own position. Human knowledge is both passive and active. It is passive in that it begins with sensation. But knowing is not simply taking a look. The active intellect renders the data of sense intelligible. "Phantasms" refer to your seeing an object. For example, you see a car. Your image of the car is not, of course, the material object itself, but the phantasm (the object possessed as sensed and imagined).

Art. 7—Again, all human knowledge is rooted in sensation, even our most abstract and speculative knowledge. "Turn to the phantasm" means attending to sensed objects directly or in memory or imagination. Abstract knowledge remains rooted here and thus we speak of the "depths" of the soul or how "far above us" is God. Thomas compares our knowledge to that of angels, who know the universal directly while we reach the universal through knowing particular material objects.

[Karl Rahner's first philosophical work, *Spirit in the World,* deals with this article. He sees here a similarity to Kant, who held that all knowledge is of sensed objects (phenomena). On this basis Kant denied the possibility of metaphysics based on knowledge. Rahner tries to think with Aquinas about Kant's problem. How is it possible to build a metaphysics if knowledge is properly ordered to material objects (as Aquinas holds here)? Rahner locates the grounds for metaphysics in the ability of the intellect to move from sensation to abstraction and judgment. This is a contemporary interpretation (retrieval) of St. Thomas. St. Thomas lived centuries before Kant and never directly addressed this question. Chapter 9 treats Rahner's interpretation of Aquinas.]

QUESTION 85:

Art. 1—Aquinas now must offer an account of human knowledge based on the premise that all knowledge begins with the turn to the phantasm, the image of the sensed object. What one knows is the knowable, the intelligible. Matter of itself is unintelligible. But the objects we encounter are always matter is some form (the form of a tree, car, etc.). The intellect must attend to the phantasm and abstract from it the form, the intelligible.

In the reply to objection 1 Aquinas points out that not all elements of the phantasm belong to the universal, the form. Thus, one might see an object and know it to be a car. The facts that it is red, two-door, dirty, etc., do not belong to the universal idea of car. No specific instance of a material nature (a car, tree, human being) exhausts that nature. Matter is the individualization of a universal. The intellect, in grasping the universal, leaves behind the specific characteristics of the individual instance of the nature, grasping the universal. This is why, for Aquinas, there is no generic angelic nature. Angels have no bodies. They are not material. Since matter is the principle of individualization, each angel is a unique nature.

Art. 2—The human intellect knows by way of abstracting the universal. But the known is the object, not the idea by which we know the object. Knowledge deals with the world of sense experience, not with our ideas. Plato, of course, made the ideas the "objects" of knowledge. Aristotle and Aquinas hold that ideas (forms, species) are the means by which we come to know concrete objects of experience.

This same point is related to modern epistemology. Thomistic realists frequently understand the entire modern philosophical project (since Descartes) as driven by the mistaken notion that ideas are the object of knowledge. When we turn to our own consciousness first we have already abandoned the proper object of knowledge, i.e., the world of physical objects. Thus Descartes must "prove" the existence of the "external" world. Berkeley, a rationalist, suggested there was no external world of physical objects. Kant held that we can only know the phenomena, i.e., things as they appear to us. About the noumenal (the physical world as it actually is) we can say nothing. The error here is the mistaken notion that we know what is in the mind rather than the real, common sense world.

Art. 3—"At the same time" here means in one act of being conscious of a form (universal). Thus, when you think car you understand all cars in that one act. But you do not also understand all trees in this act. In contrast, God understands everything, creator and creatures, in one act. That one divine act of understanding is God's very Being.

Art. 4—This very brief article takes us to the heart of Thomas' epistemology. It is helpful to see it in reference to Art. 2 of this question (85). In abstraction we are dealing with ideas, thinking. But we have not reached truth. Truth occurs in judgment when I know the sensed object in reference to its proper form.

Truth occurs in judgment when I achieve (know) the being of the object. "This is a tree." Ontological truth is the being of the thing itself. The physical object is a tree by its conformity to divine design and creation. Cognitional truth occurs when we judge what the object *is*. Truth and being coincide.

"Composition and division" refer to judgment. These are most easily understood in their spoken form. Composition is what Kant calls a synthetic proposition. "This (object experienced) *is* a tree." In judgment I come to know the proper form of the object. (Recall art. 2, the goal of knowledge is not the concept but the concrete object.)

All composition (synthetic propositions) implies division. Division is negation. This object is not a car. When I say the object is a tree by implication I negate an infinite number of other possibilities (it is not a car, a dog, a person, or *anything* else). So division can occur directly in a judgment (it is not a car) or implicitly in all composition.

Generally "composition and division" are simply referred to as judgment. Note that for Thomas' realism when we reach judgment we reach what *is*, being. This fact is fundamental to many contemporary interpretations of Aquinas.

Thomas again compares human knowledge to that of God and angels.

In judgments we work our way toward more and more knowledge, more and more of what is, being. God, for St. Thomas, is one simple act of absolute Being in that God knows everything, possesses all being, in one simple act of Self-consciousness. The hierarchy of being thus appears to be a hierarchy of knowledge. The more we know the more we are. This is Aquinas' understanding of Aristotle's position in *De Anima* (Bk. III, chap. 4 and 5) that the soul can become all things.

These brief comments on the epistemology of St. Thomas already allude to the different ways in which his thought can be interpreted today. His realism can be seen as an alternative to the modern philosophical project and its methodology of doubt. Or his thought can be placed in conversation with modern thinkers, an approach exemplified by Karl Rahner. These alternatives and their place within wider ecclesial issues are the topic of the next chapter.

## BIBLIOGRAPHY

Peter Kreeft has published *A Summa of the Summa* which is accurately described as "The essential philosophical passages of St. Thomas Aquinas' *Summa theologiae* edited and explained for beginners." Kreeft is an excellent teacher whose notes help clarify difficult material, though sometimes with rather opinionated asides. Copleston, *A History of Philosophy*, Vol. II, chapter 38 is an excellent secondary work on Aquinas' theory of knowledge.

# CHAPTER 6

# ST. THOMAS AND RECENT CATHOLIC THEOLOGY

## I. THE CONTEXT

Since the apologists Catholic Christianity has seen philosophy as an ally in the faith's quest for God. Human efforts to understand point toward revelation; revealed truth complements and completes reason. The theology and doctrine of the ancient church reflects the middle and Neoplatonism of its age. Medieval theology reached its zenith when St. Thomas placed the faith in conversation with the "new" thought of his time, i.e., with Aristotle.

The classical philosophy of Plato and Aristotle offered a rational road to God and to a world reasonably ordered. The metaphysics of these ancient traditions established both the existence of God and humanity's relationship with the divine. The world was reasonably ordered by its creator. Humanity could know that order and conform to it, thus choosing the good.

But the relationship between Catholic orthodoxy and modernity has proved less congenial. When Descartes doubted everything he drove a wedge between the knower and nature, breaking humanity's natural relationship with reality. He isolated the self and cognition (thinking, ideas). He attended to mind and its operations first (reason, rationalism), rendering the very existence of the physical world problematic (i.e., subject to doubt). Commonsense realism was abandoned.

Modern philosophy begins with Descartes and reaches its zenith in Kant. Kant's account of human knowledge excludes metaphysics. The questions of God, freedom, and the immortality of the soul cannot be answered by reason for they do not fall within its competence. The human mind can know the world of sensation but cannot move beyond this realm to metaphysics.

For example, the category of causality leads to knowledge when applied to physical phenomena. Knowing involves two poles, (1) mind applied to (2) empirical data (what we sense). So science can know the causal relationships between empirical events. But arguments for God's existence which are based on causality misuse this category. Rather than the application of the category to sense experience, these arguments reflect on causality itself (there must be a first, uncaused cause). While a natural tendency, such exercises of "pure reason" do not lead to knowledge.

Thus, Kant's epistemology excludes a rational demonstration of God's existence. The link between reason and faith is broken.

During the eighteenth and nineteenth centuries the Catholic theological response to modernity took various forms. Many theologians accepted the modern problematic and attempted to rethink the issues on that basis. Fideism abandoned the field, accepting the discontinuity between faith and reason. Ontologism argued for a direct intuition of God. Humanity in its natural state already participates in the divine. The distinction between nature and grace, the natural and supernatural, reason and faith, was thus abandoned. But, finally, at the end of the nineteenth century, papal leadership in the church rejected such efforts to accommodate modernity. Catholicism eschewed modern thought as wrong-headed and returned to Aquinas.

One element of this return was the church's formal condemnation of theological efforts to accommodate the faith to modernity. These condemnations reflected a fundamental conviction of the neo-Thomists: modern thought was in error. The turn to the subject, beginning with Descartes, was the death knell of realism. Modernity's emphasis on autonomous reason was the consequence of the Reformation and its rejection of the church's (and revelation's) authority. The remedy for this unhappy state of affairs was a rejection of modernity and a return to the realism of Aquinas.

All this occurred within a political atmosphere where the church was more and more isolated and under attack. This was the era of the French Revolution, the rise of liberal democracy and nationalism. The church had allied itself with the ancien régime, with the absolutist systems of monarchy characteristic of pre-revolutionary times. The pope was king of the papal states, a kingdom taken from him by force in 1870 by a newly united Italy. With the loss of his kingdom and the fall of Rome Pius IX and his immediate successors were physically isolated, "prisoners of the Vatican."

The church stood against modernity and all its works. This period of reaction reached its doctrinal high point in 1854 with Pius IX's promulgation of the *Syllabus of Errors*, a list of erroneous propositions. The list gathered previous condemnations and concluded by rejecting the proposition that the "Roman Pontiff can and ought to reconcile and adjust himself with progress, liberalism and modern civilization."

The Thomist revival, neo-Thomism, was in some degree the theoretical element in the church's fight against modernity. Among its advocates was Gioacchino Cardinal Pecci. In 1878 he became Pope Leo XIII. His encyclical *Aeterni Patris* (1879) made neo-Thomism *the* Catholic philosophy and theology. It was especially recommended for the preparation of priests.

Leo XIII championed Thomism because, unlike modern thought, it fit the description of philosophy and theology set forth by Vatican I in *Dei fil-ius*. Thomism provided rational arguments for God's existence, the divine attributes, the possibility of revelation, and the basis for vindicating the signs of that revelation in Christ and his church. More, according to Aristotle's model, Thomism was a scientifically organized and unified body of philosophical and revealed truths. Finally, Thomism provided the church with solid arguments against her opponents. [1]

*Aeterni Patris* treated Thomism as a unified, seemingly consistent school stemming back to Aquinas. Leo XIII, and the neo-Thomists of his day, indicate little awareness of the variety of perspectives which comprise the scholastic tradition. Among Thomas' contemporaries, and certainly among his commentators, there is pluralism of perspectives which would soon come to light. Leo's encyclical released in the church an interest in Aquinas which would renew Catholic theology and, ironically, lead toward the theological pluralism of today. [2]

The twentieth century has seen a slow accommodation of the church to modernity, culminating in Vatican II's pastoral constitution *Gaudium et spes*, "The Church in the Modern World." Philosophy and theology have followed the same path, reflecting more and more openness to modern and contemporary thought. This opening was not a rejection of Aquinas. Rather, it took the form of placing St. Thomas in conversation with modern thought. In the 1920s, for example, Joseph Maréchal sought a Thomistic response to the philosophical issues raised by Kant. But other Thomists, like Etienne Gilson, rejected such attempts as the abandonment of Thomistic realism.

Arguments over theological orthodoxy in the Catholic Church frequently reflect this issue. Can Catholic theology offer an account of the faith using modern and contemporary thought, or is orthodoxy bound to the realism of St. Thomas? Karl Rahner and Bernard Lonergan, two theological giants of the century, are correctly identified with openness to modernity. Each pursued his path by interpreting St. Thomas; each considered himself a student of Aquinas. Their interpretations make conscious use of modern thought, claiming as their precedent Thomas' own spirit of openness to the new thought of his time. In contrast, others see the introduction of modern categories into Aquinas as a compromise of his realism and, thus, a threat to Christian truth.

What follows briefly presents examples of these two approaches. Etienne Gilson insists that Thomas' realism excludes (a priori) the introduction of modern, "critical" methods. Karl Rahner uses Kant, Hegel and Heidegger to interpret St. Thomas.

## II. GILSON: THE REALISM OF ST. THOMAS

Ironically, Etienne Gilson was introduced to St. Thomas while writing on Descartes. Gilson intended to study the scholastic background to Descartes' thought. What he found in medieval philosophy, and especially in Aquinas, was a common-sense realism which stood in contradiction to Descartes and modern philosophy. Gilson concluded that modern thought was simply wrong. He spent his academic career (between the first and second world wars) studying and writing on Thomas and medieval philosophy.

The neo-Thomist revival had, by the 1920s, led in many different directions, including efforts to place Aquinas' thought in conversation with modern philosophy. For example, Joseph Maréchal, the father of transcendental Thomism, sought the grounds for metaphysics in a Kantian conversation with Thomas. Maréchal and others called themselves "critical realists." "Critical" refers to the Cartesian-Kantian project to secure a sure foundation for knowledge. The aim was a critical reading of Aquinas to recapture his realism. More simply put, critical realism was an effort to offer St. Thomas as an answer to the modern, philosophical quest for certainty.

In his work *Thomist Realism and the Critique of Knowledge* Gilson argues that the term "critical realism" is contradictory when applied to St. Thomas. The critical thought of Descartes and Kant turns to the mind, to thought, in order to guarantee the existence of the physical world and knowledge of it. This turn is already the abandonment of realism and, once taken, realism can never be regained.

Thomas does not begin with doubt. Rather, his starting point is the common-sense givenness of the physical world. Realism is characterized by the conviction that the mind immediately grasps a reality which exists independently of the mind's awareness. In sensation we are present to what is, beings. The thing (object) itself is given in sensation. In abstraction and judgment one penetrates the given to its intelligibility.

Gilson sees modern, critical thought and Thomism as two alternatives. One can begin with doubt (thought) or one can begin with being. But one cannot begin with both. Beginning with doubt, as Descartes exemplifies, means beginning with thought. One seeks in the mind for a secure foundation. But once in the mind there is no way out. There is idealism or solipsism, but realism is impossible. This is why Gilson holds "critical realism" to be a contradiction.

Descartes' methodic doubt had only one certain starting point, the mind's thinking. Doubt itself confirms this immediate given. To get out of mind, Descartes had to introduce God as guarantor that sensation was of a real world, *res extensa*. Descartes' argument for God rests on causality, i.e., that the idea of an infinite Being cannot be caused by a finite being. I, a finite being, cannot be the cause of the ideas of perfection and infinity. More, as a finite being I cannot cause my existence. Therefore, there must be a God.

Gilson points out that this argument for God presumes causality. What is the basis for this presumption? What is the source of Descartes' conviction that all things have a cause? If this conviction belongs to the doubting mind it cannot demonstrate the existence of God, for what is to guarantee the need for causal relationships? Or, if all Descartes has established is the *cogito* (I think), then he has no basis for presuming that everything is caused.

In contrast, Gilson points out that for Aquinas (against Kant and Descartes) causality is not an a priori category of mind. There are no a priori mental categories. Whatever is in the mind is first in the senses. We learn causality from the real world of physical events. Thus, Aquinas' arguments for the existence of God are based on the physical world, not on the a priori conditions of mind. His five ways are a posteriori demonstrations moving from the created world to its cause.[3]

Aquinas' position relates to his anthropology. Descartes' sharp distinction between *res cogitans* and *res extensa*, between mind and body, subject and object, does not occur in St. Thomas. Physical objects are present to us because they exist and we are physical. We know them because they are knowable and we have the capacity to grasp the intelligibility which is given in their physical being (matter in some form).

Soul is the form of human existence, not a spiritual ego inside the body. The act of knowing (sensation, abstraction, judgment) is the accomplishment of a unified human being (body and soul). Human access to being occurs in both sensation and judgment, acts which are intrinsically related. The division of subject (ego) from body breaks with the way we naturally experience things. The reality of the physical world in sensation is self-evident. We know being ("That is a tree") by a unified act of sensation and intellect.

Gilson thus rejects the entire modern project which begins with Descartes. The mind-body distinction and methodic doubt violate the common-sense world as we know it. Cast in this artificial mold, modern thought has pursued a thousand dead ends. Gilson's work is a call to return to common-sense realism.

### III. KARL RAHNER: TRANSCENDENTAL THOMISM

Chapter 9 treats Rahner's thought in detail. This section briefly contrasts his approach to St. Thomas with that of Gilson.

Rahner begins with the modern problem. Specifically, he begins with Kant's argument that human knowledge is incapable of proving God's existence. Kant's position rests on the conviction that the categories of human knowing can be properly applied only to empirical data. Rahner observes that Aquinas begins with a similar premise. All knowledge begins with sensation. There is nothing in the intellect that is not first in the senses. How then is metaphysics and a knowledge of God possible?

Rahner does not claim to see in Aquinas an explicit answer to Kant's question. This is not a question Aquinas specifically addressed. He lived six hundred years before Kant raised the question. Rather, Rahner is seeking possibilities within St. Thomas' thought that can be applied to this later question.

Specifically, Rahner asks Kant's epistemological question of St. Thomas. Kant asked about the conditions of subjectivity, of mind, which made knowledge possible. This turn to the subject is the characteristic of transcendental thought. Rahner begins with St. Thomas' description of knowing and asks about the conditions of mind which make abstraction and judgment possible. What must be true of mind for it to carry out these operations described by Aquinas? Thus, Rahner is called a transcendental Thomist.

Rahner argues (as we shall see in chapter 9) that for the mind to form a universal concept from sense experience, the mind must already possess some notion of universality. This notion of universality is the necessary condition for abstraction. It is an openness to the infinite, to infinite Being, which grounds Rahner's argument for God's existence.

Note how Rahner has thus contradicted the fundamental thrust of Gilson's Thomistic realism. Gilson underscored Aquinas' position that there is *nothing* in the intellect which is not first in the senses. Rahner's Kantian question introduces an a priori "content" to intellect as the necessary condition for knowing. The transcendental subject brings to every experience an a priori grasp of the infinite. Thus, for Rahner, there is something in the intellect which was not first in the senses, i.e. a transcendental openness to (thus, experience of) the divine.

Rahner does not hold that the transcendental openness to the infinite Being exists whole and entire prior to sense experience. Rather, it only occurs in sensation, in its awareness of the other. Sensation, spirit in the world, actuates human subjectivity. The subject only occurs through sensation and the recurring operations of abstraction and judgment. But, having said that, the human subject so actualized brings to sensation an a priori grasp of infinitude which, in Rahner's theology, proves to be an experience of God's Self-offer.

The modern character of Rahner's interpretation is manifest in his argument for God's existence. Infinite Being is the necessary condition for abstraction and judgment. God's existence is not proved inductively from reflection on causal relationships in the natural world. Rather, God is deduced as a necessary condition for the agent intellect's actions. If the mind reaches being in judgment, what is, then its openness requires a horizon of universal Being.

In contrasting Gilson and Rahner it is important to realize the nature of their difference. It is not a matter of who offers the most accurate account of what Aquinas said. Rahner was not attempting history. In his introduction to *Spirit in the World,* Rahner describes his interpretation of Aquinas as philosophy itself, a dialogue with Thomas from the modern perspective. The fact that his interpretation reflects modern philosophy is not a negative. Rahner intends to place Thomas in conversation with modern thought.

Thus, Rahner and Gilson differ in the nature of their projects. Gilson turned to Aquinas as an alternative to modern thought. To admit the modern problematic is already to have abandoned the essence of Aquinas' realism. In contrast, Rahner uses modern thought to interpret St. Thomas, developing a philosophical perspective out of a conversation between modernity and Thomism. These are two quite different approaches to Aquinas that flow out of the neo-Thomistic revival. While they are not the only philosophical approaches at work in contemporary Catholic thought, they are certainly two of the most important.

## BIBLIOGRAPHY

For the history of Catholic theology during the nineteenth century, see Gerald McCool, *Catholic Theology in the Nineteenth Century,* especially pp. 216–267. For Gilson's critique of critical realism, see Etienne Gilson, *Thomist Realism and the Critique of Knowledge.* Selections from the works of Joseph Maréchal may be found in *A Maréchal Reader.* Francis Schüssler Fiorenza's "Karl Rahner and the Kantian Problematic," the preface of the English edition of *Spirit in the World*, suggests the relationship between Kant and Rahner which I have presented in this chapter. Rahner presents his own method for interpreting Aquinas in the introduction to *Spirit in the World.*

## NOTES

1. McCool, 228–229.
2. McCool, pp. 129–144, 226–267.
3. *Summa theologiae* Part I, question 2, articles 2 and 3.

# CHAPTER 7

# BEING, GOD AND CREATION

The purpose of this chapter is not to offer a documented account of Aquinas' understanding of being, God and creation. Rather, based on what has preceded, the following remarks invite the beginning student in philosophy and theology to think about some very difficult material with St. Thomas.

To gain insight into Thomas' notion of God one must be able to think "being." One must grasp the distinction between essence and existence. On that basis one can appreciate Thomas' definition of God as the Being in whom essence and existence coincide. Creation can then be seen as God's granting existence to that which is not divine. Finally, the grounds for human knowledge of the divine mystery are established in the analogy of being.

All of this is quite difficult and abstract. But if one is really to understand Thomistic philosophy and theology it is necessary to think about these matters. The only way to do so is to begin.

## I. THINKING BEING

In chapter 5, in comments on three questions from the *Summa*, a hierarchy of being was mentioned. God, at the top, is pure being. Prime matter is at the bottom. This hierarchy suggests a picture of reality coming from God down. We, in a sense, picture all that exists. We imagine a kind of cosmic ladder with God on top, then angels slightly below, then humans, then animals, then plants, and finally rocks. Note that in this picture God is part of reality, part of what is included in our imagined hierarchy.

But, of course, this will not do. God is not one being among others. More, consider the perspective from which we imagine the hierarchy of being. That is, when drawing this picture of God and reality, where do we stand? The implicit perspective of our imagined hierarchy places us outside God and creation, looking back so to speak. Our imagined picture places us "beyond" God and creation, viewing all being. There is no such perspective.

The point to appreciate with these last considerations is that we *cannot* imagine the relationship between God and creation. If we do we make God one more thing, even if the highest and most powerful. We place ourselves above or beyond God and this is idolatry. While St. Thomas holds that everything we know begins with sensation and imagination, our thought about God cannot remain on this level. While our speech about God (in prayer and theology) evokes images, we must always be aware that these images are for us and do not grasp the divine. God remains mystery.

But Thomas' thought offers another way to think about God, one not tied to imagination. What we have learned about Aquinas' epistemology can open this way of thinking. Knowledge is not simply "taking a look," sensation. To know involves abstraction and judgment. Truth occurs in judgment and judgments of truth are expressed in propositions, assertions (e.g. "That is a tree"). This speech, judgments expressed in language, manifests a distinction implicit in the act of knowledge, a distinction which makes possible a deeper way to think about God and creation.

When we considered Thomas' account of knowing we saw that the agent intellect performs two functions. It abstracts and judges. In abstraction the intellect forms a concept, an idea. Judgment adds no new content to this concept as an idea. Judgment adds something else—existence.

If I see a strange object, for example, and ask its inventor what it is, the answer will be conceptual. The inventor will explain to me what this machine does and, perhaps, how it works. My interests, previous information, and intelligence will allow me to form a more or less adequate concept. In the future when I come across this object I will have the proper concept, I will know what it is. I might walk into an office where there are ten such machines. I look around and judge that these ten objects are such and such a machine. That is, I know these objects to be matter in the form of this machine. That is their nature. Note that these ten judgments add nothing to the concept. I learn nothing more about the machine. I simply know that there are ten instances (hypostases) of this nature in the room.

The judgment of existence adds nothing to the concept. But it does tell me something very important—it exists. I can ask if you know what a time machine is. You answer that a time machine is a device that would allow us to travel to the past or the future. That is the concept (nature, form, essence). Does such a machine exist? No. Note, the negative answer tells us nothing about what "time machine" means. But it does tell us something terribly important. This concept, essence, does not occur in the real world as the form of an existing object.

We make this distinction quite regularly in language through our use of the verb "to be." Is there a God? Are there angels? Do you know what a vampire is? Are there vampires? Your various answers to these questions imply a distinction between essence, what a thing is, and existence. When you answer (I presume) that there are no vampires, your answer implies an understanding (concept) of vampire and the judgment that this concept has no reference in reality. To say "There is no God" or "I do not believe in angels" manifests the distinction between essence and existence. To make these assertions one must know the meaning of the words (concepts) "God" and "angel"—essence. One then asserts this essence does not exist.

The question philosophy asks is, "What is this existing?" What do we mean when we say something "is"? Can we think "being" itself without reference to any essence, anything? We formulate the question this way because being itself is not a particular thing (an essence). Being is no-thing. Being is existing.

Imagine you are working with a new student of English. You do not speak this individual's native tongue but are helping her with her limited English. She asks you, "What does 'existence' mean? I do not know the meaning of this word." How would you reply? I suggest you take a moment now to formulate an answer to this question. Certainly the word "existence" has meaning to you. Explain that meaning.

If you have tried to define "existence" you probably have come up with a list of synonyms (to be, to exist). Usually when we define words we use similar objects or common categories. What is a dog? A dog is an animal with four legs, a tail, etc. Animal, legs, and tail are features common to other beings. If you know what these words mean you can construct a notion of "dog" even if you have never seen one. This is how a dictionary works. One learns the meaning of words by relating common features of known things to the unknown.

The reason for asking you to define "existence" is to point out that the normal mode of definition will not work here. "Existence" is a unique case. It does not belong to any common category of things with which it can be compared. The reason it is hard to define is that there is *no-thing* in our pool of knowledge which properly applies to "being."

Yet the word "existence" has meaning. What is that meaning? Thomas has told us that everything in our mind was first in the senses. So imagine "existence." You cannot. You can imagine things existing, that is, natures or essences (dogs, people, rocks) but you cannot imagine existence as such because *existence is not anything*. When using imagination we picture natures, essences, things. We cannot picture existence.

If you understand this last point you have grasped the essence-existence distinction. Look around the room. You will see many different kinds of things, many essences (books, doors, pens, paper, windows, etc.). What all these things, and yourself, have in common is not an essence but the fact that you exist—being. There are many different kinds of things all of which exist. You are.

Another way to grasp the distinction occurs in the fact that we can ask two questions about anything. "What is it?" asks about nature. "Is it?" (e.g.,

"Are there angels or vampires?") asks about existence. This distinction between essence and existence is critical to Aquinas' notion of God and creation.

## II. NECESSARY BEING

An important characteristic of all the beings you can think of is that these beings need not be. All the beings we encounter, including other human beings and ourselves, are not necessary. We are all contingent. Our very coming to be depended on chance (our parents might have married other people) and our going out of existence at death, while sad, will leave the world essentially untouched.

We can imagine a world without human beings. Presumably this is how it was a billion years ago. Human beings do not "have to be." Nor does any other nature we can think of. In other words, our distinction of essence and existence manifests that existence is not intrinsic to the natures we encounter within our world. It is a real distinction. All the natures (things we can know) can be understood without asserting that they exist.

The distinction between essence and existence (the ontological distinction) grounds St. Thomas' primary definition of God. God is that Being in whom this distinction does not occur. God's essence is to be. God is not a contingent being but Being itself. It belongs to the definition of God to be— necessary Being.

Thomas' notion is not solely a philosophical reflection. When asked for a name, God told Moses, "I am Who am." (Ex 3:14) For Aquinas this is *THE* divine name, Being itself. When one asks what God is, Thomas answers that the ontological distinction no longer applies. God's nature is "to be." Of course, St. Thomas' interpretation of the Exodus text is an example of the historicity of understanding. Thomas' interpretation reflects the philosophical perspective of his time, a perspective not characteristic of ancient Israel. But our interest at this moment is not the historical accuracy of his interpretation. Rather, we are concerned with the brilliant insight into the divine mystery which emerges in the fusion of medieval philosophy and the scriptural text.

Have we a definition of God? In a sense. We have said the words based on a distinction with which we are familiar. But if you have followed what has been said so far you must find yourself a bit frustrated. To assert necessary Being, that Being in whom essence and existence coincide, is not to understand. While Thomas has offered us a definition of God it is a definition in which God remains an absolute mystery.

Human knowledge is ordered toward the natural, created world. Knowledge of this world necessarily involves the distinction between essence and existence. This distinction permits us to assert of God the coincidence of essence and existence, but our finite intellects cannot understand what this means. In other words, Thomas' definition of God is true but we do not understand it.

A brief reflection on our speech about God can show how the divine always remains mystery. For example, God is eternal. What does this mean? God has no beginning or end. We can say these words but we do not understand them. We cannot conceive of "without beginning." Everything we know has a beginning. When we think "without beginning" we simply keep pushing back the start. Our minds fail. To say God is eternal is, at last, the negation of reality as we know it. It is a negative assertion. God has no beginning. To say this of God is true, but God remains a mystery. In fact, such assertions, when seriously considered, deepen the divine mystery rather than explain it.

It is important to appreciate how subtle Aquinas' theology of God is. He has offered a definition of God (pure Being) which makes a claim to truth. Yet one grasps that truth only in the realization that the divine remains an absolute mystery to us. In this sense Aquinas is sometimes referred to as "agnostic." While Thomas gave us ways to demonstrate the existence of God, and assert a definition, we never can *know* God's essence.

We must treat the question of knowledge about God a little more carefully. In fact, St. Thomas says all sorts of things about God, as do we. Let us consider how we speak of God.

First, we saw above that we can make any number of negative assertions about God which are true. God is not physical, has no beginning, has no end, and so on. While these negative assertions do not offer us clear knowledge of the divine nature, they do tell us something true, i.e., what God is not.

Second, we frequently speak of God metaphorically. God is a rock, a foundation, a king, a companion, and so on. This kind of speech is especially typical of scripture, liturgy, and piety. The key to identifying metaphorical language about God is that it can both be asserted and negated. God is not, of course, a rock, foundation, king, or companion. In fact, metaphorical speech about God is only properly understood when one grasps that God both is and is not a rock, king, etc. The truth of these assertions involves both affirmation and negation.

Thus, in the two forms of speech about God above we have language which, while true, does not speak properly of the divine nature. These statements do not assert what God actually is. But Thomas points out a third kind of speech about God which cannot be negated. That is, it consists of true propositions which speak properly about the divine mystery. This speech is analogy.

The primary analogue comes from the topic we have been considering. "God exists" is a true statement about God. It cannot be negated. But it is not a univocal statement. That is, while we can say God exists we do not really understand what we mean by this. Why?

Our knowledge of existence refers to contingent things. We know natures which exist. But their existence and their nature (essence) are not identical. We are incapable of *conceiving* of a nature the essence of which is to be. There can be no human concept of God. Thus, the statement that God exists is not like other human statements. When I say, "The book is blue" and "There is a chair," these statements are univocal. That is, for each word there is a clear and understood reference, a one-to-one correlation of word and meaning. But "God exists" is not this kind of statement because, while we have a grasp of contingent existence, we have no grasp of necessary Being.

There is an analogical relationship between our existence and "God exists." When we say that God exists we say something true, which cannot be negated, but which we do not properly understand.

What grounds this assertion? How are we able to formulate analogical assertions about the divine mystery? Our existence, which we know, is the effect of the divine existence. Existence in its full and proper sense is the divine nature. But by God's creative act we, too, exist in a derivative way. Granting this important difference, existence is something common to both God and us creatures.

### III. CREATION

Chapter 2 on the Hellenistic reception of the faith briefly mentioned the doctrine of creation *ex nihilo*. God creates out of nothing. But how are we to understand this statement? One cannot understand the doctrine descriptively, such as the artist made the pot "out of clay."

The doctrine asserts that reality is composed of God and creation. God's essence is to be; God always is. But God freely chose to grant being to natures which need not have been, i.e., angels, the natural universe and all it contains. Thus, all the beings we encounter in the universe are not necessary. There is a distinction between their essence, what they are, and their existence.

Creation is the gift of contingent existence. We cannot image creation since to do so one would have to begin with a picture of God and nothingness. If we think we can imagine either God or nothingness we do not understand their meaning. But we can grasp an insight into creation through the essence-existence distinction.

The human act of knowing can serve as model for insight into God's act of creation. The activity of the agent intellect consists of two stages, abstraction and judgment. Abstraction concerns essence. Presumably God can conceive of an infinite number of possible universes and kinds of beings—natures, essences. But God creates a specific universe.

In judgment we move from conceiving to being. If I see an object in the distance and wonder what it is, I consider concepts, ideas, essences. Is it a tree, or a man, or a car? When I finally judge the object to be a man I add nothing to the concept of humanity. Rather, I assert existence.

Our act of judgment offers an insight into what creation might be. God could conceive of an infinite number of natures but in creation God grants being to some natures by creating specific beings. The primary connection between creation and creator is, thus, not nature but existence. The primary analogue and ground for knowledge about God is being. This is why we cannot properly imagine God at the top of the hierarchy of being, as one being among many. Such a picture presumes God to be one nature from which all other natures come. But, for Thomas, creation is not primordially the emanation of natures from the divine. It is, rather, the granting of contingent being by necessary Being.

This chapter began by stating its intent to invite the reader to think some very difficult material. The topics treated here have received volumes of attention from scholars over the centuries. The accuracy, adequacy, consistency, of Thomas' thought is debated. But, whether one is a Thomist or not, these kinds of difficult subjects are at the heart of the theological enterprise. All fields within theology ultimately have their basis in an implicit or explicit stand on the issues of God and creation. Thus, while difficult, these are questions the serious student of theology cannot avoid.

## IV. BERNARD LONERGAN AND THE NOTION OF BEING

### A. Introductory Remarks

We have attempted to think the question of being by attending to the distinction between essence and existence, a distinction implicit in our acts of knowledge and in everyday speech. Transcendental Thomists observe that it is the difference between conceiving (abstracting) and judging which brings the ontological distinction to light.

We do not reach the truth, what is (being), in the formation of concepts, in thinking. Rather, we reach being in judgment, a distinct act. Understanding the nature "vampire" leaves unanswered the question as to whether vampires exist. This latter question is a matter of judgment, judgment of being.

Transcendental Thomists point out that the issue of being emerges in the act of knowing, in the distinction between abstraction and judgment. Thus, metaphysics, the study of being, must turn to the act of knowledge, to the knower in whom the distinction occurs. Here is the Thomistic form of modernity's turn to the subject, the transcendental turn.

In this section I would like to touch on the thought of Bernard Lonergan and his notion of being. Lonergan is frequently coupled with Rahner as an example of transcendental Thomism. But these are two quite different thinkers. I introduce Lonergan (we shall return to his thought in the last chapter) for two reasons. First, his approach to the question of being, while less explicitly transcendental and Thomistic than Rahner's, is more satisfying. Second, he stays closer to Thomas' realism. But, before moving on to Lonergan, let me offer a brief account of Rahner's approach, an account which might explain why we do not consider him in more detail.

Rahner's transcendental interpretation of Thomas centers on the Kantian question "What are the conditions of subjectivity which make possible the act of knowledge as Aquinas describes that act?" Rahner argues that the activity of the agent intellect in abstraction and judgment requires an a priori grasp of universality. The mind must already possess an openness to the universal in order to form concepts from sensed particulars.

In judgment the intellect achieves what is, being. Rahner contends that if this be the case then the universal horizon implicit in all acts of human knowledge must be a horizon of universal Being. If the mind is open to the universal, and reaches its goal in judging what *is*, then universal Being is its necessary condition.

Two paragraphs hardly do justice to Rahner's thought, a topic to which we will return in chapter 9. But to explore what he means by humanity's a priori grasp of being would not take us further into Thomas. Rather, Rahner's thought here reflects more of modern thinkers like Martin Heidegger. Rahner studied under Heidegger and explicitly adopts the Heideggerian approach to the question of being, i.e., studying that being (humanity) which manifests an understanding (pre-grasp) of being. Rahner's thought thus becomes a complex combination of Thomistic and modern categories. Bernard Lonergan's approach to the question is more direct and will offer the reader an easier insight into the transcendental interpretations of Aquinas.

### B. Bernard Lonergan

Bernard Lonergan was a Canadian Jesuit. His great philosophical and theological works appeared from the 1940s through the 1970s. As a teacher at the Gregorian University in Rome he had a profound influence on young theologians. The contemporary Catholic theological scene is populated by many of his students.

Lonergan's great work, *Insight*, explores human knowledge and develops a metaphysics based on the performance of knowing. While this work is not about St. Thomas, it is profoundly influenced by Aquinas. Lonergan offers an account of knowledge which reflects the contemporary practice of science and mathematics. He asks his readers to attend to what they do when coming to know. He points out that in all fields one must observe the data, question, formulate hypotheses, test them, and finally come to a judgment affirming or negating the hypothesis. In this account one hears echoes of sensation, abstraction, and judgment.

There will be no effort here to summarize Lonergan's position. In the last analysis one cannot be true to Lonergan by summary. One must think with him in *Insight*, one must find in one's act of knowing what Lonergan is about. Anything less misses what Lonergan is up to. The following remarks simply offer some reflections on how Lonergan moves from a Thomistic understanding of judgment to the question of being and metaphysics.

Through a painstaking analysis Lonergan concludes that (1) we know, and (2) that knowledge is attained through experience, questioning, understanding, and judgment. He points out that if you wish to disagree with him you must assert that we do not know, or that we are in doubt. Both assertions imply a standard of what knowledge is. More, if you wish to argue against his position you will have recourse to experience, questioning, understanding, and judgment. In brief, taking a stand against Lonergan's position implicitly affirms that position.

In *Insight*, Lonergan frequently has the practice of modern science in mind. Scientists are interested in understanding data. They want to know why things happen the way they do. They ask questions of the data. They formulate hypotheses. They test their hypotheses in the data. They judge their hypotheses to be correct or incorrect, accurate or inaccurate. Lonergan sees in this method the recurring operations of mind Thomas identified in sensation, abstraction and judgment.

Lonergan argues that people frequently overlook the nature of knowledge. They mistake moments in the process for knowledge itself. Empiricists, for example, think of sensation as knowing. Idealists mistake conceptualizing for knowing, identifying ideas with the truth. This was Aquinas' critique of Plato. Like Thomas, Lonergan holds that knowledge occurs in judgment when we attain what is.

What is, being, is the proper term (goal) of knowledge. If we know we attain being. Based on this reflection, the experience of knowing itself can become the data for understanding and judgment. Here is Lonergan's transcendental turn. Note how it differs from that of Rahner. Lonergan is not locating any a priori content in human consciousness. Rather, he is identifying recurrent operations—experience, questioning, understanding, and judgment. These operations find their natural goal in being.

From this reflection a notion of being can emerge. Lonergan carefully refers to a "notion" of being, not a concept. There can be no concept of being. Concept refers to the second operation of mind, abstraction. Being emerges in the third, judgment.

What is this being? Our access to being is in the performance of knowing. Metaphysical reflection must begin there. We attain being in judgment, knowledge. Thus, being itself must be the totality of all possible correct judgments, all that can be known, all that is. (Here again is the Aristotelian notion that the soul is possibility for all being.)

To fully appreciate the direction of Lonergan's position we must recall what has been stated about Aquinas' epistemology in earlier chapters. What gets affirmed in judgment is not a physical object or an idea. Rather, judgment affirms intelligibility. "This is a car." One does not see "car" but only an object. From the object one must abstract an idea, "car." But the truth is not that idea, concept. Abstraction is thinking. What gets affirmed in judgment is not the concept. Rather, concepts are the means by which the agent intellect renders an object intelligible.

Recall an earlier thought experiment. When I say "car" you might picture a particular automobile. You might define car. But you can also simply understand the word without either a picture in your mind or a formulated concept. The word simply has meaning—intelligibility.

Another example might help. The statement "A equals B" has meaning, intelligibility. You cannot picture it. You may picture the words but you cannot picture their reference since you do not know it. Nor can you have a concept of "A equals B" since, again, you do not have any reference. Yet the phrase has meaning, intelligibility.

Lonergan's theological example of pure intelligibility is the *homoousios* of Nicea. The Son is not the Father. Whatever is true of the Father is true of the Son, except the name "Father." The church can assert this doctrine as true without specifying its content, what it actually means to be God.

When one knows what a thing is one knows its substance, its intelligibility. Thus, it is intelligibility that is affirmed in judgment. Being and intelligibility coincide. Being is the content of all possible judgments, all that actually is, all intelligibility. One sees here the Thomistic notion of God, that Being who knows all being in one simple act of intelligibility.

Interestingly, Lonergan has come very close to Thomas' realism by entering into the modern epistemological discussion. In *Insight* he does not interpret Aquinas, but studies the act of knowledge in modern categories. Lonergan's analysis of what occurs in contemporary science finds the stages of Aquinas' epistemology (sensation/data, abstraction/questioning and hypothesis, judgment). Based on mind's recurring operations, culminating in judgment (being), Lonergan moves on to metaphysics. It is this last move, to the recurring operations of mind, which characterizes Lonergan as a transcendental Thomist.

## BIBLIOGRAPHY

For Thomas on the topics of God and creation, see the *Summa theologiae* Part I, questions 2, 3 and 44. David Burrell has written some excellent works on these topics. See *Knowing the Unknowable God,* especially chapters 1–3, and his essay "Creation and Emanation: Two Paradigms of Reason" in *God and Creation: An Ecumenical Symposium.* Robert Sokolowski's *The God of Faith and Reason* is an excellent, non-transcendental interpretation of Aquinas on these topics. For Lonergan, as indicated in the text, one must struggle with *Insight.* Short of this major undertaking, see Lonergan's *Philosophy of God and Theology* or Bernard Tyrrell's *Bernard Lonergan's Philosophy of God.*

# CHAPTER 8

# CHRISTOLOGY

This chapter considers one last topic in the thought of St. Thomas, Christology. I have chosen this topic for two reasons. First, Thomas' understanding of the incarnation is grounded in the essence-existence distinction we have been considering. Second, Christology is one of the most active and interesting areas of contemporary theology. Knowing St. Thomas' position can be a great help in grasping the content, possibilities and directions of current christological reflection.

## I. THE DOCTRINE OF CHALCEDON

The distinction between essence and existence is key to St. Thomas' understanding of the incarnation and of the doctrine of Chalcedon. The doctrine of the incarnation developed during the christological controversies of the third, fourth and fifth centuries. Reacting to heterodox speculation about Jesus, the great christological councils asserted that Jesus was fully divine and fully human, two natures, unmixed, united in one individual.

The context of the doctrine's development has already been considered in chapter 2. Parties to the christological controversies agreed that Jesus was the incarnate Logos. The first major crisis occurred when Arius denied that the Logos was divine. Arius' argument was philosophically quite simple. God is one. The Logos is not the Father. Therefore, the Logos is not divine.

From the modern perspective it is significant to note that, while denying the divinity of the Logos (and, therefore, of Jesus) Arius was still operating within the middle-Platonic context of his time. When people today say they do not think Jesus was God, they usually mean he was just a very good man. This was not Arius' view. Arius held that Jesus was the incarnation of the Logos. His heresy was that he denied the full divinity of the Logos. Arius thought of the Logos as the first of all creatures, coming from the Father before any other creature. The Logos preexisted, i.e., existed before the creation of the world and before the incarnation. Granting this preexistence, Arius taught that the Logos is nonetheless a creature. Thus, Jesus is not the incarnation of divinity.

The Council of Nicea responded to Arius by asserting that the Logos is *homoousios* with, the same substance as, the Father. The core intuition behind this assertion is that only God can save. If Jesus is our savior he must be divine. With the *homoousios* the church took a major step toward the trinitarian doctrine in that it asserted both the oneness of God and the true divinity of both Father and Son.

Nicea did not end the Arian controversy. For the sake of simplicity, however, we will only trace the direction of orthodox speculation about the Christ. With the divine nature of the Logos established, attention soon turned to the question of how divinity and humanity come together in Jesus. Two major christologies emerged: the Logos/sarx and the Logos/anthropos.

The Logos/sarx Christology is generally associated with the city of Alexandria. Sarx means flesh. The image suggested by this approach is that in the incarnation the divine Logos took on a human body. This Christology can be exemplified by one of its most extreme proponents, Apollinaris (d. 390). Apollinaris taught that Jesus had no human soul. The soul of Jesus, his form, was the divine Logos. Jesus was, to put it simply, God wearing a human body.

Appolinaris, in denying that Jesus had a human soul, was denying that Jesus was fully human. This is the weakness of the Logos/sarx Christology and the heterodox element in Appolinaris' teaching. Lacking a human soul, Jesus had no human consciousness, no human self. However, the strength of the Logos/sarx Christology is that Jesus is one, unified being. The importance of this strength becomes clear in considering the Logos/anthropos alternative.

The Logos/anthropos Christology is associated with Antioch. Anthropos means human. This way of understanding Jesus insisted on his having two full natures. The Logos incarnate in Jesus is fully God. The divine Logos is united with a full human nature. Jesus is human, body and soul. The strength of this Christology is precisely its insistence on the two full natures—divine and human.

The weakness of the Logos/anthropos is that it seemingly asserts a duality in Jesus, two beings brought together. This weakness is exemplified by the heterodox teaching of Nestorius (d. 451). Nestorius taught that one ought not call Mary the "Mother of God." Mary is a creature of God, not the mother of divinity. One should say that Mary is the mother of the human part of Jesus, but not the mother of God.

Of course Nestorius is correct in saying that Mary is a creature of God. But Nestorius' error was to divide Jesus. He wanted to talk about Mary being the mother of the human part of Jesus, not the divine. This division of Jesus is seemingly implicit in the Logos/anthropos Christology. But such dividing of Jesus was rejected by the Council of Ephesus which condemned Nestorius and proclaimed Mary the mother of God.

The Council of Chalcedon finally brought about the orthodox formula for speaking about Jesus. Chalcedon gave us a language for speaking about the incarnation and, thereby, set the parameters for an orthodox Christology. Chalcedon took the strengths of each of the two Christologies mentioned above, and excluded the weakness of each. It asserted that Jesus had two full natures (unmixed), united in one hypostasis, one prosopon. The "two full natures" asserts the strength of the Logos/anthropos and excludes the weakness of the Logos/sarx. Conversely, the "one hypostasis, one prosopon" asserts the strength of the Logos/sarx and excludes the weakness of the Logos/anthropos.

What does this language of nature, hypostasis and prosopon mean? How are we to think about and imagine the incarnation? What does this actually tell us about Jesus? What are the orthodox boundaries for Christology? These kinds of questions are naturally raised by the contemporary Christian. The following presents St. Thomas' interpretation of the Chalcedonian formula. Considering Aquinas on this topic allows us again to see the importance of the essence-existence distinction for his thought. More, Aquinas' interpretation of Chalcedon, his understanding of the incarnation, shows us both the limits and possibilities for a contemporary understanding of the incarnation.

## II. AQUINAS ON THE INCARNATION

What follows is based on the *Summa theologiae* Part III, questions 2, 5 and 9. I suggest the reader stop here and read these three questions before continuing.

In question 2 Thomas approaches the topic of the incarnation by asking about the mode of unity between humanity and divinity in Jesus. In a sense he asks about "where" in Jesus does the unity occur. He suggests two possibilities. The essence–existence distinction offers these possibilities. Does the unity between humanity and divinity occur in the essence (in the natures) or in the act of existence?

Article 1 of question 2 asks whether the unity occurred in the natures (essence). Nature refers to what a thing is. In the case of Jesus there are two answers to this question. When we ask, "What is Jesus?" we answer, "Fully God and fully human." But this would not be the case if unity occurred in the natures. Thomas points out that, if you mix humanity and divinity, the human simply disappears into the divine. It is absorbed into divinity, like putting a drop of water into a flagon of wine.

Thus, if the incarnation occurred through a mixing of natures there would cease to be a real incarnation since the humanity of Jesus would disappear into the divinity. This is the error of the Logos/sarx Christology.

Having excluded a union of natures (essences), Aquinas turns to the act of existence as the "locus" of unity. In this he is interpreting the language of Chalcedon through his understanding of the essence-existence distinction.

Article 2 is the key to Aquinas' Christology. To grasp his position we must consider his understanding of the terms hypostasis, suppositum and person.

Having excluded nature (essence), Thomas concludes that the act of existence, the hypostasis must be the locus of unity. For Aquinas, like Aristotle, reality is constituted by the individual things which exist. The mind grasps the nature of things (what they are) through concepts. But, in contrast to Plato, concepts (forms) do not occur in the order of the real (save in the mind of God). They are the means by which created mind attains the real. Reality is made up of individual things. While we understand these things through the universal concept, only individual things exist.

I may wonder what a strange piece of office equipment is. I ask about its nature or essence. Its inventor explains the nature of this strange object and through her explanation I formulate a correct concept or idea. But in constructing the concept (abstraction) I do not attain what is, being. The concept has no existence beyond my thinking. What is real, what exists (being) is the object at hand. In judgment I achieve being, I know what *it is*.

When encountering any real thing we can thus distinguish between what it is and the individualization of that nature. For example, here is a human being. Human is the nature, the essence of this being. But what exists here is not human nature in general (the concept) but an individual occurrence of human nature who is female, 5' 8", blond, slim, English, etc. Thomas calls this individualization of human nature "suppositum" or "hypostasis."

The distinction between essence and existence, between abstraction and judgment, makes it possible to grasp Thomas' point. One must think of existence as "happening" or "occurring," as an event. If you look up from this page you see a variety of kinds of things. There are many natures before you (books, walls, windows, etc.). What all these things have in common is that they are existing, occurring. They are the hypostasis of some nature.

In article 2 St. Thomas exploits this distinction. He observes that in material objects we distinguish between nature and individualization. For example, if you see a car outside your window you see a specific hypostasis of the nature car. But there are characteristics of this object which do not properly belong to the nature "car." It is red. Of course cars need not be red. It is two-door, but there are four-door cars, etc. The fact that this individual existent (being) possesses characteristics not intrinsic to the nature "car" points to the difference between nature and its individualization, its actual occurring. The terms "suppositum" and "hypostasis" refer to this act of occurring, this individualization. While having wheels and a motor belong to the nature car, red and two doors are characteristics of this particular hypostasis.

The word "person" has a very technical meaning here and must be distinguished from its common use in English today. To us "person" means the self, the center of consciousness. For Thomas this term is a name one can give to the hypostasis of a nature with the use of reason. When the being occurring is rational, has intelligence, one may call this hypostasis a person. Aquinas cites Boethius' definition of person, "an individual substance of rational nature." Thus the term "person" may be used of both human beings and of God. The eternal Word, therefore, is a Person (a hypostasis of divine nature).

Recall the distinction made above between nature and individualization. A human being exists. She is blonde, slim etc. Blonde and slim do not belong to human nature as such but occur in its individualization, in this particular hypostasis. Thomas uses this distinction to locate the unity of humanity and divinity in Jesus. The Logos is an eternal hypostasis, Person. To this divine hypostasis is united a human nature which does not belong to its divine essence. The locus of unity between humanity and divinity is the hypostasis, the act of existence of the eternal Word.

By locating the unity in the hypostasis Aquinas has protected the integrity of the two natures. They are unmixed, as Chalcedon asserts. Jesus is fully God and fully human. But there is only one being here. Jesus' human nature has no being of its own but only occurs in the hypostasis of the Logos. To employ previous examples, red has no being of its own but only occurs in the hypostasis (existing) of this car. Blonde has no being of its own but only is in the hypostasis of this woman. It is an error, therefore, to imagine the incarnation by picturing two separate natures brought together. This imagined picture grants a separate existence to the humanity of Jesus, apart from the hypostasis of the Logos. This is the error of Nestorius. Chalcedon, and Thomas' account of its doctrine, prohibit such a move.

How then are we to imagine Jesus? Neither Chalcedon nor Thomas tell us. The formula of Chalcedon, and Thomas' account of the incarnation, simply assert that when treating the incarnation we must say that Jesus is fully God and fully human, but there is only one individual here—a hypostatic unity of unmixed natures. Rather than a complete Christology, Chalcedon and Aquinas give us a rule of speech, the boundaries within which an orthodox Christology must operate. This last observation can be clarified if we consider St. Thomas' position further.

## III. SPEECH ABOUT THE INCARNATION

In article 3 of question 2 Aquinas argues that in speaking about reality the reference of language is not nature in the abstract, but a hypostasis. Again, Aquinas is no Platonist. Forms, concepts or natures do not exist as such. The real are individualizations, things, actual occurrences. One cannot say that human nature reasons or laughs. Rather, concrete, real people (hypostases) reason and laugh. The reference of language, of true assertions, is not nature in general but the hypostasis, suppositum.

This rule of speech governs what we say about Jesus, i.e., Christology. When speaking about Jesus our reference is the one divine hypostasis to which is united a human nature. The human nature does not have its own hypostasis and, therefore, cannot be the reference of speech. Here again is Nestorius' error. Thomas cites the Council of Ephesus: "If anyone takes the words of the Gospel or of apostolic writings—whether said of Christ by the saints or by Christ himself—and applies them to two persons or hypostases, to a man understood precisely in contrast to the Word and the rest to the Word of God the Father, as being proper to God alone, let him be anathema."

When speaking about Jesus we are speaking about one individual, one act of existence, one individualization of two natures. We may not divide Jesus up, speaking about this nature, then the other, as if there were two things (hypostases) in him. There is one individual here. Thus, in response to Nestorius we can set forth the following series of statements. Jesus is God. Mary is the mother of Jesus. Therefore we can say that Mary is the mother of God.

In a very real sense Thomas' Christology is simply an extension of this rule of speech. In question 5, for example, Thomas deduces that Jesus had a human body, soul and intellect. Jesus is human. Human beings have bodies, souls and intellects. Therefore Jesus must have these human properties.

A common modern question about Jesus deals with his knowledge. Christians frequently deduce from the doctrine of Jesus' divinity that he must have known everything. Yet human beings learn. More, Jesus admits not knowing, for example, the exact time when the kingdom will come. St. Thomas' approach to the question of Jesus' knowledge exemplifies his Christology and suggests possibilities for contemporary reflection.

In question 9, Thomas deals with Jesus' knowledge. His method is to deduce conclusions from the hypostatic union. He predicates about the knowledge of Jesus based on the rule of speech mentioned above. That is, when speaking about Jesus the reference of our assertions is the hypostasis of two full natures. Thus, did Jesus possess the beatific vision (article 2)? The beatific vision is, of course, the vision of God possessed by those in heaven. It is a participation in God's Self-vision, in the divine Being, in truth itself.

Humanity has the potential for the beatific vision. Since the humanity of Jesus occurs in unity with the eternal Word, Jesus must have possessed the beatific vision.

Did Jesus have created knowledge (article 1), did he learn from experience (article 4)? Jesus is human and human beings learn from experience. Therefore, Jesus learned from experience. The point here is simply to observe that Aquinas carries out his Christology by deducing from the Chalcedonian formula, the hypostatic union, what we must properly say about Jesus. As moderns, absorbed in epistemological questions, we want to know how an individual human consciousness can both possess the beatific vision and learn from experience. What did Jesus know and when did he know it? St. Thomas does not answer these questions. He simply asserts what one must predicate about Jesus. He carries out a rule of speaking about Jesus based on the hypostatic union.

## IV. POSSIBILITIES

In this last, brief section we will consider some possibilities for contemporary Christology related to St. Thomas' thought. First, Aquinas' explication of the incarnation allows for a full human consciousness in Jesus, a consciousness which learns from human experience. The fact that Jesus was divine need not mean that he was all-knowing in his human nature. Like us, Jesus learned from his world and his knowledge was limited by the normal human conditions of time and place.

More, Jesus' human consciousness offers contemporary Christology a starting place for reflection. Here is something we hold in common with the Lord, a common ground which ties us to the incarnate Word. Karl Rahner, for example, begins his philosophical-theological project here, in consciousness. Where do we encounter God? If Jesus is human like us, the "locus" of the incarnation ought to be in that "place" where we encounter the divine. Rahner locates the meeting place of humanity and divinity in transcendental consciousness.

Finally, consider the words in quotation marks above. "Locus" and "place" are spatial terms. The language of doctrine suggests these spacial images. *In*carnation, two natures are united *in* one Person. Does the unity of humanity and divinity occur in the natures or in the hypostasis? Of course the tradition never understood the incarnation as a spacial event. "He came down from heaven" and the "Word in flesh" are metaphors. The incarnation is not a spatial event, as if the eternal Word moved from one location to another. The eternal, divine Word has no location, does not exist in space. Location is a function of material existence.

Yet the language of the tradition suggests spatial metaphors. How does one unite two natures in one individual? Above we noted that one cannot imagine the humanity of Jesus existing apart from the hypostasis of the Logos. Here imagination fails.

Contemporary thought suggests a different metaphor for understanding the incarnation which, perhaps, better expresses what the Chalcedonian formula sought. The key to this metaphor is the notion of human existence as freedom. Karl Rahner's anthropology is an example of this common understanding of human existence.

In modern thought freedom is not an attribute of human existence, not a property or ability. To be human is to be freedom. Human beings are not fixed things, not settled natures. Rather, to be human means to become. What do we become? That is determined by where we exist. An example might make the point most simply.

Imagine a child born today in a local hospital. It is possible that this baby could be put on a jet and flown anywhere in the world. Say the child is flown to China and adopted by a family there. Or, the child could be adopted in France, or Angola, or Mexico, and so on. In each instance that child would become a different person, learning a different language, living with different kinds of families, in different cultures, with different religious beliefs, and so on. The point of the example is to indicate that what a person becomes is, to a great extent, determined by his or her context. Another way of saying this is that the world we relate to (our families, country, language) determines who we are. Relating, interacting, determines our being.

Based on this insight many contemporary christologists suggest that we understand the incarnation relationally. Who Jesus was, what he became, was determined by his relationship with the Father. Living within the context of a first century, Palestinian Jew, Jesus always related perfectly with God. He determined his being by that relationship. In Rahnerian terms, he always said yes to God's Self-offer. In the language of Boff, he sought not his own self (being) but determined his being in service to the Father and humanity. Jesus became who and what he was by these relationships. He became the perfect incarnation of the divine, the perfect human image of God.

Treating the incarnation through the modern notion of freedom suggests a relational rather than spacial metaphor. God creates a nature (humanity) that is capable of this kind of relationship with the divine (an obediential potency for incarnation). The divine nature is a triune relationship. God creates a nature that can enter into this divinity of relationships. In Jesus this potential is perfectly actualized through Jesus' perfect exercise of human freedom. He becomes the Word incarnate.

This relational imagery gets past the spacial problem of putting two natures together in one individual. The divine and human are relational realities. Humanity is not a fixed essence, but "freedom for" through how one relates. In Jesus this freedom actualizes humanity's highest potential. Jesus defines his very being by his relationship with God. It is in this sense, which I suggested above, that the contemporary notion of freedom might better express what the church sought to say in the dogma of Chalcedon.

With these last observations we have moved beyond St. Thomas' categories into modern thought. Theologians of different persuasions will evaluate this move positively or negatively. But, approved or not, much of Catholic theology has entered into an open conversation with modern thought.

We will conclude our reflections on St. Thomas by attending to one of the most influential, contemporary interpretations of his thought. Karl Rahner's retrieval of Aquinas, briefly mentioned in the last three chapters, can now be presented in some detail. These considerations serve as a bridge between Thomas and some of the most influential minds in modern and contemporary philosophy.

## BIBLIOGRAPHY

*Summa theologiae* Part III, questions 2, 5, and 9. For a brief survey of this material see chapter 13 of Richard McBrien's *Catholicism.* J.N.D. Kelly, *Early Christian Doctrines,* chapters 9–12 offer a more detailed account. Jaroslav Pelikan treats the development of the christological dogma in chapter 5, Vol. I of *The Christian Tradition.* The classic work on the development of the Chalcedonian dogma is Aloys Grillmeier's *Christ in Christian Tradition.* For Rahner's notion of freedom, see "Theology of Freedom" in *Theological Investigations* 6:178–196 and chapter 1 of *Foundations of Christian Faith.* Rahner explicates the relationship between freedom and incarnation in *Foundations of Christian Faith,* pp. 212–228.

# CHAPTER 9

# KARL RAHNER'S RETRIEVAL OF AQUINAS

Karl Rahner is the most influential Catholic theologian of this century. He is a transcendental Thomist. His early philosophical works, which serve as the foundation for his theology, were an interpretation or a retrieval of Aquinas.

The term "retrieval" indicates the complex and eclectic character of Rahner's philosophy and theology. He does not simply repeat St. Thomas' position. Rather, Rahner thinks with Aquinas about modern questions and perspectives. He places Thomas in conversation with the entire tradition, with contemporary problems and with modern thinkers like Kant, Hegel and Heidegger. The theology which emerges from this conversation is both traditional and modern. Rahner has the same goal as the apologists and Aquinas—to offer an account of the faith which makes sense to his contemporaries.

Rahner's primary theological interest is pastoral. He seeks to make the faith credible for people in the twentieth century. His profound influence reflects his success in this task.

Catholics believe in the scripture, in the creeds, in the dogmas and doctrines taught by the church. Yet these beliefs frequently assert strange, seemingly mythic events. The gospels tell us that the dead Jesus was raised to new life. The creed of Nicea says that the eternal Son of God became human. The dogma of the assumption states that Mary was assumed body and soul into heaven.

Must Catholics today suspend their normal experience of the world in order to believe? Does our faith insist that the world was once a quite different place in which bodies rose into the sky and God entered history in human disguise? It is not uncommon for Christians to question, and even abandon their faith because they cannot accept what seems to be asserted in these various beliefs.

Rahner's goal is to interpret the teachings of the church in a manner that can make sense to people today. He pursues this end by returning to one of the oldest themes in western philosophy, Plato's notion of knowledge as memory.

In Rahner's view, the core Christian truth is that God offers each human person a share in the divine life. God is near to each of us. Where or how do we encounter this divine Self-offer? Certainly not in the world of physical events. God does not appear to us and talk with us. Rather, God is within each of us, part of us. There is an inner experience of God. Christian doctrine speaks about, makes explicit, this inner experience of God's Self-offer. The faith brings to language, reminds us of what all humanity already implicitly knows. We understand the meaning of scripture and doctrine when we find within ourselves the God about whom Christian faith speaks.

The aim of this chapter is to indicate some of the philosophical notions intrinsic to Rahner's theology. Specifically, the chapter argues that Rahner retrieves a Platonic notion of knowledge as memory through a modern (Kantian) interpretation of Aquinas. This complex, philosophical achievement results in a perspective that is not Platonic, Thomistic or Kantian. Rahner establishes his own philosophical-theological position, and in doing so reaches toward his goal of making Christianity credible today. He identifies the reference of all Christian teaching in the universal experience of the divine Self-offer.

## I. EXPERIENCE OF GOD

### A. The Act of Knowing

Rahner began his philosophical and theological journey by interpreting St. Thomas' description of knowledge. But he does not simply repeat Aquinas. He asks a question about Thomas' description of the act of knowing, a question that comes from the modern philosopher, Immanuel Kant. We begin with a brief review of Aquinas' account of human knowing.

Thomas argues that all human knowledge begins with sensation. We see, hear, touch something. But mere sensation is not knowing. A dog sees what we see but does not know and understand as do we.

Human beings question experience. We ask, "What is that?" To answer this question involves the introduction of an idea, a concept, a universal. I see a figure and ask, "What is it? A tree? A man? I am not sure." In other words, I am seeking the correct concept (tree, human being), to know the object experienced in terms of the right idea. I study the object, get closer, improve the light, until I reach the correct judgment, "That is a man."

In this last act of judgment ("That is a man") I reach what is (being), the truth. The act of knowing thus consists of three steps: sensation, abstraction and judgment. What I know is first of all in the senses. But knowing is not simply looking. To know is to judge an object of sensation in terms of an idea, a universal, a concept. I abstract the universal from the sensed. But to reach an idea is not yet truth. I am still thinking. We have all had the experience of being mistaken, of mistaking, for example, a distant man for a tree. Truth occurs in judgment when I judge an object to be an instance of the correct universal—human being.

According to Thomas the intellect is both passive and active in this performance of knowing. It is passive in sensation. I receive the object. But abstraction and judgment involve activity by the mind. We are doing these things—questioning, thinking, conceiving, and judging. To return to an earlier observation, both human beings and dogs sense. What makes us different is that human beings move beyond sensation, in abstraction and judgment, to knowing. Abstraction and judgment are the work of what Thomas calls the agent or active intellect.

Now let us see how Rahner brings Thomas' description of knowledge into conversation with modern thought, with Immanuel Kant. Kant was a modern thinker and not a follower of St. Thomas. But Rahner sees similarities between Kant's thought and that of St. Thomas. Both hold that all knowledge begins with sensation and that the intellect is active in the attainment of knowledge. The characteristic question of Kant's epistemology is, "What are the conditions for the possibility of knowing?" That is, Kant asks about what in the human intellect makes it possible for it to do what it does in the act of knowledge (the transcendental method).

To understand the nature of Kant's question it might be helpful to introduce an analogy. Hearing involves two elements, sound waves and the ear. A doctor studies the structure of the ear in order to understand what makes hearing possible. If a patient cannot hear, the doctor examines her ear to identify what in its structure is faulty. The act of hearing is dependent on the healthy structure of the ear.

Analogously, for Kant, knowing involves two elements, objects of sensation (phenomena) and the structure of the mind (the subject). Kant seeks to study the structure of subjectivity which makes the act of knowing possible.

In the history of philosophy this is called the transcendental turn, or the turn to the subject. Knowledge is the act of a subject (the human being) knowing some object. Kant seeks to offer a description of the conditions of subjectivity which make the act of knowing possible. This is what is meant by the turn to the subject.

Rahner is called a transcendental Thomist because he asks Kant's question of St. Thomas. What are the conditions for the possibility of knowing as Aquinas describes the act of knowledge? It is important at this point to alert the reader to the complex nature of Rahner's use of Aquinas and Kant. Thomas never asked the transcendental question within his own thought. He lived five hundred years before Kant. And Kant was certainly no Thomist.

Rahner's transcendental Thomism is, in the historical sense, neither Thomistic nor Kantian. It must be thought of as Rahner's own position resulting from the creative combination of these two quite different thinkers. This method of interpretation is called "retrieval" and reflects the influence on Rahner of his teacher, Martin Heidegger.

In answering his transcendental question of St. Thomas, Rahner comes to the universal experience of God. Rahner looks to the activities of abstraction and judgment. What are the conditions for the possibility of these acts? What must be true of the human intellect for it to abstract and judge?

In abstraction the mind attains an idea, a concept. In the example given above the knower questions whether the object seen is a tree or a human being. "Tree" and "human" are ideas, concepts, universals. The idea "tree" implies no specific tree and carries with it no limitation as to the number of possible trees. The concept tree could apply to an infinite number of possible objects. A concept is universal.

Similarly, when the knower judges this object to be a human being a universal concept (human nature) is applied to an object of experience. This act of judgment involves a negation. I judge this to be a human being and nothing else. This is a human being and not a tree, not a car, not a dog, and so on infinitely. The act of judgment specifies the nature of the object over and against an infinite number of negated possibilities. Again, judgment implies some notion of the infinite or universal.

Rahner argues that St. Thomas' description of the active intellect's performance in abstraction and judgment implies a notion of universality. How else could the mind abstract a concept (universal) and judge a sensed object to be a specific nature, negating an infinite (universal) number of other possibilities?

It is here that Rahner asks Kant's transcendental question. How is this activity of the intellect possible? Recall that all knowledge begins with sensation. But there is no sensation of universality. We only sense specific objects. We do not sense human nature or tree as such. I never see the concept tree, but only specific objects which I classify within the universal idea "tree." How is this possible?

Rahner argues that for St. Thomas knowledge is achieved by the activity of the agent intellect. If the universal as such is not experienced in sensation, then the only alternative left is that the intellect itself must have some notion of universality which makes possible abstraction and judgment.

Rahner's point here is quite difficult and must be approached with care. First, he is not saying the mind already has a concept of tree or human nature which it applies to specific sensed objects. Rahner is in the tradition of Aristotle and Aquinas on this point, not Plato. Thomas holds that all knowledge begins with sensation. Concepts are abstracted (learned) from the objects we see, hear, etc. But for the mind to move from a specific, sensed object to a universal concept requires, as its necessary condition, some notion of universality.

Second, universality itself is not a concept or idea. Try to think universality or infinity. We cannot. When thinking about universality or infinity we basically negate our experience. We say "without limit," or "no limit." We know what limits are because everything in the physical world is limited. We experience nothing without limit. The objects of experience are always specific and finite.

Concepts and ideas are extensions of these experiences. Tree or human nature are concepts which can be specified, described, exemplified. Universality cannot. Universality can only be spoken of through negation. It is without limit or specification. It cannot be imagined or exemplified.

Yet some notion of universality remains the necessary condition for what we do when we know. How else could we produce concepts, universals? If universality is never sensed, and is the necessary condition for abstraction (conceptualization) and judgment, then it must belong to the knowing subject prior to (as the necessary condition for) these acts. We must have some grasp of universality logically prior to any act of knowing. Some notion of universality must belong to the very structure of subjectivity.

In treating this notion of universality Rahner makes two rather difficult points which we must consider. First, the notion of universality is not a direct object of experience, but is manifest in the intellect's movement toward knowledge—in the activity of the agent intellect. It is a kind of know-how, a competence, an active capacity. Rahner understands the activity of the intellect as a dynamism, a movement to know everything that exists. Our grasp of universality is manifest in that movement as the dynamism's necessary condition.

One cannot look within oneself to find one's openness to the universal as if it were something we possess within like an idea, feeling, or imagined picture. But we have a grasp and experience of the universal which is manifest in our performance of knowledge. It is a competence manifest in our activity.

An analogy might help. When we ride a bike we know how to balance without thinking about it. In riding we manifest a competence, an ability, a knowledge which is not explicitly formulated in our thoughts or words. We simply do it. Our knowledge, know-how, is manifest in the act of riding.

If someone asks, "How do you do that?" we would have to attend to what we are doing. That is, we would have to pay attention to what we do without thinking and make explicit (offer a description) of how we maintain our balance. The description would bring to words what we already know, though perhaps have never thought about.

So in his description of our grasp of universality Rahner hopes to elicit from us something about which we already have an awareness. He is bringing to explicit terms what we already implicitly grasp. To hear and understand Rahner's description of our grasp of universality is to "remember" what we already possess.

Second, what is this universality we grasp? Is it merely empty potentiality, our moving out toward limitlessness? Centering his argument on the nature of judgment, Rahner argues that it is a movement toward universal Being, toward God. The dynamism of the intellect, which manifests our grasp of universality, moves toward and makes judgment possible. In judgment one asserts what a thing is, "That is a man." Judgment attains what is; it reaches being.

Recall that judgment asserts what a thing is against an infinite horizon of what it is not. Judgment requires, as its necessary condition, a grasp of the absolute range of all knowable objects. More, the range of the intellect is unlimited. It is ordered toward knowing all reality. Judgment occurs within the horizon of the universal's infinite range of possible applications, and the intellect intends all that is. If judgment really attains what is (being) the absolute range of universality must be absolute Being.

This last point introduces the notion of absolute, infinite, pure Being. It suggests that we think about Being itself, that which all existing things have in common, existence. We considered this topic in chapter 7. Suffice it to say here that in attaining a notion of absolute Being Rahner has reached the goal of his retrieval of Aquinas. His transcendental analysis of Aquinas' description of knowledge has concluded that a notion, a grasp of universal Being is the necessary condition for the activities of abstraction and judgment.

In brief, Rahner argues that all human beings must have an openness to God, an implicit grasp of infinite Being, to do what we do in abstraction and judgment. Here is the universal experience of God which will serve as the reference of Christian doctrine. But before treating this experience more carefully, and indicating how it guides Rahner's interpretation of Christian faith, let us consider Rahner's transcendental argument in a less technical form. We can do this by looking to what Rahner means by human transcendence and freedom.

## B. Human Freedom and Transcendence

Rahner's notion of freedom was introduced in chapter 8. We now consider it in more detail. To understand Rahner's account of freedom and transcendence readers must see if they can recognize the experience of self Rahner describes. We usually think of freedom as the ability to choose this or that. I am free to study or not, to marry or not, and so on. Rahner argues that this freedom to choose is derived from a more primary freedom. To be human is to be freedom.

Human existence is different from anything else we experience. Trees, dogs, chairs, rocks, etc., are what they are and can be no other. They are fixed things, set natures, existing in the way determined by what they are (their nature).

Human beings are not so fixed. To be human is to be free for an infinite number of possible ways of being. This being free for possibilities is not something we choose; it is our unavoidable way of being.

In chapter 8 I suggested the example of a newborn child. That child could be flown to any part of the world to be raised in very different places. The child could be taken to Mexico, China, France, Africa, Russia, and so on. And if the child is taken to one of these places she becomes a different kind of person than if taken elsewhere. What we become reflects the culture in which we grow up, the language we learn, the kind of family we have. To be human is to be potential for an infinite number of ways of being.

At some point in an individual's life one starts to become responsible for who one becomes. This was once called the age of reason by Catholics. This simply means that as children grow toward adulthood, they slowly take responsibility for who they are and what kind of lives they live.

Our capacity to make the specific choices which determine the direction of our lives (to choose a profession, to marry, to have children, to practice the faith) is based in our being possibility, freedom. Because we are not fixed and totally determined, not a thing, we are free to make ourselves, to become through our choices.

This is what Rahner means by freedom. To be human is to be a becoming. We are handed over to ourselves to become, to choose what kind of person we will be. We work out our freedom through the specific choices we make during our life.

Another way of saying this is that as human beings we are always transcending ourselves, going beyond what we have been. We are always becoming. Rahner argues that there are no limits to this becoming. The only time we stop being free for possibilities, stop transcending what we have been, is when we die.

Rahner places his description of human existence as freedom over and against what might be called a deterministic behaviorism. This behaviorism treats human existence as if it were just one more thing. To be human is to be the creature of an environment. We are no more than the result of what has happened to us. There is really no freedom. What we are and do is determined by the environment in which we live.

Rahner argues that there is an inherent contradiction in this deterministic description of human existence. To say I am simply the product of an environment is already to have stepped beyond that environment, transcending it. To even think about myself is to view my totality from beyond it, to transcend everything I can say about myself by standing beyond.

In brief, Rahner argues that human existence is unavoidable transcendence, a transcendence without limit. I cannot hand over my being as freedom by saying I am simply this and no more, because to know what I am is already to stand beyond what I have become. Nor can I set limits on my possibilities for being, my freedom. Setting such limits is to stand beyond, to transcend them.

Rahner argues that this being as freedom, as unavoidable transcendence, requires (as its necessary condition) an openness to infinite possibility, to a horizon of infinitude. To deny such a horizon is implicitly to affirm it. If I say humanity is finite and limited to a set of possibilities I already transcend the finitude asserted. To be human is to exist within a horizon of the infinite, of universality.

Rahner's argument is transcendental. He describes human existence as freedom, as unavoidable self-transcendence. He then asks the transcendental question. What are the conditions for the possibility of such an existence? His response is that to be human freedom is to have an implicit grasp of an infinite horizon of being. An openness to God is a constitutive element of human existence. To deny this is to implicitly affirm it.

It is important to note here that Rahner's transcendental deduction of God is not the deduction of a concept. The infinite horizon that is the necessary condition for human freedom is an absolute mystery to us, always ahead and receding. But that there is such a mysterious, infinite horizon must be affirmed as the necessary condition for us to be what we are—freedom.

In the transcendental arguments presented thus far Rahner has been trying to lead us to an experience of God. He has argued that to do what we do as human beings (know), to be what we are (freedom) we must have some grasp of infinite Being, of God. Rahner is not suggesting we have an idea or a concept of God as the necessary condition for our being human. Rather he is suggesting that an openness to God is a constitutive element of being human. This openness is not an object of experience (like a thing in the material world), or an idea. Rather it is an experience of God which belongs to our experience of ourselves—the transcendental experience. We can now turn to what Rahner means by our transcendental experience of God.

## C. Knowledge of God: The Transcendental and the Categorical

For Rahner, all human experience has two intrinsically related poles, the thing experienced and the self experiencing. Another way of saying this is that we always have an experience of ourselves when experiencing anything else.

If I see an object, *I* am seeing. I experience myself as over and against the object. Even when I think about myself, make myself the object of reflection, there is a horizon of self within which this reflection occurs.

The distinction between self and the objects of experience is called in philosophy the subject-object distinction. Rahner's transcendental thought follows the suggestion of Kant to turn our attention to the subject (the self) and ask what must be true about subjectivity for us to do what we do.

Thus far we have seen Rahner's transcendental argument that some openness to infinitude, to God, is the necessary condition of subjectivity for human knowledge and freedom. We can now come to an understanding of what Rahner means by our transcendental experience of God.

The transcendental conditions of subjectivity are implicitly experienced in the performance of knowledge and freedom. Rahner is not describing a static, self-conscious ego that looks out to the material world. The transcendental is only experienced as the horizon within which knowledge and freedom are performed.

Consider an analogy to clarify this difficult, but crucial point. If we reflect on our experience of time and space, a little thought makes it clear that we never experience them directly. I do not see pure space, but always things arranged spatially, in space. I have no experience of time as such, but only of the sequence of events. Things happen sequentially.

Try to imagine space. What most of us do is to think of a limitless void, a vacuum. But try to imagine a limitless void. It is impossible. The best we can do is to imagine an empty space with ever receding boundaries.

Try to imagine time, pure time. We cannot, for time is always sequence. It is the sequence of something, hands moving on the face of a clock, thought occurring in impatient anticipation.

Can we conclude from these exercises that there is no experience of time and space? Not at all. All our experiences of the material world are spacial and temporal. Things are somewhere and we see them in some sequence. The experiences of time and space belong, not to the objects of experience, but to the horizon of subjectivity within which our experiences occur. In this sense there is an experience of time and space in that they are the horizon, the background of all experiences of the material world.

Rahner's notion of a transcendental experience of God must be understood in a similar manner. We have no direct experience of infinitude, as if it were an object out there or within. Rather, infinitude is the necessary horizon for human freedom and knowledge. It is experienced as the infinite horizon of subjectivity within which all other experiences occur.

In Rahner's terminology, one can distinguish between transcendental and categorical experience. The things I experience (dogs, trees, people), the thought I consider, and the language I use, are the categorical. All these experiences and activities are performed by a subject (me). They occur within the horizon of my subjectivity. This subjective pole of experience Rahner calls the transcendental.Rahner thus argues that an experience of God (our openness to the infinite) occurs as the transcendental horizon for all categorical experiences. When I know, I know something (the categorical). When I exercise my being as freedom it is always in relation to a specific (categorical) possibility. These categorical events require, as their necessary condition, the horizon of infinitude. Here is the universal experience of God. Since all human beings know and are freedom, the transcendental experience of God is implicit in all categorical experiences.

Locating the experiential reference for the word "God" in the transcendental determines the direction and method of Rahner's theology. All language about God, all religious expression refers to the transcendental experience of the divine. One interprets statements about the divine by referring them back to our transcendental experience of God. It is in this sense that Rahner's interpretation of the Christian faith is memory. The faith tells us what we already are, what we already possess in the transcendental.

As indicated above, the transcendental is never directly experienced but is background for all categorical experiences. The categorical also provides the language for speaking about the transcendental. We take elements from our experience of the world and use them to speak about the transcendental. Thus our speech about the transcendental is always analogous and metaphorical.

Consider what has been said so far. The transcendental is the horizon for all experiences of the material world. Horizon is a word drawn from the physical world. It says something true about the transcendental, but only if we understand the word metaphorically. We are not using the word in the same way as when I observe, "There is a ship on the horizon." Similarly, we have taken the term "background" from categorical experience to speak of the transcendental, but are using the word in a different (metaphorical), though related way.

For Rahner all religious claims, including those of the Christian faith, are categorical expressions which point metaphorically to the transcendental. The truth of Christian teachings is found not in understanding such expressions as literal descriptions of categorical reality, but rather the truth of these categorical expressions is attained by relating them to our transcendental experience of God.

Based on what has been established thus far we can now introduce Rahner's understanding of Christian revelation and his interpretation of the Catholic faith through memory. All human beings have a transcendental experience of God. To be human is to have a relationship with God. What is the nature of this relationship? The infinite is absolute mystery.

Religious language attempts to interpret our transcendental experience of God, to tell us the nature of our relationship with God, through the use of categorical language and images. Christians believe that in Jesus God has offered the divine answer to the question about our relationship with God. Jesus tells us the nature of our experience of God.

## II. THE CHRISTIAN FAITH

### A. The Revelation of Jesus

Rahner's understanding of Christ's revelation is guided by his notion of the transcendental experience of God. Language about God is categorical expression of a transcendental reality. Thus, Jesus' message about God must be understood as a categorical interpretation of humanity's transcendental relationship with absolute mystery.

Rahner accepts the general consensus among scripture scholars that the core teaching of Jesus was that "the kingdom of God is near." In the apocalyptic categories of Jesus' time this seems to have meant that the end of the world is near, that God's final judgment is about to occur. But Rahner's theology is not concerned with a literal, historical understanding of these categories. Categorical language about God refers metaphorically to the transcendental. Christ's message must be interpreted accordingly.

Rahner has established that to be human is to have a relationship with God as the necessary condition for the constitutive human activities of knowledge and freedom. This relationship with God is an openness to absolute mystery. But what is the nature of our relationship to mystery? God could simply be distant horizon which makes possible our activities as subjects, our being as freedom and knowers.

Jesus reveals quite a different relationship. He reveals that God is near offering the divine Self. God seeks to be one with us. The nearness of God's kingdom, which Jesus proclaims, is the nearness of God's very Self. It is a divine Self-offer which enables us to choose eternal union with God or to reject it.

Jesus thus reveals our transcendental experience of God to be an experience of God's Self-offer. We have an experience of God's very Self. Here is Christianity's central truth and, for Rahner, all Christian language, practice, and imagery amounts to categorical expressions of this transcendental reality and its implications for our freedom.

Eternal life with God is the final possibility for human freedom. For union with God to be a possibility for human existence God must make the offer. God must be present to us for how else could we choose or reject union with the divine? And, since the church teaches that God wills the salvation of all humanity, God's Self-offer must occur to every human being.

That offer is experientially present in the transcendental openness of every-one. All human beings are the event of God's Self-communication.

In this way all human beings already participate in the divine life. God is present to all. Our participation in God is manifest and experienced in the transcendental. The language of Christian faith expresses this reality categor-ically. It tells us what we are. It interprets our transcendental experience of ourselves to us. It makes explicit our transcendental experience of ourselves to us. It makes explicit our participation in the divine. It reminds us of what we are.

Rahner is generally, and correctly, placed within the tradition of Aristotle and Aquinas. His anthropology and account of knowledge come from this tradition. But with the notion of God's Self-gift, our constitutive participation in the divine mystery, Rahner evokes Plato's anthropology. The fundamental human truth, and the ground for all truths, is our participation in the divine. We must already "know" in order to hear and comprehend God's revelation in Jesus.

The final truth of Christian teachings does not occur by making a his-torical study of their categories, though such a study is an essential part of Christian theology. We do not grasp Jesus' message by simply studying what the words "kingdom of God" meant to a first-century Jew. Rather, we grasp the truth of Christ's message when, through it, we recognize God's transcen-dental Self-offer to us and say "yes" to it. Truth occurs in our correlating the categorical expression of Jesus with the transcendental experience of God, when we experience God's very Self in the transcendental.

The message of Christ does not bring God's Self-offer to us for the first time. Rather, it interprets to us what we already are. It makes explicit our implicit, transcendental participation in the divine. In this sense Rahner's interpretation of Christ's message is memory. It tells us on an explicit, cate-gorical level what we already are in the transcendental. It brings to language and interprets what we already possess in what might be termed our tran-scendental memory.

This appeal to transcendental memory is Rahner's consistent method for interpreting Christian teachings. We have seen this method at work in Rahner's interpretation of Christ's message about the nearness of the king-dom. The foundational Christian proclamation that Jesus is risen from the dead can serve as another example.

## B. The Resurrection of Jesus

It was observed at the beginning of this chapter that Rahner seeks to offer a credible account of the faith. Some Christian teachings seem mythic and incredible for people today. Rahner's interpretation of Jesus' resurrection is a good example of how he seeks to make doctrines accessible to his contemporaries by correlating them with experience (transcendental memory).

The nature and meaning of Christ's resurrection is a controverted issue in contemporary theology. Some of the questions about the resurrection were raised in chapter 2. Can one know that Christ rose through historical study, or is belief in the resurrection simply a matter of blind faith? What happened to Jesus' body in the tomb? What was the nature of the apostolic experience which led to the conviction that he was alive and Lord?

Rahner does not approach these questions historically. Rather, the meaning of resurrection must already be possessed in the transcendental memory. Belief in the resurrection is made credible through a correlation between the doctrine and the transcendental. The material set forth in the preceding sections is adequate for understanding Rahner's interpretation of Christ's rising.

Rahner describes human existence as freedom. The ability to make specific choices is grounded in our being as possibility. To be human is not to be a fixed nature, but to be a becoming. We are always becoming someone.

Rahner calls this basic condition of becoming transcendental freedom. Human beings determine their being by the specific, categorical decisions they make. If I choose to tell lies I become a dishonest person. If I choose to share what I have with those who have less I become a generous person. I determine my being by the choices I make.

The exercise of freedom constitutes human existence. Everyone must choose. Some may flee their freedom by simply going along with what everyone else does, but that, too, is a choice as to what kind of person I am to be.

Rahner argues that within the unavoidable exercise of freedom an unavoidable question occurs. "Does it make any difference? What's the sense of it?" This question especially arises when we confront the knowledge of our own death. We are freedom toward death. Is there any meaning to the choices I make or do I simply die into nothingness?

In Rahner's view every human being must make a fundamental choice (option) concerning the validity of human life. One can opt for the view that life is without meaning. Whatever I do and become in freedom has no meaning. It makes no difference. This option manifests itself in a life lived in selfishness. I do what is good for me at the expense of other people.

The other option, which necessarily occurs to transcendental freedom, is that there is some meaning, some validity to human existence. There are human beings who live life as if it were of some meaning, of some validity. They give of themselves for the good of others. They choose to be honest when lying might seem to their advantage. They try to build a better social-economic order for the good of all.

Rahner terms this second option hope. It is a choice to live one's life in the hope that there is some meaning to human existence. The choice for hope need not be religious. Nor need this hope take the form of belief in life after death. It can, in fact, be quite unspecified—simply a life lived for the good of others in the conviction that this is the right way for a human being to exist.

Christ's message was that God is offering humanity an eternal share in the divine life. Death is not the end of existence. There is meaning, validity to a life lived for others. Jesus' own life was lived in perfect freedom toward God's Self-offer. He always gave himself for those in need. He always trusted and hoped in the God he proclaimed. Christ's life for others led to the cross. Yet even there he trusted and hoped.

In the resurrection God validates Jesus' life. God confirms the truth of Jesus' trust and hope.

What specifically does this mean? What happened to Jesus after Good Friday? Rahner holds that we can have no clear, categorical answer to these questions, since Christ's risen state is the validity of a human life beyond history, beyond space and time. Since our experience is within history we have no way of knowing what the final meaning of our existence might be beyond history, beyond the grave.

But we do have access to the meaning of the resurrection in our experience of transcendental hope. The possibility of some meaning occurs to every human being in the anticipation of death. Every human being lives life with an implicit option for its meaning or not. To say, "Life is meaningless," implies a notion of what meaningful life might be.

Hope is our access to the meaning of Christ's resurrection. When we correlate the church's proclamation that Jesus is risen with our transcendental hope for some validity to our existence in freedom, we have the meaning of Christ's resurrection.

The point at issue here is not a clear and complete understanding of Rahner's interpretation of the resurrection. Rather, it is simply to indicate that Rahner interprets the resurrection by asking us to find in our own transcendental memory the possibility for hope. When we correlate the doctrine of the resurrection with that hope we attain the meaning of the church's proclamation that "Jesus is risen."

## CONCLUDING REMARKS

As must be clear by now, Rahner's position is a complex combination of a number of thinkers into his own synthesis. While beginning with Aquinas, his philosophical-theological perspective includes insights from

Plato, Kant, Heidegger and others not mentioned. His goal is to establish a credible account of the faith for his contemporaries.

Why is faith difficult for people today? This chapter began by indicating some of the problems for belief Rahner addresses. Christian scripture and doctrines were formulated in different historical periods. They frequently reflect worldviews quite different from our own. Jesus' message about the kingdom, for example, suggests an apocalyptic vision of history. The world is about to end. The resurrection is similarly tied to apocalyptic categories. As indicated in chapters 3 and 8, the dogma of the incarnation reflects the philosophical categories of previous ages. Are contemporary believers bound to the ancient and medieval worldviews which gave rise to these doctrines? Must we suspend our own experience of the world? Does orthodoxy bind us to the philosophical categories of doctrinal formulas?

These questions manifest one of the fundamental givens of contemporary experience—our awareness of history. We know that different ages and cultures think about, and experience the world differently. The questions about the faith mentioned above ask, finally, about the relationship of Christian faith to human historicity.

This chapter has briefly presented Karl Rahner's answer to these questions. His method of correlating doctrine with the transcendental experience bypasses historical questions. What unites the faith is not its historical categories of expression, but the universal experience of God's Self-offer.

One can view Rahner's entire project as a response to the questions historical consciousness presents to the faith. His is but one theological response. All contemporary philosophers and theologians must grapple with the fact of human historicity. The next three chapters address this topic.

## BIBLIOGRAPHY

The philosophical background of Rahner's thought is very complex. Plato develops his notion of knowledge as memory in the *Phaedo*. Aquinas' epistemology was treated in chapter 5 of this work. For Kant's epistemology see his *Critique of Pure Reason*. Copleston's treatment of Kant in volume six of *A History of Philosophy* is excellent. For the influence of Martin Heidegger on Rahner, see *Rahner, Heidegger and Truth* by this author. Rahner develops his philosophical perspective in his two early works *Spirit in the World* and *Hearers of the Word*. These works are quite difficult. The introduction and early chapters of *Foundations of Christian Faith* present much of this material in a slightly more readable fashion. Also, see chapters 4 and 6 of *Foundations of Christian Faith* for Rahner's interpretation of the historical Jesus and his resurrection. Mary Hines' *The Transformation of Dogma* is an excellent introductory work to Rahner's thought.

# PART III
# HISTORY

Faith and reason are compatible. This is the premise underlying the conversation between philosophy and theology which is our topic. In recent centuries the intellectual tradition of the west has become profoundly aware of human historicity. We know that human existence, mores, language and thought are intrinsically related to historical context. Modern theology continues to struggle with the implications of this knowledge for Christian faith.

Chapter 9 introduced some of the questions historical consciousness raises for the faith. The next three chapters pursue this topic. They treat the nature of historical consciousness, the historical-critical method, some consequent theological problems and possibilities. Contemporary philosophy, and its awareness of history, suggests both questions and solutions for theological reflection. The reader is invited to enter this theological conversation.

# CHAPTER 10

# HISTORICAL CONSCIOUSNESS AND DOCTRINE

## I. HISTORICAL CONSCIOUSNESS

It is generally accepted today that people from different times and places will look at things differently. We anticipate such differences in travel or when people move to our country. American family structures (or lack thereof), the place of women, the importance of individual rights and expression are not universal. Other cultures, with different histories and traditions, have different values and structures.

Similarly, we frequently anticipate that older people will have points of view (musical taste, social-moral values, etc.) different from the young. Or, when we study art and literature we place works within their historical context, knowing that artists reflect the values, controversies and perspectives of their time.

Each of these instances is an example of historical consciousness. People reflect the historical period and cultural context in which they live. This way of looking at things is so familiar to us we can overlook the fact that it is a recent development in western consciousness. An awareness of human historicity, and the critical study of history which flows out of that awareness, became intellectually significant only in the eighteenth century.

Thinking historically about human existence and, therefore, all manifestations of human life (including the church), is a characteristic of the contemporary intellectual life. Philosophers now debate whether there is anything but history, whether there is anything like an enduring human nature or lasting truths. Our concern in this chapter is the profound effect historical consciousness has had on theology.

Scripture and church doctrine are texts (language) which reflect human historicity. As Catholics we accept their truth; as theologians we must try to understand that truth within the context of history. This chapter does not call the truth of scripture and doctrine into question. Rather, accepting the truth of church teaching, a task of contemporary theology is to give an account of that truth in view of history.

The importance of history for theology is clear in contemporary study of scripture. The historical-critical method dominates the field. A new theology student studying the gospels will soon find herself immersed in questions about the sources of the evangelists' stories, the authenticity of Jesus' statements, the influence of later church beliefs on the gospel narrative, etc. The method's critical approach to the story of Jesus frequently has students wondering if anything about the gospels can be trusted to be true.

But historical questions cannot be avoided in Christian theology. To be a Christian is to believe that God's Self-revelation and offer of salvation occur in a historical figure. Jesus lived, preached and died at a specific time and in a specific place. His message and manner of life are comprehensible only within the context of first-century Judaism. The apostolic witness to his resurrection took place within the same context. Our knowledge of Jesus comes from documents (the gospels) subject to the normal canons of critical research.

The study of church doctrine also requires historical awareness and criticism. The Council of Chalcedon, for example, teaches that Jesus is two natures (fully God and fully human) united in one hypostasis, one prosopon. A serious study of this dogma requires an analysis of what the terms "nature," "hypostasis," and "prosopon" meant in the context of fifth century, Hellenist philosophy, and how these words can be translated into contemporary terms.

The results of historical consciousness and critical research have raised serious questions for orthodox, Catholic belief. Much of contemporary theology addresses these questions and, thus, one cannot understand this theology without an appreciation of the issues raised by history.

## II. THE HISTORICAL-CRITICAL METHOD [1]

That there are historical problems in the scripture is not a modern idea. Patristic writers in the early centuries of the church were well aware of historical inconsistencies. For example, in the third century Origen knew that the accounts of Jesus' cleansing of the temple could not be harmonized. The synoptics place the event at the end of Jesus' ministry while John's gospel has it at the beginning. To resolve the conflict Origen treated the story as a spiritual allegory rather than an historical event. The cleansing of the temple is an allegory for Jesus entering and cleansing the soul.

Treating the narrative of an event as a spiritual allegory seems an unsatisfactory method for interpreting the gospels today. We are curious about what really happened. But it must be kept in mind that the fathers lived within a world dominated by Platonic and Neoplatonic thought. The world of physical things and historical events is but an imitation of another, more real world—the spiritual world of the forms. Thus, the allegorical was a common patristic hermeneutical tool. This difference between ourselves and the fathers is one more example of human historicity.

During the Middle Ages St. Thomas Aquinas, perhaps reflecting his Aristotelian perspective, urged a more literal interpretation of the scriptures. But the roots of the historical-critical method are found later, in the Renaissance and Reformation, in rationalism, and in the Enlightenment.

The Renaissance (literally "rebirth") sought to recapture the art and wisdom of the ancient world. To this end it involved study of the languages of scripture (Hebrew and Greek). Ancient texts were collected, critically studied and compared. For example, in 1440 Lorenzo Valla demonstrated that the Decree of Gratian, attesting to Constantine's donation of lands to Pope Sylvester I (d. 325), was a forgery. Valla used linguistic evidence and legal history to make his case—an early example of historical-critical argument.

The Reformation also played a part in the method's development in that it refocused Christian attention on scripture and its interpretation. Luther's rejection of church authority, and the magisterium's power to interpret the Bible, led him to assert that the meaning of scripture is available to any believer who reads it. The Protestant emphasis on reading the Bible, free of dogmatic authority, led not only to a wider study of scripture, but also showed the need for some hermeneutical method to control and evaluate the variety of interpretations which flowed out of the Reformation.

Luther held that the texts of scripture could be understood by any believer because they mean exactly what they say. There was no need of an authoritative interpreter (i.e., the magisterium). What resulted was a proliferation of interpretations reflecting various interpreters' different perspectives and the pluralism of theological perspectives present within the biblical texts. Luther met this problem in some degree by establishing a canon within the canon. To put the matter simply, for Luther and classical Protestant thought, Paul's letter to the Romans is *the gospel* which interprets the rest of scripture.

The seventeenth century marks the beginning of the modern era. Scientific developments, like Copernicus' revolution, soon challenged the biblical view of reality. Cartesian doubt and rationalism, which held reason to be the sole criterion for a truth claim, raised serious problems for those who held the Bible to be God's revealed word. Stories about the sun stopping in the sky, angelic visitations, ascending bodies, miracles, and the like, seemed to describe a childlike world now superseded by reason.

The Enlightenment proclaimed human liberty from the ignorance institutionalized in state and church. The world can be known by reason. Thought is only "critical" when it can account for its positions, grounding itself in solid, rational foundations. God, for Enlightenment thinkers, was needed only to explain the origin of a well-ordered universe which worked like a machine—deism. Scripture's descriptions of supernatural events were at best doubted, and more commonly rejected.

In this atmosphere of critical reason historians developed their own methods to date and authenticate historical texts. Tradition's attribution of authorship to famous persons, and texts' description of miraculous events, were systematically doubted. Vocabulary and style, for example, could help identify when a text was written and, frequently, whether it was written by a specific author. For example, in 1753 Jean Astruc identified four separate sources in the Pentateuch based on variations in the divine name. Or, critical scholars began to question why the synoptic gospels were so similar, a debate that gave rise to source theory.

Freed from church dogma and an uncritical reading of the gospels, nineteenth-century scholars set out to write a history of Jesus. The Jesus of John's gospel is obviously not the Jesus of the synoptics. Were these texts written by eyewitnesses? Do they not reflect the faith of the post-Easter church read back onto a historical figure? Scholars sought to discover the historical figure who stands behind church dogma and gospel narratives. Led by the presupposition of a world naturally ordered, supernatural events, like miracles and angelic visitations, were frequently excluded by the very nature of the historical method.

The nineteenth century abounds with efforts to write a critical history of Jesus. These efforts culminated in Albert Schweitzer's landmark work, *The Quest for the Historical Jesus* (1906). Schweitzer chronicles the efforts of scholars to find the Jesus of history. He argues that, rather than describing Jesus as he actually was, liberal European scholars generally re-created him in their own image.

Schweitzer himself concludes that Jesus was an apocalyptic preacher who proclaimed God was about to put an end to history and establish the divine kingdom. In this Jesus was obviously wrong. While Jesus can be honored as a great figure who stood against the evil of history, his actual teaching about the end of the world has nothing to say to moderns. Schweitzer's work put an end to the "first quest" and scholars did not return to this topic in earnest until the middle of the twentieth century. But Schweitzer's conclusion demonstrates the kind of difficult theological questions history can present. How can this ancient, Jewish rabbi have a claim on the modern world?

The vast majority of nineteenth-century theologians who took part in these historical studies were Protestant. The question of history barely touched the Catholic Church until the beginning of this century. The first theological attempts to place historical consciousness and the results of historical research in conversation with Catholic doctrine were a factor in the

Modernist crisis at the beginning of this century. The nature of Modernism, and of the church's response, are complex topics beyond the scope of this chapter. But the practical result of the crisis was that Catholic scholars were not allowed to pursue the historical-critical method. For example, a Catholic had to hold that Moses wrote the first five books of the Old Testament, despite critical evidence to the contrary.

But this did not solve the questions history raises for orthodox Catholic belief; it delayed and exacerbated them. Much of the theological tension within the church today reflects the continuing question of the relationship between history and orthodoxy.

Pius XII began the process of opening the church to historical-critical studies. The full freedom of Catholic scholars to address the issues raised by history did not occur until Vatican II.

Instead of treating the issue of history and theology in the abstract, we will now consider two doctrines which seemingly are challenged by the results of historical-critical studies—the resurrection of Jesus and the church's doctrine about its origins in Christ. Having noted the questions historical research raises about these doctrines, we will see how some theologians go about resolving them.

## III. THE RESURRECTION OF JESUS

No one seriously doubts that there was a Jesus of Nazareth, a first-century rabbi who preached the nearness of God's kingdom and who was crucified by the Roman authorities. Christians are those who believe God raised this Jesus from death and made him Lord. Christian faith is, first of all, belief in Jesus' resurrection.

If this be the case, one would think that the first Christians would have recorded an accurate account of the events following Jesus' death. But when one turns to the gospel accounts of Easter the testimony is quite confusing. I suggest that the reader study the endings of the four gospels, noting their similarities and differences.[2]

Mark (16:1–8), the earliest gospel, ends with the discovery of the empty tomb. A young man proclaims the crucified has been raised and asks the women to tell the apostles that Jesus goes ahead of them to Galilee where they will see him. The story concludes by stating that the women said nothing to anyone because they were afraid.[3]

Matthew (28) and Luke (24) add to Mark. What they add is inconsistent. The most obvious difference is that Matthew, seemingly following the tradition of which Mark was aware, places Jesus' apparition to the apostles in Galilee. Luke places his stories about Jesus' apparitions in Jerusalem. Luke tells us about Jesus appearing to two disciples traveling to Emmaus on

Easter Sunday. He also recounts an Easter Sunday appearance to the eleven in Jerusalem, a story which concludes with Jesus' ascension. Interestingly, when Luke continues his story, in Acts of the Apostles, he places the ascension forty days after Easter.

John narrates two independent accounts of Jesus' appearances. Chapter 20 of John's gospel occurs in Jerusalem with an apparition to Mary Magdalene at the tomb, and two appearances to the apostles which tell the story of Thomas' doubt and faith. Chapter 20 ends with a conclusion to the gospel. Chapter 21, making no reference to what has preceded, tells the story of Jesus appearing to the apostles at the lake in Galilee.

A critical reading of these accounts leaves one conclusion sure. They cannot all be literal accounts of what happened that first Easter. While the risen Christ might be able to be in both Jerusalem and Galilee, the apostles could not.

Why, if the resurrection is fundamental to the faith, is the Easter testimony so apparently confused and contradictory? If we cannot depend on the accuracy of scripture, where are we? How can we say the Bible is true if its narratives are contradictory? And how can this be the word of God if God cannot make mistakes? In brief, it does not take long to realize why a critical study of scripture can be so disturbing to believers.

Of course, the historical-critical method excludes the possibility of a dead person returning to life. As we saw, critical history has its origins in rationalism and the Enlightenment. The world operates by natural laws accessible through reason. Supernatural events are excluded a priori. That is, the method does not admit such events as possible and thus negates them as historical. It is not methodologically possible to investigate a supernatural event historically.

In historical research this a priori exclusion is called the canon of analogy. The world has always operated according to the natural processes with which we are familiar. Thus, any narrative of a supernatural occurrence is presumed to be non-historical, i.e., one cannot assert such an event on the basis of historical research. It is in this sense that theologians sometimes say that Jesus' resurrection is not a historical event. They mean that one cannot get to the resurrection through historical research alone, since the canon of analogy disallows such a supernatural occurrence. What historical research can show is that Jesus' followers, with the exception of a few women, abandoned him when he was arrested. Later they proclaimed that he had been raised from the dead. There is no "historical evidence" to account for this change.

Thus, one cannot "prove" the resurrection and the truth of Christianity by historical research alone. This is hardly surprising since Christian belief, by definition, requires faith. The gospel stories themselves seem to indicate a struggle between doubt and faith on the part of the apostolic witnesses (Mt.

28:17; Jn 20:24–29). But our original question remains. If Christian faith depends on the apostolic witness to the resurrection, why is the scriptural evidence so confused?

There is more scriptural material to help the believer with this question. In 1 Corinthians 15, Paul writes to the church of Corinth about the resurrection. 1 Corinthians was written at least ten years before the first gospel. Paul has heard that some members of the church at Corinth deny the future resurrection of believers. In this context Paul speaks about Jesus' resurrection. His comments are of special interest because this is the only record we have on the topic by one of the witnesses (apostles) to the risen Christ.

Paul observes that denying our future rising strikes at the very heart of the faith. If we do not rise from the dead then Jesus did not rise. And if Jesus did not rise "your faith is worthless (17)." Paul reminds the Corinthians that he had taught them what he had been taught. The formula Paul uses, "I handed on to you first of all what I myself received (3)," indicates a credal formula he had been taught at the time of his own conversion. Thus we are dealing with material dating from the first ten years after Jesus' death and resurrection. The early creed states:

> Christ died for our sins in accordance with the Scriptures; that he was buried and, in accordance with the Scriptures, rose on the third day; that he was seen by Cephas, then by the Twelve. After that he was seen by five hundred brothers at once, most of whom are still alive, although some have fallen asleep. Next he was seen by James; then by all the apostles. Last of all he was seen by me, as one born out of the normal course (3b–8).

Paul has added his own experience to an earlier list(s) of witnesses. Our purpose here is not to exegete this passage. Volumes have been written on it. Rather, one observation is in order. This early proclamation of the resurrection contains no stories about Jesus' appearances. That Jesus was raised and seen is simply proclaimed. In this it resembles the early ending of Mark's gospel.

It is widely held that the absence of stories in the earliest levels of the tradition reflects the character of the apostolic experience and, thus, the nature of Jesus' resurrection. Again, 1 Corinthians 15 can help us.

In verse 35 Paul observes that some ask the question, "How are the dead to be raised up? What kind of body will they have?" It is reasonable to presume that Paul will answer this question based on his experience of the risen Christ. That is, he will tell us what a risen body is like by reflecting on the risen body of Christ revealed to him.

Paul's response to his questioner: "You fool!" (36a). Why is the questioner a fool? Paul first writes of a seed that must die so God can give it the body of a full-grown plant. He then speaks about the many different kinds of bodies there are, human, animal, heavenly (stars, planets). So it is with the resurrection.

> What is sown in the earth is subject to decay, what rises is incorruptible. What is sown is ignoble, what rises is glorious. Weakness is sown, strength rises up. A natural body is put down and a spiritual body comes up (42b–44a).

What is Paul trying to say? What is a spiritual body? Body is one thing, spirit another.

Paul seems to be insisting that one cannot describe a risen body by the very nature of the case. If Jesus' risen state could have been described in imaginable terms Paul would have had a basis for answering the Corinthians' question. (For example, a risen body glows, can walk through walls, has height, etc.) In contrast, Paul says one cannot imagine (picture) what a risen body is like. We can imagine ghosts. Movie-makers do it all the time. But Paul says we have no basis in our everyday experience for picturing the risen Jesus. Can you tell from a seed what the plant will look like? No more can you tell from our present body what its risen nature will be. The questioner is a fool because the question, asking for a description of the risen body, misunderstands the very nature of resurrection.

If our interpretation of Paul is correct, we now have a basis for understanding why the Easter stories are so apparently confused and contradictory. To tell a story about Jesus appearing on Easter Sunday involves imagining him. That is, when we read the stories of Jesus appearing we must picture him talking, walking, eating, etc. But this is exactly what Paul says we cannot do. The risen body cannot be pictured. If it could Paul's answer to the Corinthians' question would have been much simpler. Thus the early proclamation of the resurrection involved no stories. The earliest material (Paul's credal formula and Mark's gospel) simply proclaims Christ has risen and has been seen by the apostles.

The stories in the gospels about Jesus appearing developed in the later church. The proclamation that Jesus was seen by Peter and the eleven was put into concrete narratives in which Jesus enters rooms, speaks and eats. Since these stories developed later, i.e., they did not belong to the original proclamation, they took on different forms in different churches. That is why the stories, when compared to each other, are contradictory.

Let us now consider for a moment where these historical-critical reflections have taken us. Perhaps we have always presumed that the gospel stories about Easter are literal narratives of historical events. A brief, critical comparison of the texts raises serious questions about this presupposition.

Seemingly the critical method is an attack on our faith. But theologians argue that this critical analysis of the texts has forced us to consider again the nature of the resurrection. To picture Jesus' body as a resuscitated corpse is to misunderstand the Easter event. Paul certainly rejects any notion of resurrection as mere resuscitation, like Lazarus returning from the dead. Yet, if we take the Easter stories as literal narratives we must imagine Jesus' risen body as a resuscitated version of what he was before his death (even if it can pass through walls, appear and disappear).

But, on another level, we already know something different about the risen Christ. If asked, "Where is Jesus?" Christians will normally offer two responses together: "He is in heaven," and "He is here with us." If the risen Christ were a resuscitated body he could hardly be here with us, and with all other Christians around the world. Bodies have specific location. They can only be in one place at one time. Yet Christians know that Jesus is really present with us all the time. Why else would we speak to him in prayer or celebrate his presence in the eucharist?

But if Christ is really present to all Christians of every age (Matthew 28:20) then his body must have been radically transformed in the resurrection. And is this not exactly what Paul tells us in 1 Corinthians 15?

In contrast, if we insist on keeping Jesus in a body similar to our own all sorts of problems result. We have already seen the inconsistencies within the scripture which flow from such an understanding. Another example from church history will point up the theological difficulties flowing from such a view.

Catholic doctrine about the eucharist has insisted on the real presence, i.e., that the bread and wine become the body and blood of Christ. As is always the case, this doctrinal insistence reflects past theological controversies. Questions about the real presence date back to the ninth century, to scholars like Ratramnus. The issue was argued by the scholastics in the Middle Ages and was a source of doctrinal division in the Reformation.

While the controversy over eucharistic presence is quite complex and beyond the scope of this chapter, the nature of Christ's state is fundamental to the doctrine. One reason why scholars like Ratramnus raised the question was that they understood Christ's risen body in an imaginative fashion. This body was in heaven. How, then, could it be really present on all the altars of the world?

The point of these observations is to indicate that this questioning of the doctrine of real presence is rooted in an understanding of the resurrection. If, in contrast, one understands the resurrection as a radical transformation of Jesus' body, a transformation that renders Christ really present to believers for all time, then the eucharistic problem of real presence is itself transformed. The eucharist does not render an absent Christ present, but makes sacramental the enduring presence of the risen Lord.

Recall Augustine's eucharistic theology treated in chapter 4. Augustine warns against the desire to cling to the earthly body of Jesus. For Augustine, the body of Christ is the risen Jesus, united with all his members, ascended to the eternal banquet with God. Perhaps these reflections on the resurrection of Jesus can help retrieve this patristic understanding of the sacrament. I suggest this not as an alternative to the doctrine of real presence, but to situate the doctrine in a broader and richer context.

This section began by indicating the apparent problems for faith raised by a historical-critical look at the resurrection stories in the gospels. My suggestion is that what first appeared problematic ends by offering rich possibilities for theological reflection. A critical study of scriptural texts on the resurrection has led to a deeper appreciation of the mystery of the risen Lord.

## IV. JESUS AND THE DIVINE ORIGIN OF THE CHURCH

Our second example of how historical criticism can trouble orthodox belief concerns the founding of the church. We begin with Catholic doctrine. The first and second Vatican Councils offer the clearest, and most authoritative teaching on the topic. In its dogmatic constitution *Pastor aeternus* the First Vatican Council taught,

> The eternal Shepherd and Guardian of our souls, in order to render the saving work of redemption lasting, decided to establish his holy Church....He placed St. Peter at the head of the other apostles that the episcopate might be one and undivided...that the whole multitude of believers might be preserved in unity of faith and communion by means of a well-organized priesthood (DS. 3050).
> If anyone says that it is not according to the institution of Christ our Lord himself, that is by divine law, that St. Peter has perpetual successors in the primacy over the whole Church; or if anyone says that the Roman Pontiff is not the successor of St. Peter in the same primacy: let him be anathema (DS. 3058).

Vatican II reasserted the teaching of Vatican I on the primacy of the pope and went on to teach about the episcopacy, the bishops. In its dogmatic constitution *Lumen Gentium* the Second Vatican Council taught that "Christ the Lord set up in his Church a variety of offices"(18), and

> That divine mission, which was committed by Christ to the apostles, is destined to last until the end of the world, since the

Gospel, which they were charged to hand on, is, for the Church, the principle of all its life for all time. For that very reason the apostles were careful to appoint successors in this hierarchically constituted society (20).

The councils cite Matthew 16:17–19, John 20:21–23, and John 21:15–17 (and other texts) in presenting their teaching.

One need only be vaguely familiar with the Catholic Church to be aware how important these texts are for church life. The teaching authority of the pope and hierarchy, the magisterium, is a constant theme in theology and the press. May Catholics disagree with the teaching of pope and bishops? Are the magisterium's pronouncements on the ordination of women final? As the council texts make clear, the church teaches that God has divinely instituted in the church offices with authority. The practical question at issue in current disputes concerns the nature and breadth of that authority. Behind these disputes lurks the question about the grounds of the claim to divine institution of ecclesial office. Again, historical questions are crucial.

The quotes cited above could give the impression that Jesus clearly foresaw the age of the church between his resurrection and the end of the world. He thus foresaw and designed an institution in which the office of the twelve, headed by Peter, would continue to run the church through the bishops and pope. But the evidence of history militates against such a simple understanding of Church doctrine.

The first historical problem with this understanding of the relationship between Jesus and the church concerns Jesus' conscious intention to found a church. The gospels do not tell us about Jesus actually designing a church. Matthew 16:16b–19 is the only place in the gospels where Jesus speaks about establishing a church. The passage is much debated because of its later connection with the papacy. If the words actually go back to the historical Jesus, and many scholars think they do not, at most they can be said to refer to an apocalyptic community waiting for the end.[4]

The last point brings us to the crux of the discussion. Scholars generally agree (and have for some time) that Jesus' historical message pivoted around the proclamation, "The kingdom of God is at hand." The kingdom meant for Jesus the end of the world as we know it and the establishment of God's rule. The Son of Man would come, the dead would rise for judgment, and the just would enter the kingdom.

While it can be argued that Jesus foresaw a period of time between his death and the coming of the kingdom (e.g., his injunction to "do this in memory of me" to the apostles at the last supper), it is generally agreed that he anticipated the end was near. This is certainly how early Christians understood his message and the significance of his resurrection. Paul in 1 Thessalonians

(4:15), for example, expects the end during his lifetime.

If Jesus anticipated an early end to the world it seems unreasonable to think that he intended to found and design an institutionalized community. It would be like a group of terminal patients arguing over the by-laws of their new club. It is not something people standing before the end do. If the end is at hand there is no need for an institutionalized community.

One might theorize that the establishment of ecclesial structures and offices by Christ occurred after the resurrection, during his forty days with the apostles. Our remarks above about the risen Christ makes this thesis problematic. But, granting the possibility, were this the case then one would anticipate that the church's structures would have appeared at once.

The second historical problem with the notion that Jesus consciously established a church, is that the institutional structures referred to by the two Vatican councils developed historically. If the Jesus of history had designed an ecclesial structure for his new community, one would think that the community would have employed that structure from the beginning. That is, each local church would have been headed by one presbyter-bishop appointed by an apostle.

This is demonstrably not the case. The church Paul writes to at Corinth does not have such a structure. The church at Rome does not seem to have developed the structure of a single bishop until the middle of the second century. Thus, while St. Peter died at Rome in the mid 60s, it is anachronistic to refer to him as "bishop of Rome."[5]

What is clear in the historical record is that the church's structure developed. Structures emerge in the pastoral epistles which date from the end of the first century. This is to be anticipated, for these and other later texts, reflect the church's adjustment to the delay in the Lord's return.

Similarly, the place of the bishop of Rome within the universal church develops, as does the practice of holding episcopal councils as a way to establish orthodoxy. Thus, the structures of the Catholic Church, and the authority belonging to its offices, cannot be traced back to the conscious institution of Jesus.

How, then, are we to understand the teaching of the two councils? If church structure develops, can it not develop further? Why not a more democratic structure? Is the church free to change its practice of ordaining only men? One can see at once the practical ramifications that historical consciousness presents to the church.

As Catholic theologians we accept both the teaching of the two Vatican councils and the results of historical critical research. The theological question is, "How do we hold these two positions together?" Theological efforts to answer this question, the topic of chapter 11, allow us to see once again how philosophy plays an essential role in the theological enterprise.

## BIBLIOGRAPHY

The comments in this chapter on the development of the historical-critical method follow Edgar Krentz, *The Historical-Critical Method*, pp. 6–32. For the condemnation of Modernism see the decree of the Holy Office, *Lamentabili,* and the encyclical *Pascendi.* Dermot Lane's *The Reality of Jesus,* chapters 2–5, offers a good account of positions commonly held by scholars about the historical Jesus and the resurrection. The questions treated in this chapter about Jesus' resurrection are developed further in Raymond Brown's essay, "The Resurrection of Jesus" in *The Jerome Biblical Commentary.* Or, see Reginald Fuller's *The Formation of the Resurrection Narratives.* Citations within the preceding text to DS. refer to a compilation of doctrinal texts in *Enchiridion Symbolorum,* first edited by Henricus Denzinger. The work is commonly referred to as "Denzinger" and references frequently take an abbreviated form like DS or Denz. Most of Denzinger is in Latin, though the Greek texts of the early councils are also included. The English texts of Vatican I cited in this chapter come from *The Church Teaches.* The texts from Vatican II come from *Lumen Gentium* and are taken from *Vatican Council II,* ed. by Austin Flannery. An excellent account of the development of the early Church can be found in Frederick Cwiekowski's *The Beginnings of the Church.* Also see *Antioch and Rome* by Raymond Brown and John Meier. For an excellent discussion of Matthew 16:16b–19, see *Peter in the New Testament,* ed. by Brown, Donfried, and Reumann.

## NOTES

1.  In this section I am following Edgar Krentz's *The Historical-Critical Method,* pp. 6–32.
2.  See Raymond Brown, "The Resurrection of Jesus," *The Jerome Biblical Commentary.* The first edition, 78:146–149, pp. 791–795; Second edition, 81:118–134, pp. 1373–1377.
3.  Scholars generally agree that Mark 16:8 is the end of the original gospel. This is obviously a rather unsatisfactory conclusion. Verses 9–20 were later added to many versions of the gospel and appear to be a compilation of material from the other gospels. These latter verses are part of the canonical text.
4.  *Peter in the New Testament,* pp. 83–101. The word "church" appears only twice in the four gospels, Mt. 16:18 and Mt. 18:17.
5.  The points made here are commonly held among scholars. See, for example, Raymond Brown and John Meier, *Antioch and Rome,* pp. 162–165.

# CHAPTER 11

# THE DIVINE ORIGIN OF THE CHURCH

We saw in the preceding chapter how critical history raises questions concerning the church's doctrine of its origin in Christ. Vatican I and Vatican II teach that the church and its hierarchical structure (pope and bishops) were established by God in Christ. Yet the historical evidence suggests that 1) Jesus did not consciously intend a church, and 2) the church's structure developed during the first century after the Christ event. How, then, are we to understand the conciliar doctrine?

This might seem a rather obscure question, but it has practical ramifications for the life of the church today. What in church structure can change? Here is the critical issue. Seemingly, what God has designed for the church is unchanging. Church structures which are *de jure divino,* set by divine law, cannot change. Consider the implications of this question for the ecumenical movement, the effort of Christian communities for a unified church. What papal functions and authority are divinely instituted and, therefore, cannot be compromised for the sake of unity? Is the episcopal structure willed by God, or could a united Christian church include communities with congregational structures? What can be changed or compromised for the sake of unity? Or, all would agree that celibacy is not required by divine law for ordination. The church is free to change this discipline. But is the church free to change its unbroken tradition of ordaining only men?

One's stance on these current questions is determined, in no small part, by how one understands the origin of the church and its constitution. If Jesus, during his ministry or as risen Christ, had given the church a specific constitution, the church would be permanently bound to that structure. Again, the historical evidence indicates this did not happen. Christians, of course, believe that the Spirit guides the church. The decisions taken about ecclesial organization are, therefore, divinely assisted. But why cannot the church take new decisions about its structure? On what basis can it be asserted that certain historical decisions about the church's constitution are divinely intended and, therefore, unchangeable?

Theologian Jean Galot underscores this point in his book *Theology of*

114

*Priesthood.* Galot argues that grounding the divine origin of ecclesial office in the Spirit's guidance, rather than in the conscious intention of Jesus, gives the church greater freedom in how it structures itself. Offices which rise from within the church, even under the Spirit's guidance, have their authority from the church rather than from Christ. Galot contends that, while such a scheme might appeal to our democratic spirit, church doctrine teaches that the offices of pope, bishop and priest come from Christ himself and cannot be changed.

Galot holds that church offices are grounded in the conscious intention of the historical Jesus. He argues that Jesus identified himself as shepherd. This image contains within it the three functions identified with ecclesial office—priest, prophet and ruler. Not knowing when the world would end, Jesus chose the twelve, and coworkers, to carry on his mission as shepherd. Galot maintains that there is evidence of the offices of bishop and priest in the earliest days of the church. For example, in Acts of the Apostles (chapter 6), seven men are chosen for the distribution of bread. Galot sees this as the twelve (bishops) choosing coworkers to celebrate the eucharist (priests).

While we shall not pursue Galot's position further, it is significant to note for two related reasons. First, he clearly indicates the significance of our topic for church life. Second, his interpretation of the historical evidence is quite different from that of most scholars. He argues that Jesus intended the church and designed its constitution. While this position is certainly congenial to one understanding of church doctrine, it does not reflect the general consensus among historical-critical scholars on this topic. The presupposition of this chapter is that one cannot deduce history from doctrine. In this writer's opinion, such an approach amounts to an ecclesial fideism and, thereby, contradicts the church's basic teaching about the relationship of faith and reason.

Our goal is to consider how theologians give an account of church doctrine in view of the more widely accepted interpretation of the historical evidence. As Catholic theologians we are not questioning the truth of church doctrine. We accept the teaching of the two Vatican Councils. Nor can we flee the hard questions raised by historical evidence. We seek to offer a reasonable account of church doctrine in view of the data.

Following the example of theologians since the first centuries of the church, contemporary thinkers turn to philosophy for help in explaining church teachings. In this chapter we will see how two Catholic theologians use philosophy to explicate the church's teaching about its divine origins. Specifically, we will see how Karl Rahner employs a form of Kant's transcendental thought while Francis Fiorenza utilizes the insights of hermeneutical philosophy. Drawing these two positions together we can see at least a partial explanation of the teaching of the Vatican Councils, an explanation which takes the results of historical research into account.

### I. A TRANSCENDENTAL DEDUCTION OF THE CHURCH

The word "transcendental" indicates that Rahner's position has its roots in the way of thinking suggested by Immanuel Kant. "Transcendental" refers to Kant's theory of knowledge. Kant's epistemology sought to ground scientific knowledge in the face of Hume's observations about causality. For the sake of brevity I will simplify the point at issue with an example.

Imagine you are watching your classmates play pool. You see the table before you with balls on it. You watch one lad take his turn. The ball ("a") he hits moves across the table and comes up next to another ball ("b"). The first ball stops, the second begins to move. Hume points out that while we see this series of events we do not see the first ball cause the second to move. How then do we know that the first causes the second's motion?

Hume's question has profound implications. He is asking about the epistemological grounds for the physical sciences. The sciences seek to understand the relationship between empirical events. For example, does virus "x" cause a specific illness? Hume asks about the grounds for asserting causality. This is the question Kant seeks to answer. That is, Kant wants to establish an epistemological foundation for scientific practice.

Of course I know that ball "a" causes ball "b" to move but I do not see the causality. What I see is a sequence of events. But not all sequential events involve causality. Despite their frequent coincidence, getting into a shower does not cause the phone to ring. So how is it that I attribute causality to one sequence of events and not to another?

Kant, like most of his contemporaries, presumed the subject-object distinction introduced into modern thought by Descartes. What Hume's question points out is that causality does not belong to the realm of objects. I do not see it out there. If causality is not an object of sense experience (empirical) then it must be provided by the subject, by the knower. Kant's epistemology thus turns to the subject, to the knower. He asks a very specific question: What are the conditions (of subjectivity) which make possible the act of knowing? This question is the distinctive characteristic of the transcendental method, or the transcendental turn (the turn to the subject). What must be true of subjectivity for it to do what it does in the act of knowing?

Consider again the analogy suggested in chapter 9. Hearing involves two elements—sound waves and the structure of the ear. A medical student studies the conditions (the structure of the ear) which make possible the act of hearing. If a patient cannot hear, the doctor looks at her ear to see what is wrong. The ear must have a specific structure for hearing to take place. So Kant sought to establish the conditions of subjectivity which account for the act of knowing. Part of Kant's answer is that the category "causality" must be an a priori condition of subjectivity. That is, the mind must bring some grasp of causality to the visual experience of the two pool balls. Logically this competence of the subject must exist prior to the empirical events it understands causally.

Thus, Kant deduces the conditions of subjectivity which make possible the act of knowing. The classic form of Kant's transcendental method is the question: What are the necessary conditions for the possibility of knowing? The answer is a "deduction" because, unlike that doctor looking at the ear, the conditions of subjectivity are not empirical. They are implicit in the act of knowing itself. One must deduce them from the act as its necessary conditions.

This way of thinking drives much of Karl Rahner's theology and he employs it to explain the doctrine of the church's divine origins. The issue here is, of course, not the act of knowledge. But the form of the transcendental question suggests a way of understanding the divine origin of the church which does not depend on the explicit design of Jesus Christ.

The major premise for Rahner's deduction is the fundamental Christian belief that God offers all humanity salvation in Jesus. Rahner asks: What are the necessary conditions for the possibility of Jesus being universal savior?

The answer to this question can be found in our own experience as believers. How is it that we experience salvation in Jesus? How did we come to this faith? We believe in Jesus because he was proclaimed to us. Our families, or friends, or whoever brought us to knowledge of Christ, made our faith possible. In other words, a necessary condition for Jesus being our savior is a community of believers who told us about him. By extension, the necessary condition for Jesus being the savior of people in all times and places is that there be a community of believers to proclaim him—a church.

So if one believes that God offers all people of all times salvation in Jesus, one must conclude that God wills a community to live and proclaim the faith. Without church Jesus would be just one more individual in history, not an object of faith. The church is a necessary condition for Jesus being universal savior. Whether Jesus consciously intended to found a church is not terribly important. God willed the church in offering all people salvation through Jesus.

Transcendental argument can also establish that God wills institutional structures within the church. Human communities necessarily organize themselves. Since God wills the church, a human community, God also wills ecclesial offices. This, of course, does not bring us to specific forms of office, e.g., it does not establish the *ius divinum* (divine law) character of a single bishop leading each local church. One cannot demonstrate from a transcendental deduction alone that God wills the hierarchical structure which developed in the church's early centuries. The deduction only establishes that God wills a structure because, as a human community, the church requires some manner of organization.

However, transcendental argument can demonstrate God's will for a papal ministry, i.e., the essential character of an office symbolizing the unity of the universal church. Believers generally agree that the Christian community ought to be united worldwide. Since human communities require an office for the sake of such unity (as countries have a monarch or president) so the church requires a unifying office.

Let us sum up what has been said thus far. Both Vatican councils teach that the apostolic offices of bishop and pope are divinely instituted by Christ. If these offices could be traced back to the conscious design of Jesus Christ, the meaning and implications of the councils' teaching would be clear. But evidence indicates that these offices developed in the history of the church after Easter, Pentecost and Ascension. Rahner's transcendental deduction can establish God's will for a church with offices, including the papal office for the unity of the universal church. But human communities can organize themselves in many ways. The deduction cannot establish that God wills the specific offices spoken about by the two Vatican councils. How, then, are we to understand the church's teaching?

In other words, Rahner's deduction offers some rather abstract principles about the divine origin of church and its structures. It is not, however, very helpful in connecting the concrete, historical structures of the church with Jesus and God's will. The abstract nature of Rahner's position reflects the transcendental character of his thought. Hermeneutical philosophy suggests another way of thinking about the church's origin in Jesus which takes greater account of the relationship between the historical Jesus and ecclesial structures.

## II. A HERMENEUTICAL ACCOUNT OF THE CHURCH'S ORIGINS IN CHRIST

### A. Background: Hermeneutics

When we looked at the results of historical-critical studies concerning the founding of the church we saw the difficulty of connecting the church with the conscious intention of the historical Jesus. Hermeneutical thought suggests that this is the wrong way to state the issue.

Hermeneutical theory deals with the meaning of texts. The question of textual meaning rose within the context of western philosophy's obsession with epistemology. How do we know? Kant had offered an answer to that question for the physical sciences. But what about the humanities? When reading historical texts or literary classics, is there a method to assure an accurate reading and to referee conflicting interpretations?

If you receive a note from your boss instructing you to perform some task, and if sections of the note are unclear, you might ask a coworker what she thinks the note means. If the two of you cannot agree, and the opinion of others fails to resolve the confusion, how do you settle the question? Obviously you ask your boss what she meant. The true meaning of this text, the note, is determined by the intention of its author.

In the first stages of the hermeneutical thought "author's intent" was assumed to be the goal of interpretation. The historical-critical method comes out of this presumption. The practitioners of the method are generally trained in the languages and history of the period they intend to study. The goal of the method is to understand the vocabulary, usage, customs, perspectives, values, etc., of the time in which the text was formulated. In this way interpreters can avoid simply imposing the contemporary meaning of words onto an ancient text.

Examples might help. A characteristic of fundamentalism is that it is uncritical in reading the scriptures. Twentieth-century, conservative Americans read the Bible and find in it the values they hold dear. Capitalism, anti-feminism, divine punishment on victims of AIDS, etc., are all supported by a "Scriptural Christianity." The fact that the scriptures were written over a period of one thousand years, reflecting a variety of theological perspectives and stages of development, is overlooked. So, too, is the fact that terms like justification and righteousness had meanings in the context of first century Jewish-Christian thought that are difficult to retrieve two thousand years later in a very different context.

The same kind of uncritical thinking can also occur within Catholicism. John 20:22–23 can be viewed as Jesus founding the sacrament of reconciliation. Or questions about women's ordination can be settled with the assertion that Jesus did not ordain any women. Each instance is anachronistic in that it imposes later questions and ecclesial forms onto the past.

Historical criticism seeks to avoid this kind of imposition of meaning through method, the scientific manner of controlling research. In science one follows a method to avoid distorting the evidence. In the scientific method the researcher must follow established procedure accepted by her colleagues. To test a hypothesis an experiment must be devised which isolates a specific matter from other influences. For example, if a scientist is studying the effect of temperature on a given material, all other factors (humidity, air pressure, etc.) must remain constant as the temperature is changed. One thus isolates a specific variable to see its effects. The experiment must be repeatable by other scientists. Whether those scientists are communists or capitalists, white or black, religious or atheist, makes no difference. The very purpose of method is to exclude variables like the cultural, ideological, and religious prejudice of the one performing an experiment. Method guarantees the integrity of an experiment and the validity of its results.

The historical-critical method developed in the nineteenth century when the physical sciences seemed to offer *the model* for certain knowledge. Hermeneutical thinkers sought to do for the humanities what Kant had done for the physical sciences. That is, they set out to establish the grounds for assuring the correct interpretation of classic, historical texts. How do we attain the true meaning of an ancient text? What method can we use to assure an accurate interpretation? How do we attain the meaning the text had for its original author and audience?

As with the philosophy of science, theorists attempted to offer grounds for what practitioners were already doing. There were scientists successfully carrying on science before Kant attempted to establish firm, epistemological grounds for their project. So the eighteenth and nineteenth centuries abounded in historians and biblical scholars critically studying texts. As mentioned earlier, the nineteenth century produced many attempts by scholars to write a critical history of Jesus' life.

The problem with these studies, unlike the physical sciences, is that there continued to be a wide variety of interpretations of the same material and there seemed no way of deciding who, if anyone, was correct. Schweitzer's book chronicling the history of the quest for the historical Jesus concluded that, despite all their critical efforts, scholars kept finding in Jesus the values and perspectives they themselves held. The "Jesus of history" consistently seemed to look like a nineteenth-century, European liberal. Schweitzer's own interpretation of Jesus, as an apocalyptic prophet, remains only one among many conflicting interpretations.

It seems obvious that theology, and the other humanities, need some method to control and referee these conflicting views. The effort to achieve such a method, and its grounds, is called the hermeneutical movement. Frederick Schleiermacher and Wilhelm Dilthey are the names most commonly associated with its beginnings in the nineteenth and early twentieth centuries.

To grasp the problem at issue it is helpful to distinguish the kinds of claims a text can make and the consequent problems in interpretation. When the gospels tell us that Jesus went up to Jerusalem and died, there is no difficulty in understanding the meaning. But when we are told Jesus died for our sins interpretation becomes quite problematic. What is the meaning of this last assertion? This is the kind of claim, found in canonical texts, which gives rise to conflicting interpretations.

In recent years hermeneutical thought has moved in new directions. Many hermeneutical philosophers have abandoned, as misguided, the whole effort to attain the mind of the original author. For the sake of brevity we will consider the thought of one of the most influential hermeneutical philosophers, Hans-Georg Gadamer, to get a sense of why this approach is so important in contemporary theology.

Gadamer's key work is titled *Truth and Method*. The title is ironic. As noted above, the physical sciences developed method to assure validity and truth. By methodically disengaging the personal-cultural interests of the scientist from her experiment, method assures objectivity and validity. Gadamer argues that such method is precisely how one does *not* interpret a text. The interpretation of classic texts is not carried out by methodical disengagement, but by participation in the matter at issue. Against the fundamental thrust of Enlightenment thought, with its emphasis on the integrity of autonomous reason, Gadamer argues for the rehabilitation of prejudice. By this he means that our cultural, linguistic, historical circumstances are not the enemy of interpretation, but its possibility. An example might clarify this critical point.

We are going to the theater this evening to see *Hamlet*. How shall we understand this classic work? We might spend the afternoon reading sections of the play and commentaries on it. We might go to a dictionary to get help with some of the Elizabethan terms used. What did these words mean in Shakespeare's time? English usage has changed a great deal since then. Our modern English usage is quite different from that of Shakespeare. Methodical preparations can surely help in understanding the play and what Shakespeare meant when he wrote the text.

But how do I really understand *Hamlet*? If I continue my methodical approach while the play goes on I will have a dictionary in my lap, scanning its pages for precise definitions. I will consider how the director has staged the play, and evaluate how the actors have interpreted their roles. Perhaps I will compare them with previous performances I have seen, or with the commentaries I read earlier in the day. And through all this methodical attention I will fail to see *Hamlet*. More precisely, all this methodical study will finally prevent me from grasping what *Hamlet* is really about.

*Hamlet* is a classic work not only because it is a good story in beautiful English, but because it has something to say about being a human being. As with any classic, it makes a claim on us. When Hamlet wonders "To be or not to be..." he confronts a question we all face and must decide upon. Unless that question strikes home, unless I know within what Hamlet suffers, unless I have something in my own experience of that question, I cannot grasp the meaning. Methodical separation and distance is not the means to the text's truth; it makes that truth impossible. Personal participation in the matter at stake is the grounds for understanding, not its foe.

The truth of *Hamlet* is not found by a methodic reconstruction of its author's intent. The play is a classic because it has made a claim on audiences since the seventeenth century. In differing contexts and conditions the play has made its claim, taking on as many unique meanings as people who have appreciated it and seen their own lives through it. *Hamlet's* meaning goes on and to limit it to the intention of Shakespeare is simply to misunderstand the nature of its claim. The truth of *Hamlet* is its continuing effect in history, what Gadamer calls the effective history of the text.

This example makes Gadamer's central point. The truth of a classic work is not attained by method (the irony of his title) but by participation and application of the work's claim to life. Gadamer does not mean that the historical critical-method has no role. He argues that we must let the text stand in all its historical uniqueness. The world of a classic text (its historical context) is frequently strange to us. We must let that strangeness challenge our present. But, finally, we grasp the text's meaning only in application. Thus, we cannot leave our own historical context to take on another (the mind of the author) since our own context is the grounds for understanding (application).

## B. Hermeneutics, Jesus and the Church

Central to the observations above is that a text's meaning is not limited to the conscious intention of its author. Meaning occurs as a text is applied in the countless contexts of history. Francis Schüssler Fiorenza applies this insight to the question of Jesus' founding of the church. Fiorenza argues that to limit the question to the conscious intention of the historical Jesus (Did Jesus intend to found a church?) is to misunderstand the meaning of human actions.

All historians know that the meaning of an event is not limited to the intentions of the actors involved. In 1914 the assassins at Sarajevo certainly did not grasp the significance of their act and its meaning (which we are still living out). Or, you might consider specific choices you made in your life and recall your conscious intentions at the time. The meaning of those choices has probably gone in unanticipated directions. Ask a couple married fifty years what their vows meant on their wedding day and what their vows have meant since. I suspect you will get a smile, a shake of the head, and "I had no idea!"

We are also familiar with this dynamic in the history of God's revelation. For example, the suffering servant songs of second Isaiah had their original meaning in the context of the exile, five hundred years before Jesus. But these texts took on a new meaning within the context of Jesus' suffering and exaltation. Or, Jesus' life and resurrection gave God's promise to the house of David new meaning.

In similar fashion Fiorenza argues that the acts and words of the historical Jesus have meanings beyond his conscious intention. Jesus' choice of the twelve, the place of Peter with Jesus and the twelve, Christ's table fellowship, his words and actions at the last supper, and so on, all take on new meaning in view of his death and rising. These words and acts have the effect in history of giving rise to the church, its structures, the variety of eucharistic practices over the church's history, etc. As a classic text, the words and actions of Jesus have an effective history which constitutes their meaning. To limit the question to Jesus' conscious intention is to misunderstand the nature of meaning.

Fiorenza thus ties the concrete historical forms of ecclesial office to Jesus. The offices of pope and bishop are the effect of Jesus' life, message and fate. After Easter and Pentecost the acts and words of the historical Jesus took on new meaning in a new context. His choice of the twelve and the position of Peter had effects beyond Jesus' original intention (whatever that might have been). These actions have had the effect of giving rise to specific ecclesial offices. One can thus accept both the conclusion of historical research, Jesus did not consciously intend or design the church, and church doctrine about the origins of its structures in Christ.

### III. CONCLUDING REMARKS

Combining the insights of transcendental and hermeneutical thought can bring theology a long way toward explaining the doctrine that God founded the church and its structures in Christ. God's offer of salvation to all humanity occurs in the life, message, death and rising of Jesus. The proclamation of the Christ requires a community of witnesses—the church.

The church has its roots in the community formed by Jesus' historical ministry. As all human communities, it requires a structure. The church's first leaders were those who knew Jesus best and were witnesses to his resurrection. These naturally had authority in the community formed by the Christ event. They guaranteed continuity between the historical Jesus, the paschal event and the faith of the church. This apostolic function was continued by presbyter-bishops. Jesus' choice of the twelve has this effect in the history of the church, i.e., the episcopacy.

Peter's position in the early church reflected his relationship with the historical Jesus and, perhaps, his priority as witness to the resurrection. The function of symbolizing the unity of the entire Christian family has thus been characterized as Petrine, i.e. an extension of Peter's place in the early church. Thus the community's need for a unifying office (transcendental) is met by the effects of Jesus' historical relationship with Peter (hermeneutical). This effect continues in the history of the church. The church at Rome became the locus of this unifying function through the combination of its central position in the empire and the fact that it could claim Sts. Peter and Paul. In 325 the Council of Nicea recognized Rome as the first see in Christendom.

Thus, transcendental and hermeneutical theology offer a way to understand church doctrine about its origins, without attributing a conscious, ecclesial plan to the historical Jesus. But the attentive reader will also have noted that these theological perspectives do not establish the permanent character of any specific ecclesial form. In other words, there is nothing in the logic of these positions which would exclude the possibility of changing the concrete forms of ecclesial offices.

Our discussion of this topic ends without final resolution. While we can understand the church's teaching about its origins in Christ, the practical questions about what can and ought to change are left unanswered. As noted at the beginning of this chapter, this question lurks beneath many contemporary debates within the church. This work seeks to introduce students to the theological dialogue, not to resolve it.

## BIBLIOGRAPHY

For the argument that the church's structures can be traced to the conscious intention of the historical Jesus, see Jean Galot's *Theology of Priesthood*. Patrick Dunn repeats Galot's position in more popular fashion in his book *Priesthood*. For Rahner's transcendental deduction of the church, see chapter 7 of *Foundations of Christian Faith*, especially sections 1–5. Fiorenza's hermeneutical account of the church's origins can be found in his *Foundational Theology*, pp. 108–154. Part II of Hans-Georg Gadamer's work *Truth and Method* is important background to Fiorenza's proposal. The next chapter returns to Gadamer's thought. *Truth and Method* is a difficult work. A good summary of Gadamer's position can be found in David Linge's "Editor's Introduction" to a collection of Gadamer's essays titled *Philosophical Hermeneutics*.

# CHAPTER 12

# HUMAN HISTORICITY

The section in chapter 11 on hermeneutics raises a central issue in contemporary philosophy and theology—the radical historicity of human existence and knowledge. Gadamer criticizes the Enlightenment notion of reason, and the historical-critical method which flows out of it, for failing to fully appreciate human historicity. This might seem an odd critique of the historical-critical method. The goal of the method is precisely to span the historical gap between interpreter and text. But herein lies Gadamer's problem with the historical method. The method's goal is to free the interpreter of contemporary prejudice and, through study of ancient culture and language, offer access to the original meaning of the text. This approach is profoundly aware of the historical character of the text, i.e., that the text comes from a very different historical context. But the method, in its effort to free one from contemporary prejudice, neglects the historicity of the interpreter.

Gadamer's hermeneutic exemplifies an emphasis on human historicity typical of much of contemporary (sometimes called postmodern) thought. This emphasis on historicity has profound implications for theology.

Gadamer owes his fundamental insight into human historicity to his teacher, Martin Heidegger. In the first section of this chapter we will consider the thought of the early Heidegger. Heidegger's book, *Being and Time,* is arguably the most influential philosophical work of the century. My goal is to present Heidegger's notions of human historicity and truth. The second section treats the implications of these notions for the interpretation of texts. The chapter's final section relates these observations on historicity to theology.

## I. THE EARLY HEIDEGGER: HISTORY AND TRUTH

The questions of historicity and truth appear within the context of the early Heidegger's wider concern. Heidegger sought to retrieve the question of being, a question which he thought had been long neglected by philosophy. The purpose of *Being and Time* was to lay a foundation for thinking about being. What follows treats but a few topics which occur within Heidegger's effort to establish a basis for ontology.

## A. Truth and World

The traditional definition of truth is an *adaequatio intellectus et rei,* a conformity of intellect to the thing known. Heidegger challenges this notion of truth. Or, more accurately, he sees this conformity as derived from a more primordial truth.

1) *World:* Heidegger's critique of the traditional notion of truth deals, for the most part, with modern philosophy. Since Descartes philosophers have tended to take the subject-object distinction as a given. We are knowers, subjects. Knowledge occurs when we have in our mind a correct understanding of an object or of the relationship between objects. But how do we know that our understanding actually conforms to the object "out there"? Descartes' method of doubt raised the question. Any student of modern philosophy is familiar with the variety of answers that have populated the philosophical landscape since.

Heidegger suggests that the premise of the question, the presumed subject-object distinction, is erroneous. He offers an alternative, a description of human existence which seeks to get behind or beneath the subject-object distinction. To evaluate his description readers must see if it is an accurate account of their experience.

We can take as our example the familiar act of walking into a classroom, sitting down and listening to a lecture. The notion of truth as conformity of mind to objects suggests that I know when I look around the room and judge objects to be desks, pens, lights, windows, etc. That is, I judge an object to conform to the correct mental concept: "That (the object there) is a desk (concept)." But is that really what happens?

Rather, I walk into a classroom, flop into a desk, take out pen and paper, listen and write. In all these activities I give no direct attention to desk, pen or paper. I simply use them. They are equipment for the task I have undertaken—education. Heidegger points out that we do not attend to these objects unless they fail. If the desk collapses, or my pen runs out of ink, they draw attention to themselves by failing to function. But in the normal course things simply are what they are by fitting into an environment, by being ready for use.

Heidegger argues that this environmentality, this being functionally deployed within a context, determines what things are. Truth occurs when an environment uncovers what things are for. Things are what they are because they have a function in an environment. In our example, they have a place in the world of education.

In the course of a day I am present in a variety of such contexts. In church, at home, on the bus, and so on, I encounter a multitude of objects all of which are what they are by having their place (use) within an environment. The unity of all these various environments form my world. World, thus, refers to the contexts in which I live or, more accurately, the unity of the various contexts which make up my life (e.g., the worlds of education, parish life, family, America, work, neighborhood, etc.). Truth, what things are, happens because things occur within a world.

2) *Freedom:* Worlds, in turn, reflect human projects. The classroom is for education, home is for shelter, the bus is for transportation.

These various projects point to the unique character of human existence as freedom. Freedom is frequently thought of as a human capacity, an ability we have to choose this or that. Heidegger argues that the ability to choose is derived from a more primary freedom. Dasein (the human existent) does not have freedom; Dasein is freedom.

Chapters 8 and 9 introduced this notion of human existence as freedom. To be human is not to be a fixed nature. Dasein is not a thing, like a chair or a tree. Things are fixed natures. They simply are what they are and can be no other. In contrast human existence is constituted by its becoming.

Heidegger indicates that Dasein always already finds itself in a world becoming in the manner prescribed by that world. To repeat the example offered in chapter 9, a child born today could be flown to any location on earth and adopted by parents there. The child will become according to the possibilities offered by the world in which he finds himself. If the child is flown to Africa he will become quite a different person than if he is adopted in China. These are very different worlds, with different languages, religions and occupations. These various worlds offer the child different possibilities and what the child can become is determined by his world.

Note the intrinsic relationship between world and freedom. A world is an environment where things are functionally deployed for Dasein's projects (becoming). In turn, these various projects (education, recreation, professions, etc.) reflect Dasein's being as freedom. And, in turn once more, Dasein is free to become because it finds itself in a world which offers possibilities.

3) *Truth:* This section began with the traditional definition of truth as a correspondence of mind to object, a correspondence manifest in human judgments. (This is a desk.) Heidegger's description of human existence, freedom-in-the-world, establishes the grounds for this correspondence. Things are uncovered by their occurrence within a world. The classroom reflects the world of education. That context uncovers what objects are for. Pens, desks and blackboards are what they are within this environment, this world.

When I enter the classroom the world of education has already uncovered what all these things are. This is the primordial event of truth. When I pick up a pen and use it, or state, "This is a pen," I only make explicit what world has already uncovered. Thus judgment, the assertion of correspondence between mental concept and object, is not the primary locus of truth, but a derivative. In judgment I make explicit what world has already uncovered.

The subject-object distinction occurs not in the primordial event of truth (world) but in the derivative act of judgment. In Heidegger's description of human existence, the distinction of subject and object only emerges when equipment fails, when the pen runs out of ink. In failing to work the pen becomes a mere object at hand, calling attention to itself precisely by no longer being equipment for the project.

Let me suggest another way to grasp Heidegger's position. The definition of truth as correspondence of mind to object creates in the modern imagination a picture of two different kinds of things. One is a thinking-knowing thing (*res cogitans*) and the other a physical object (*res extensa*). Heidegger asks us to think about human existence in a different way. Being human is not being a thinking thing. We are not primordially subjects looking out onto objects.

The term "Dasein" literally means "there-being." With this term Heidegger wants to suggest that we always already find ourselves "there," i.e., in a world becoming. The "there" is a unified given in which everything has its place. The distinction of an I-here over and against objects (out-there) is derived from this primordial givenness.

One can get a glimpse of Heidegger's point in our unreflective willingness to imagine the earth prior to human existence. We picture the earth free of people and human artifacts. Is this a "worldless" earth, an object free of humanity? Of course not, since I imagine it. When I so imagine the earth it is I, with my language, values and all else that is my world. I am constituted by my world and to think that I can imagine the earth without humanity (a worldless nature, a neutral object, an "in-itself") simply misunderstands human existence.

This last point is the one Gadamer exploits in his critique of the historical-critical method. To methodically try to disengage myself from my world mistakes the grounds for human knowledge. Worldhood is not the foe of historical knowledge, it is its very possibility. To grasp Gadamer's point we must first attend to the historical character of world.

## B. The Historicity of World

Kant's explication of knowledge, treated in chapter 11, suggests that knowing is a combination of two things—empirical data and the categories of mind. Sensation presents the subject with a sequence of events. Mind provides the category of causality by which we understand those events. In this scheme, which presumes the subject-object distinction, understanding and meaning are the achievement of the subject.

Heidegger's description of truth suggests something quite different. Understanding and meaning are not the projection of mind onto objects. Rather, they are implicit in the world in which Dasein always already finds itself. World is not a private possession or a personal projection. Dasein is born into a world with other human beings. The world in which Dasein finds itself is a public reality which occurs in how others speak and act. Truth and meaning are already deposited in this public realm which is Dasein's "there."

So, too, what Dasein becomes is derivative of world. Human existence amounts to the appropriation of possibilities offered by one's world. What Dasein can be depends on what is deposited in the language and in the modes of behavior which characterize a community.

The preceding paragraphs may sound rather abstract but, in fact, the point is quite simple. How did I become who I am?. I was born into a home where English was spoken, where the Catholic religion was practiced, where education was valued, and so on. Becoming a person amounts to appropriating what one's world offers by becoming according to the possibilities at hand. These are possibilities first experienced within the family and later in the wider world of which the family is a part.

The world into which we are born is a community with a history. The language we learn, the customs we practice, the vocations we pursue, the structure of family life, the political order, our religious beliefs and practice, our moral code, all these, and everything else in our world, are creations of our community's history. When we are born into a community, appropriating its language and customs, we take on that history. We participate in what the community is and has been. More, our world is not the static creation of the past. History continues.

Thus, world is not something we have; it is what we are. To be human is to be constituted by a world, to be historical. Chapter 10 began our consideration of historical consciousness with the observation that people in different times and places see things differently. They live in different worlds, are the products of different histories. Here is where the hermeneutical question appears. When confronted with a text from a different time and culture, how do we understand it? With the notion of world we have the basis for grasping how Heidegger and Gadamer answer the hermeneutical question.

Before addressing the question of interpretation we should mention one other topic. The reader might feel offended by these reflections. We are, after all, individuals, not mere robots created by social order. Does Heidegger's description of our worldly existence end in a determinism?

Heidegger's description suggests that to take hold of our freedom we must first be aware that what we are and do comes from our world, that we have become who we are by simply going along. This realization grounds the possibility of authentic existence. By authenticity Heidegger means we can accept responsibility for who we are, we can begin to choose who we become rather than simply going along.

But if we overlook the basis of our existence in world we thoughtlessly take the perspective handed onto us as our own. We simply repeat what "they" speak and do, even though that repetition may involve the rhetoric of individualism and freedom.

## II. METHOD AND TRUTH

The preceding section provides the anthropological foundation for Gadamer's critique of the Enlightenment and of the historical-critical method. Chapter 2 briefly noted the Enlightenment's prejudice against tradition and prejudice. Autonomous reason alone offers access to reality. The rational individual must be free of the prejudices that abound in traditional societies. The aim of method is to achieve this freedom. But Heidegger's anthropology suggests that the Enlightenment has misunderstood the nature of human knowledge and reason.

While Gadamer's work encompasses a wide range of interests, our treatment applies his work to theology and the interpretation of classic Christian texts. The church was one of the Enlightenment's chief targets. Institutionalized religion was seen as institutionalized ignorance, imprisoning reason and thwarting its drive toward knowledge. The church taught, for example, that death is the result of sin rather than part of the natural order. Mental illness is demonic possession. Humanity had to free itself from such mythic thinking and face reality reasonably.

The Enlightenment presumed that the natural world operated by rational patterns. Reason, and reason alone offers access to reality (autonomous reason). Thus, reason must be freed from all prejudice to pursue the truth, i.e., the conformity of mind to the real. The scientific method is the model for, and the most successful example of, reason's systematic exclusion of prejudice from the human project to know.

The historical-critical method is similarly a systematic attempt to attain the meaning of ancient texts. The method presumes historical consciousness in that it is aware that the text reflects a different world. By the study of the text's original language, philology, archeology, history, etc., the historical critic seeks to understand the text in its original context.

Hermeneutical philosophy sought to offer philosophical grounds for this task, as Kant had offered an epistemological foundation for the practice of the empirical sciences. But this task proved problematic. While the physical sciences treat concrete data which any scientist can "consult" through experiments, historical-critical studies attempt to attain the meaning of an author long dead. When scientists disagree about a hypothesis they return to the data, contriving experiments to referee their differences. When historical critics disagree, whom do they consult?

For example, it is generally agreed that Jesus' central message concerned the coming of the kingdom of God. What did he mean? Interpretations abound. Did he mean a kingdom within? The final resting place of the soul? Is the world about to end? Is paradise going to be established on earth? Does he want us to work for a more just social and political order? Is there a real physical resurrection? Is the church the kingdom? The rapture? Is the nearness of the kingdom the nearness of God's Self-offer? All these, and others, are interpretations of Jesus' message. Which one, or combination, is correct? How would one decide? Why do scholars, studying the same texts, using the same method, come up with such a variety of interpretations?

The anthropology of Heidegger and Gadamer offers an answer to this last question. All human knowledge is grounded in one's world. The particularity of one's world is the basis for understanding anything at all. The multiple interpretations of Jesus' message reflect the variety of worlds within which interpreters live. One ought to anticipate rather than be surprised by such pluralism.

When we read about Jesus in the New Testament we understand out of our own experience, out of our world. When the text states that Jesus took a trip to Jerusalem, was arrested, tried and killed there is little difficulty in understanding since all of these events (trips, arrests, trials, death) are familiar elements in our world. But when we read, "The kingdom of God is at hand," how do we understand the phrase? Our world provides the resources for whatever interpretation we might offer. We must consider this point more carefully.

Perhaps you become fascinated with the New Testament and want to understand it more deeply. How would you pursue such a project? An obvious first step would be to master the original language of the text—Greek. How would you go about this task? One studies a new language by learning its vocabulary and syntax. How? By use of a dictionary one finds the meaning of these strange words. That is, one uses familiar English words to open up the meaning of ancient Greek words.

If you have studied a foreign language you know how complex this task is. With the exception of concrete nouns (and frequently not even then) words of different languages rarely have a one-to-one correlation. One must become accustomed to how words are used in a new language. We can embarrass ourselves by failing to realize the more subtle meaning of a word or phrase. A friend of mine once concluded a speech in French, "Je suis fini." In literal English, "I am finished." In French the phrase implies that I am dead.

The point of the example is that one learns ancient Greek through contemporary English. Speaking standard American English is not the enemy of our understanding ancient Greek. It is the necessary condition for learning that ancient language. This is what the Enlightenment's prejudice against prejudice overlooks. The goal of autonomous reason, free of culture and history, misunderstands the nature of human knowledge. One's world (i.e., culture, language and history) are the very possibility of understanding. The attempt to leave my world behind, and understand the author's intent, is like the attempt to imagine a "worldless" nature, a world without humanity.

We saw this point in chapter 11, in the example of watching *Hamlet*. To concentrate on methodological questions prevents the play from making its claim on us. Both *Hamlet* and the New Testament are more than stories. They express human truth; they have something to tell us. Their truth can only be heard if we connect them with our own lives, if we apply their claim. If we fail to let that claim be made, by methodically disengaging ourselves, we cannot grasp the texts' truth.

The goal of method is to be an objective, neutral observer. Such neutrality requires that I have nothing at stake, that I am not personally involved in the matter at hand. Consider one more example. Your family has rented a movie, a love story. As the family watches the movie there is only one uninvolved, neutral observer, your five-year-old brother. He is neutral, uninvolved and bored because there is nothing in the movie with which he can connect. He is innocent of the matter involved. He lacks the experience and resources to connect with the movie. The movie can make no claim on him. He can only wonder at your mother's tears. But his neutrality is not an advantage for understanding the movie. It is a deprivation which puts the movie beyond his grasp. Participation, having a stake in the matter at hand, is not something to be methodically overcome. On the contrary, it is the very possibility of understanding.

Understanding is achieved, not by leaving my world behind and grasping the world of the ancient author, but through a mixing of worlds, what Gadamer calls a fusion of horizons. The interpreter's world is an intrinsic element of understanding because it is understanding's necessary condition.

While Gadamer thinks the goal of method, author's intent, mistakes the nature of human understanding, he does not jettison the method's critical tools. The fusion of horizons requires a critical moment. The distant horizon of an ancient text must be allowed to stand in its strangeness. The tools of historical research (the study of ancient languages, customs, philology, archeology, etc.) present the interpreter with a very different world or horizon. One must allow the world of the text to emerge in its strangeness, in its historical distance. One must permit the text to make its claim. The interpreter must not simply absorb the ancient text into the present. Fusion of horizons means that the interpreter's world is changed through a conversation with the text. The meaning that emerges from this conversation is, thereby, something new. In this way the text has its effect in history and, for Gadamer, the truth of a text is precisely the history of its effects.

## III. SOME QUESTIONS

Gadamer's account of interpretation has its critics. In this last section I would like to introduce two important criticisms to which we will return in the final chapters of this book. First, Gadamer's critique of method overlooks one of the most important achievements of the Enlightenment—its suspicion of tradition. Second, Gadamer's notion of interpretation seems to exclude the possibility of lasting truth. All seems reduced to history. Does not Christianity presume a unity of and, therefore, a permanent character to truth?

### A. A Hermeneutic of Suspicion

Perhaps the most common critique of Gadamer's hermeneutic comes from the German thinker, Jürgen Habermas. Habermas argues that Gadamer's account of interpretation amounts to an uncritical submission to tradition. Gadamer presumes the truth claim of classic texts. The interpreter must let the classic text make its claim. The truth of texts occurs when the interpreter applies that claim in the present, within her or his world.

Habermas' perspective reflects what is commonly called a hermeneutic of suspicion. This way of thinking is associated with Marx, Nietzsche and Freud. Marx, for example, argued that one ought not accept a society's account of itself at face value. The ideology of a society, its explicit interpretation of itself, reflects and frequently covers deeper interests. One should be suspicious of what is beneath the surface.

The United States, for example, has long proclaimed an ideology of individual rights and equal justice. Yet our history and our present condition involve enormous inequality and exploitation. Political efforts to correct inequality by hiring from groups that have been systematically excluded (e.g., minorities, women) are countered with the language of equal rights. All citizens should be treated equally and without discrimination. The law ought to be "color blind." This language of "rights" and "equality" in fact covers an economic and political system that favors men who are white, heterosexual and wealthy. A hermeneutic of suspicion requires that one look beneath the rhetoric of rights and equality. It suspects that this ideology hides and, thereby, fosters a distorted social, political and economic system.

Here is Habermas' critique of Gadamer. The fusion of horizons which

Gadamer describes presumes the authority of traditional texts. Habermas suggests that the interpreter ought to be suspicious of both the horizon of the text and of one's own worldview. Texts from the past reflect the distorted, unjust social systems within which they were written. To submit to these texts, as Gadamer's hermeneutic describes, is to perpetuate distortions and unjust systems. Habermas argues for a hermeneutic of suspicion. Interpretation ought always involve a critical moment which seeks to uncover distortive elements in both the world of the text and the world of the interpreter.

Gadamer responds that suspicion is, in fact, an element of the contemporary interpreter's world. Thus, Habermas' suggestion is another example of fusing horizons. But our interest is not the debate between these two thinkers. Rather, Habermas' critique of Gadamer introduces an important insight within contemporary philosophy and theology.

Texts, theory and ideology reflect the social, political and economic structure of a society. Interpretation is a fusion of worlds, the world of the text and the world of the interpreter. The hermeneutic of suspicion suggests that the interpreter turn a critical eye to both these worlds. One ought to suspect that underneath surface speech and ideology there lurks a distorted social order. In chapter 14 we shall see this hermeneutic of suspicion at work in the liberation theology of Leonardo Boff.

## B. Truth and History

Gadamer's account of interpretation, and Heidegger's anthropology which grounds it, seem to exclude the possibility of a permanent truth claim. If humanity is radically historical, as these thinkers suggest, there is no way for us to attain permanent truths. Rather truth is always intrinsically related to world. There is no way to stand above history, to identify transhistorical truth.

This perspective presents a profound challenge to Christian faith. Do not Christians hold to the same truth? Does not the faith require a unity of truth, truth proclaimed in scripture and dogma?

To return to our earlier example, Jesus' preaching centered on his proclamation that the kingdom of God is at hand. What is the lasting truth of this proclamation? What does it mean? Which interpretation is correct? How can we speak of a unity of faith when we cannot agree on the meaning of Jesus' central proclamation?

The next chapter takes up the specific question of the relationship between Jesus' historical message and lasting, Christian truth. Wolfhart Pannenberg offers one way of thinking about the relationship between history and truth. His perspective exploits the thought of both Hegel and

Gadamer, allowing us to see once more the intrinsic relationship between philosophy and theology.

The final chapter returns to the question of the relationship between history and Christian truth. It indicates how this question drives the magisterium's most recent teaching about the relationship between philosophy and theology.

## BIBLIOGRAPHY

For the early Heidegger's description of Dasein's being-in-the-world, and his notion of truth, see the first division (the first 44 sections) of *Being and Time*. This is very dense material. Richard Palmer's *Hermeneutics* offers an excellent account of the history of the hermeneutical question, including the contributions of Heidegger and Gadamer. *The Hermeneutical Reader*, edited by Kurt Mueller-Vollmer, is an anthology which includes relevant selections from Heidegger and Gadamer. Habermas' critique of Gadamer is also found in this volume.

# PART IV
# PHILOSOPHERS AND
# THEOLOGIANS

These final chapters offer specific examples of the place of philosophy in the practice of contemporary theology. Chapter 13 examines how the Lutheran theologian Wolfhart Pannenberg uses the thought of Hegel to interpret the historical Jesus, the resurrection and the doctrine of Christ's divinity. Chapter 14 argues that the thought of Karl Marx grounds Leonardo Boff's theological method and Christology.

Chapter 15 returns to the church's teaching about the relationship between philosophy and theology. The chapter sets forth recent magisterial teaching on the subject and exemplifies how a number of contemporary theologians work out that teaching.

# CHAPTER 13

# HEGEL AND THE THEOLOGY OF WOLFHART PANNENBERG

The focus of this chapter is the influence of Hegel on Wolfhart Pannenberg's Christology. Pannenberg's thought also gives us the opportunity to return to some important questions. Specifically, we will take up again the relationship of reason to Christian faith. The question of history and Christian truth also recurs as we see how Pannenberg uses Gadamer's hermeneutic to develop a conception of truth.

Wolfhart Pannenberg is a Lutheran theologian whose thought reflects his own journey to faith. His was a journey of the intellect. Religious belief was not an important part of his life until he began the study of philosophy as a university student. Philosophical reflection led him to an intellectual affirmation of Christianity and to theology. Pannenberg's theology mirrors this journey. He contends that rational arguments can lead one to Christian faith. We begin our consideration with Pannenberg's understanding of the relationship between reason and faith.

## I. PANNENBERG'S THEOLOGICAL PROJECT

Can reason help us toward Christian belief, or is faith totally God's work of grace? Chapter 2 considered the Catholic understanding of the relationship between faith and reason. In Catholic doctrine faith is a divine gift and cannot be achieved by intellectual effort alone. Yet reason can help lead one toward faith by demonstrating the existence of God and by identifying signs that point toward divine revelation.

Protestant theology in the first half of this century tended to fideism. The thought of Karl Barth and Rudolf Bultmann dominated the scene. Both rejected attempts to justify faith through reason. Such attempts are human efforts to achieve the faith that saves. Evoking the classic Protestant principle that faith alone saves, such efforts were eschewed as human works.

Pannenberg rejects this fideism. He argues that there must be some reason for holding that Jesus is God's full and final revelation. After all, history is replete with figures making religious claims. Why believe in Jesus?

Pannenberg's response to this question is quite simple. One must go back to Jesus and see what his claim was. What was this man about? Having established what Jesus taught, Pannenberg asks if there are any reasons for believing him. The answers to these questions set the grounds and direction for Pannenberg's theological project. Reason precedes and offers a basis for faith.

For Pannenberg, a reasonable argument for belief in Jesus must be a historical argument. Jesus is a historical figure who made a claim. The nature and possible verification of that claim are accessible to the historian. What can historical studies tell us about Jesus of Nazareth? What was his message? Does history offer any reasons for asserting that Jesus is God's revelation?

Pannenberg insists that, if he is God's revelation, we must accept Jesus' historical message. That Jesus was an apocalyptic prophet is a widely accepted position among historical scholars. Jesus of Nazareth was a first-century Jew who proclaimed that God was about to establish his kingdom on earth. The end of history was near.

A good deal of modern theology has struggled with the apocalyptic character of Jesus' message. Can people today believe in Jesus' proclamation about the impending arrival of God's kingdom? After all, it has been two thousand years since Jesus proclaimed the nearness of the end. More, the images of the end of history and the establishment of God's rule can seem hopelessly mythic to the modern mind. The Son of Man coming in the clouds with angels, a general resurrection and judgment suggest a more primitive way of looking at the world, a way now superseded by science.

Over the past century Christian theologians have spent a good deal of effort offering credible interpretations of Jesus and his message, i.e., interpretations which replace or demythologize Jesus' apocalyptic categories. Bultmann is the best known example of demythologizing Jesus' proclamation. According to Bultmann, Jesus was bound to a pre-scientific worldview which thought of history as having a real beginning and end. Bultmann demythologizes Jesus' message by interpreting it as a mythic way to call people to a decision for or against God. We must decide now about Jesus' message of meaning and hope. The apocalyptic is interpreted existentially. Faith does not require that we live in Jesus' pre-scientific world. The apocalyptic was a primitive way to assert a divine meaning for human existence. The proclamation of the gospel requires that we decide for or against that meaning.

Karl Rahner similarly demythologizes Jesus' message. The nearness of the kingdom is a categorical way to express the transcendental truth that God is near. Rahner holds that Christianity's core truth is God's Self-offer to every human being. Jesus' eschatological proclamation is a call to decision about that offer.

In these, and many other contemporary interpretations of Jesus, theologians supply an acceptable, modern interpretation of Jesus' message. This seems, to Pannenberg, a distortion of Christianity's fundamental claim that Jesus is God's full and final revelation. If Jesus is God's revelation ought we not listen to his word? Should we not submit our lives to his claim, rather than submitting his claim to our contemporary perspectives?

Pannenberg concludes that to be a Christian is to believe in Jesus of Nazareth. Jesus was an apocalyptic preacher who proclaimed God was coming to establish the divine kingdom. One either believes that proclamation or not. It remains for us to see: 1) how Pannenberg interprets "The kingdom of God," 2) how reason demonstrates the truth of Jesus' claim (and thereby calls forth faith), and 3) how Jesus' fate establishes him as divine. Exploring these three topics brings Hegel's influence on Pannenberg into view.

## II. THE KINGDOM OF GOD

Hegel's influence becomes obvious when Pannenberg sets out to explain Jesus' message about the coming kingdom. Jesus identified the kingdom with the end of time and identified God with that coming reign. Hegel's notion of history allows Pannenberg to think of this eschatological message as an ontological event. It is not that a distant God will be fully manifest at the end. Rather, God's coming rule at the end of history is God's coming to be. God and the end of history coincide.

What does the word "God" mean? God is the all-powerful, the ruler of all that is. God is the divine reign.

This obvious and accepted definition of God raises problems for believers. If God is all-powerful, why is there evil and suffering? Why do the good suffer? For example, if the reader had the power to cure cancer and chose not to, we would think you a monster. Pannenberg recognizes how difficult faith is for many people today. A common problem is the question of evil. How can one believe in a good, all-powerful God when there is so much that is evil?

Pannenberg's response to these questions is that they presuppose a notion of God that comes from Greek philosophy rather than revelation. Again, Pannenberg seeks to retrieve Jesus' word about God, to free his message from later philosophical accretions.

Jesus identifies God's rule with the future. In God's reign there will be no more suffering, no more death. There will only be the good. That is what God's reign means, the rule of good and the end of evil. But this rule is promised for the future. In Jesus' message God's rule is yet to be established.

It is here that Pannenberg offers a Hegelian interpretation of Jesus' message. The move is quite simple. If God is the all powerful, and the divine rule does not yet exist, then, from within history, one must conclude that God does not yet exist. Jesus identifies God's rule with the end of history. Therefore, God is God only at the end. From within history we can say God does not yet exist.

Pannenberg argues that to be a Christian means to accept Jesus' message. His message is that the kingdom of God is coming at the end of history. Hegel's identification of God and the end of history allows Pannenberg to interpret Jesus' message as an ontological event. God is not simply going to assert the divine power at the end of history, putting an end to all evil and establishing the kingdom. The future coming of the kingdom is God's very coming to be.

## III. WHY BELIEVE IN JESUS?
## THE RESURRECTION AS THE GROUND FOR CHRISTIAN FAITH

One of the most controversial elements in Pannenberg's theology is his argument that historical reason can attain knowledge of Jesus' resurrection. The normal canons of history exclude the possibility of an extraordinary event in history. According to the rule of analogy the world has always operated by the same natural patterns. People in our world do not rise from the dead. Therefore, the resurrection of a dead person cannot be asserted as historical, i.e., historians cannot assert it as a fact in history. Historical research excludes, a priori, such an occurrence.

Pannenberg addresses this rule of historical research head on. He recognizes that if the resurrection of Jesus is to be available to history he must set aside the rule of analogy. Pannenberg's thesis is that if one does not methodologically exclude the possibility of a resurrection a priori, then resurrection is the best hypothesis for explaining the historical data we have about Jesus and his fate. That is, if one does not begin with the assumption that there can be no resurrections in history, then resurrection is the best hypothesis to explain the historical data about the cross and Easter. Pannenberg's Hegelian interpretation of history offers him the key for breaking out of the rule of analogy.

People commonly imagine creation as an event in the past. Cosmic history has its beginning in the big bang, or some such event. All the building blocks for physical evolution, down to human consciousness, are present from the beginning. The history of the universe is a story of more and more complex combinations of what has always already been. There is not anything new coming onto the scene. All is reducible to what has been.

Pannenberg's Hegelian notion of God suggests to him a different model for creation, one that he argues better explains reality as we know it. God does not create from the past but from the future. Every moment in history is not merely a new combination of what has always been. Rather, each present has a righteously new element, a unique character not reducible to what has been.

The emergence of human consciousness might serve as an example. Why ought we slavishly work out of a hypothesis that consciousness is simply a complex combination of already existing elements? While requiring a biological-chemical base in the brain, human consciousness is also related to the use of language. Whence language? What comes first, the capacity for language or the use of language which forms consciousness? From where does the mind's linguistic capacity come? Is not the emergence of language and consciousness something new, i.e., not reducible to what has been? That human consciousness and the use of language are not reducible to what has already been, that they are something new, is at least an arguable hypothesis.

Or, recall an instance when you came to understand something. You might have been puzzled by some problem or struggled to grasp a topic studied in school. The data were all there but you simply did not see the answer. Then, frequently unexpectedly, the lights come on. You see it. You understand. That understanding is something new. It is not merely an accumulation of data. Some people will have the data for years and never understand.

The creation and acceptance of a new scientific hypothesis is another example. Scientists may be troubled by data that contradict the accepted paradigm. Then comes an Einstein or a Freud. They see in a new way. Our understanding of the physical world and of human nature are profoundly changed.

Thus, Pannenberg argues that history is not reducible to what has been. The righteously new occurs. There is a creative element, something new and unique, in every present. If one accepts this position then one need not exclude, a priori, the possibility of the new and unique in history, e.g., a resurrection.

Having argued for the possibility of such a unique event in history, Pannenberg turns to the historical evidence surrounding Jesus' fate. It is not necessary to present his argument in detail. Essentially he points out the historicity of the apostles' betrayal of Jesus on Good Friday and their later proclamation of him as Lord. Why this change? They explained themselves by proclaiming that God had raised Jesus from death. The empty tomb is further historical evidence.

The preceding paragraph lists historical data. Pannenberg argues that, if one has not excluded the possibility of a resurrection a priori, then resurrection is the best hypothesis to explain the historical data. With this move Pannenberg has reached one of his chief goals. Historical reason shows that God has raised Jesus from death. Jesus is thereby confirmed as God's revelation and it is reasonable to place one's faith in him.

Critics of Pannenberg frequently concentrate on his argument for the historicity of the resurrection. Doing so, one can miss the depths and possibilities in his theology. These possibilities emerge when we draw together what has been said so far.

## IV. THE RESURRECTION AND THE DIVINITY OF CHRIST

We began our consideration of Pannenberg by presenting his method. Christians claim that Jesus is God's full and final revelation. Pannenberg argues that theology must clarify who this Jesus was. What was his claim? Why believe in him? We now have the basis for offering Pannenberg's answers to these questions.

Jesus proclaimed the coming kingdom. God would come at the end of history. There would be a resurrection and judgment. The kingdom is God's reign, God's rule. To rule is God's nature, what it means for God to be God. Thus, Pannenberg offers a Hegelian interpretation of Jesus' message in which divinity and the end of history (God's rule) are identified.

Jesus' resurrection occurs within this context. The meaning of the resurrection is intrinsically related to Jesus' message about the end. Theologies which remove the apocalyptic from the Easter proclamation leave Jesus behind. Such interpretations supply some other perspective for that of Jesus. For Pannenberg, to be a Christian is to believe in Jesus. Jesus was an eschatological prophet who died and rose. The context of eschatological expectation is intrinsic to Christianity and cannot be replaced.

Why believe in Jesus? Because he was raised from the dead. Jesus was not simply a prophet with a message. His message was confirmed in his resurrection. More, his message was fulfilled in his resurrection. The promised kingdom occurs in Jesus.

Resurrection belongs to the end. It happens at the end when the Son of Man comes. Resurrection is an eschatological event and that is how Jesus' rising was interpreted by the first believers. Jesus' resurrection means the last days are at hand. In his resurrection Jesus is identified with the end of history. The end of history has occurred for Jesus in history. In his resurrection we get a glimpse of the end. Jesus' message about God and the kingdom are confirmed in that they are realized within history. Jesus' rising, which anticipates the end, occurs within history as promise and fulfillment.

The identification of Jesus with the end of history constitutes his divinity. God, the end of history and the risen Christ coincide. Jesus reveals God in that his resurrection is a glimpse of the end of history. Jesus' divinity refers to his eschatological identification with the end of history.

## V. HEGEL, GADAMER AND PANNENBERG

These brief remarks intend only to point toward the importance of Hegel's thought for Wolfhart Pannenberg's theology. Pannenberg wants to go back to Jesus, identify his claim and see if there be any reason to believe in this ancient Jewish rabbi. Pannenberg comes to the common conclusion of historical research. Jesus was an eschatological prophet who proclaimed the nearness of the coming kingdom.

Hegel's thought permits Pannenberg to interpret history and Jesus' message in a new manner. Pannenberg sees a commonality between the message of Jesus and Hegel's notion of history. Hegel views history as Absolute Spirit coming to itself. Absolute Spirit occurs only at the end of history.

Pannenberg uses Hegel's identification of God and the end of history within the context of his interpretation of Jesus. One way to grasp his position is to consider the questions of meaning and truth. The question of God is, at root, a question about the final meaning and truth of human existence. Is there any meaning or are we all merely a cosmic accident?

Pannenberg argues that Jesus, like Hegel, identifies final meaning and truth with the end of history. In this context Pannenberg turns to the hermeneutical philosophers Dilthey and Gadamer. Dilthey (1833–1911) theorized on the occurrence of meaning within history. What he saw was that the meaning of any particular event, person, text, etc., was dependent on its place within the whole. An example will make this critical point clear. A student might choose to attend a specific school with a particular goal in mind, e.g., medical school. That choice is part of the individual's life story no matter what happens later on. The student might give up the idea of a medical career and become a teacher. Or the student might continue in medical school and become a great surgeon, or a psychiatrist, and so on.

Dilthey's point is that one does not know the full meaning of the choice to attend medical school until the individual's life story is complete. The meaning of our actions and decisions is determined by their place within our personal history. The same is true of historical events. The meaning of the assassins' action at Sarajevo in 1914 is still being determined by the course of western history.

Pannenberg combines Dilthey's insight with the thought of Gadamer and Hegel. Gadamer argues that the meaning of a text occurs in application, when the interpreter applies the claim of the text within her present horizon. Returning to an earlier example, the meaning of *Hamlet* is not determined by Shakespeare's intention when he penned the manuscript. Rather, the play's truth occurs as audiences in different times and places apply its meaning within their own lives. The play's truth has a history, i.e., its continuing effect within ever changing circumstances.

Or, what is the truth of the Servant Songs of Isaiah? The prophet proclaims:

> See, my servant shall prosper, he shall be raised high and greatly
> exalted (53:13)....Yet it was our infirmities that he bore, our suf-
> ferings that he endured (54:4)....he was pierced for our offenses,
> crushed for our sins (54:5)...through his suffering, my servant
> shall justify many (54:11b).

This text had meaning five hundred years before Christ, a meaning within the context of its composition—Israel in exile. But it took on a new meaning, a new truth after Jesus' cross and rising. The text offered a way to understand Jesus' fate and, in doing so, took on a new meaning, new truth.

The same history of effects can be seen in Jesus' parables. Recall the parable of the great supper (Matthew 22:1–10). In this story Jesus describes an individual who sends out his servants to tell the invited guests that the banquet is ready. The guests offer excuses for why they cannot come. The host responds by sending his servants out again to bring in anyone they find. What does this text mean? Scholars suggest that it was originally Jesus' response to his critics, those who attacked him for being in the company of tax collectors and sinners. The invited guests refuse to come, while tax collectors and sinners are entering God's reign. The story takes on new meaning when it is repeated in different circumstances. Thus, in Matthew's church, the story has become an allegory for the history of salvation. Most Jews, the invited guests, have not accepted Jesus, while Gentiles have.

What, then, is the final meaning of these texts, their full truth? That final truth will occur only when the history of their reception is finished, when the history of their effect is complete. The final truth occurs only at the end of history when everything has its place within the whole story, within universal history.

This is the philosophical perspective Pannenberg uses to interpret the historical message of Jesus. The coming of the kingdom refers to the end of history. Only at the end of history will final truth and meaning occur. At the end God will occur as the final truth, the meaning of all that has been. God will be manifest as the goal and power over all history. But only at the end will God be God. From within history we must still wait on the future for final meaning and truth. This is Jesus' message. Within history sin and evil still have their power. But at the end God will come in power and establish that rule which will banish all evil and grant final meaning to all that has been.

The resurrection of Jesus not only confirms the truth of his message, but is a proleptic event, an event which anticipates the end. Final meaning and truth occur in Jesus' resurrection. It is in this sense that Pannenberg asserts the divinity of Jesus.

How is a resurrection in history possible? Pannenberg's use of Hegel has allowed him to imagine God at the end of history. We normally imagine creation as a divine act in the past which sets the world on its course. Pannenberg's Hegelian view suggests that we imagine God at the end rather than at the beginning. With this image he suggests that we view creation not as an action in the past, but from the future. Each present is a creative moment in which the final future (God) is creatively present. This metaphysics of the future offers Pannenberg the grounds for overturning the historical method's rule of analogy mentioned above. History is not reducible to what has always already been. Rather, each moment in history contains a new and creative element. Jesus' resurrection is the instance of this creative power *par excellence.* The divine future posits itself and is manifest in the risen Christ.

We conclude with an observation on how Pannenberg has used the thought of Hegel (Dilthey and Gadamer). He is not simply Hegelian. Rather, Pannenberg has used elements in Hegel's philosophy to interpret the historical message of Jesus. He gives Jesus, especially the resurrection, a meaning quite different from Hegel's understanding. He has retrieved Hegel's thought to new purposes. This creative use well exemplifies how theologians use philosophers. It also exemplifies how the history of thought occurs.

The story of philosophy and theology is a conversation within history. The work of earlier thinkers is placed in conversation with later problems and perspectives. In this process new possibilities occur and, frequently, old insights gain new life. Of course this is exactly what Pannenberg describes. The final meaning of any thinker's work will only occur at the end of history when the story of humanity's continuing conversation comes to an end. When history is complete (universal history) everything will find its place within the whole. Each truth will have its meaning within the One Truth.

## VI. IS PANNENBERG ORTHODOX?

Pannenberg is a Lutheran theologian, not a Roman Catholic. His position that, from within history, God does not yet exist hardly seems an orthodox notion of God. What can such a notion say to Roman Catholics?

First there is Pannenberg's qualification "from within history." He insists that we are finite and historical. We have no access to the divine mystery as it is in itself (what the tradition calls *Deus ut in se est*). Perhaps Pannenberg's radical assertion can give us pause as to how much we know about God. Any image we have of God's relationship to creation (at the beginning, present or end of history) is inadequate. Consider again the comments in chapter 8 about St. Thomas' agnosticism.

Second, it seems to this writer that Pannenberg's association of God with the final meaning of human existence, the final meaning of human history, is insightful, accurate and pregnant with possibilities. More, his understanding of Jesus as the revelation of the final meaning of history, that mystery hidden from all eternity, seems quite traditional. Is not the resurrection of Jesus the ground of our faith? Does not God's revelation in Jesus wait on the eschaton to be complete? These are all quite traditional and orthodox positions.

I am not recommending Pannenberg. The chief goal of this chapter is to indicate how Hegel's thought is essential to his theology. However, having made this disclaimer, there remains a wealth of insight and possibility in what Pannenberg has accomplished.

## BIBLIOGRAPHY

For Pannenberg's argument identifying God with the end of history see chapter 1 of his *Theology and the Kingdom of God*. He develops his notion of creation in the same work, pp. 61–68. Pannenberg's argument that the resurrection can be demonstrated historically occurs in *Jesus—God and Man*, pp. 88–106. His explication of Jesus' divinity is found in the same work, pp. 133–141. For his notion of truth as universal history see *Basic Questions in Theology* 2:21–23. E. Frank Tupper's *The Theology of Wolfhart Pannenberg* is a very good introduction. For Hegel's thought, see his introduction to the *Phenomenology of Spirit*. Hegel is difficult to read and secondary material can prove a helpful guide. Peter Singer's *Hegel* is an excellent introduction to his thought. Copleston's *A History of Philosophy* volume 7, chapters 9 and 10 are also good.

# CHAPTER 14

# MARX AND LIBERATION THEOLOGY: LEONARDO BOFF

The purpose of this chapter is to indicate how Marx's anthropology undergirds and unites the Christology of Leonardo Boff. I suggest that the reader study chapters 2–4, 7 and 10 of *Jesus Christ Liberator*. Boff does not explicitly claim Karl Marx in *Jesus Christ Liberator*. But when one reads Boff's account of the Christ with a Marxist anthropology in mind, his thought attains a remarkable unity and simplicity.

To assert that a theologian uses a Marxist anthropology is a red flag to many. Let me clarify Boff's "Marxism" from the start. Boff does not reduce reality to materialism. Boff does not advocate class warfare or violence. Boff is not a naive utopian thinker who believes we can build heaven on earth. Boff is a Catholic Christian who holds firmly to the conviction that, finally, only divine intervention and grace can transform our world into the promised kingdom. The Jesus presented by Boff is a man of peace who calls upon humanity to cooperate with God's transforming grace by working for true community among people with God.

In what sense, then, can Boff be "Marxist"? My thesis is that Boff accepts Marx's view of human existence as primordially a creation of social existence. This chapter attempts to demonstrate that thesis. Boff's hermeneutical principles for interpreting scripture and the doctrinal tradition will first be presented. Second, I will offer a Marxist interpretation of these principles. Finally, we will consider key elements of Boff's Christology, indicating how his interpretation of the Christ reflects a Marxist anthropology.

## I. PRINCIPLES FOR INTERPRETING JESUS THE CHRIST

Boff establishes his hermeneutical principles in chapter 2 of *Jesus Christ Liberator*. He begins by embracing the historical-critical method, offering a brief description of form, tradition and redactional criticism.

But Boff's embrace of the historical-critical method involves a proviso typical of many contemporary thinkers. He rejects the naive epistemological view that one can attain, through the method, the "objective" reality of the

historical Jesus. Echoing Gadamer's thought, Boff asserts that Jesus' message makes a claim on the reader and one cannot encounter that claim
through methodological disengagement. Rather, one must be involved in the
matter at hand (salvation, damnation, meaning). So the conditions of the
interpreter in the present, the human condition experienced today, are the
context of pre-comprehension which makes it possible for the interpreter to
understand.

In interpreting Jesus we are actually defining ourselves. "[T]o really
comprehend who Jesus is, one must approach him as one touched by and
attached to him....We cannot escape our life, our culture, and situation to
touch Jesus as he really was" (39). The gospels themselves offer interpretations of Jesus which reflect the concerns and perspectives of the evangelists'
churches. So today interpretations of Jesus find their roots in the faith community, in the church.

Having taken a common hermeneutical position about the nature of
interpretation (i.e., that it always reflects the communal context of the interpreter), Boff makes a critical move in a brief, two-paragraph section entitled
"The Hermeneutics of Political Existence." An interpreter exists within a
church and a church always exists within a political context. This political
context is intrinsic to the interpreter's (and church's) world. If this fact of
human existence is not recognized the ideological perspective of one's political environment can silently determine one's interpretation of Jesus. In this
last observation Boff exemplifies the hermeneutic of suspicion mentioned at
the end of chapter 12.

Jesus did not come to establish any particular political order or culture.
The trouble is that the church sometimes has neglected this fact and has identified a particular culture or political ideology with Jesus and his gospel. This
is a powerful fact in the history of the Latin American church, a church long
dominated by the ideology and interests of the western, European church.
The values and interests of western culture were identified with Christianity
itself. A truly critical interpretation of Jesus will recognize such social-politi-
cal factors and, thereby, begin to free Jesus from the domination of one culture's interpretation.

No one cultural-historical context can exhaust the divine reality offered
in Jesus. Different cultures and perspectives illuminate different aspects of
what God has done in Jesus. Granted this insight of contemporary hermeneutical thought, Boff, a Brazilian, proposes to offer an interpretation of Jesus
from the unique perspective of Latin America. He delineates the characteristics of Latin American culture which will be intrinsic elements of his interpretation of Jesus.

Boff first observes that the church in Latin America has been essentially European. "The general horizon was one that dogmatically interpreted

canon law and juridically interpreted dogma" (44). Latin America must now develop its own interpretation of Jesus. The decisive factor in this interpretation is not the past but the utopian promise of the future. The key is Jesus' promise and achievement of the utopian kingdom to come.

Faith promises a utopian future and that promise prevents the absolutizing of any present structure or model. This promise introduces a critical element into theological reflection which resists the church's natural tendency to stagnate, defend its present forms, and repress all criticism. Every present must be criticized in view of the promise of the kingdom (utopia).

The promise of utopia has special relevance midst the poverty and oppression which characterize Latin America. In this context social questions have priority over personal. A call for individual conversion has little significance in an area permeated by distorted social, economic and political structures. Rather, the church, like Jesus, must reach out to liberate the poor and the weak. Thus, the central mission of the church, and the essential element in its interpretation of Jesus, is to work for the establishment of the kingdom, utopia (orthopraxis). In the past the church has concentrated on correct thought about Jesus (orthodoxy). Now the emphasis moves to "correct acting in the light of Christ" (46).

What has been said thus far appears to be a series of general principles one can accept or reject. The decisive factor in approving or disapproving Boff will most likely be one's political and ecclesial opinions. A conservative will disagree; a liberal will be more sympathetic. But why accept Boff's principles for interpretation? Is this merely a matter of political or cultural preference? The answer lies in the anthropology which undergirds these principles. My suggestion is that the basis of Boff's hermeneutical principles becomes clear when placed in conversation with Marx's anthropology.

## II. MARX'S ANTHROPOLOGY AND BOFF'S HERMENEUTIC

One of the most familiar "tags" placed on Marx is that he is an economic determinist. Marx did not think that people always acted on economic motivations. His economic determinism is, rather, an anthropological principle. The means of production within a society determine everything else—ideology, religion, political structures, forms of consciousness and personal existence. A closer examination of this Marxist position can help us understand Boff's theology.

Let me first observe that Boff does not take over Marx's position whole and entire. But what Marx means by economic determinism can enlighten Boff's epistemology and hermeneutic.

According to Marx, humanity began like all animals, living off what was available and depending on what nature provided. Truly human existence did not emerge until people began to shape the world, reorder it for their own needs. This happened when groups, for example, began to cultivate crops and herd animals. These are social activities which mold the environment for human ends. Social existence (language and forms of social organization) developed for these common purposes. In other words, to perform these tasks people had to communicate in more complex ways and communities had to organize. Forms of social existence were determined by common economic tasks, e.g., providing food for the group. As these tasks became more complex, as more complex economies developed, more complex forms of social organization were required.

In this way the means of production determine the forms of social existence. Political systems, religious beliefs, family structure, etc., all serve a society's economic structure in that they reflect the manner of social organization which makes forms of production possible. For example, the French Revolution proclaimed an ideology of personal freedom and individual rights. In fact, France was moving from an agricultural to an industrial economy. While an agricultural society needs workers scattered across the countryside, an industrial society needs a pool of cheap labor collected in the cities. The "freeing" of the masses served the purpose of throwing the peasants off the land and forcing them to collect in the cities where they would be available as a source of cheap labor.

Marx does not mean that the philosophers of individual rights were conspirators with the industrialists. That their philosophy reflected the changing economic structure of their society simply exemplifies Marx's principle that thought follows economic structure. This is the nature of human consciousness and thought. Forms of thought are created and directed by the underlying structure of the society which gives them birth.

When Boff asserts that orthopraxis has priority over orthodoxy I think he has something like this in mind. It is not that what we do is more important than what we think. Rather, what we do gives rise to thought. In turn what we do is determined by the social, political and economic structures of the society in which we live. Change social structures, the patterns of activity and interrelationships, and thought will change. Here, I believe, is the key to Boff's hermeneutical principles and his Christology.

The social and political (praxis) have priority over the personal and orthodoxy. This priority is not a matter of preference but the nature of human existence. Thought always follows praxis. For example, first-world scripture scholars insist that the historical critical method can locate the objective reality about Jesus. This objectified, neutral Jesus serves the interests of the first world in that he does not disturb the existing order. The first world prospers at the expense of the poor nations. Scholarly debates about whether Jesus understood himself to be the Son of Man, or whether Jesus had siblings, leave the issues of justice and exploitation untouched. In this way these scholars serve the interests of the society from which they benefit. Their "serving the interests" is not a matter of bad intentions. Theory always reflects societal structures.

If one recognizes this anthropological principle one gains some freedom. It is possible to begin to choose, modify or reconstruct the societal context within which one lives. Boff's hermeneutical principles amount to a conscious choice by a Catholic theologian in Latin America to move away from the long established, social, political and economic structures. These established structures first served the interests of European colonialism. Now they serve the interests of an exploitive world economic order and of indigenous oppression. Boff's hermeneutic, in contrast, chooses to root itself in the context of the oppressed rather than the oppressor.

The manner of Boff's option for the poor is manifest in his "utopian principle." Boff understands Jesus' message about the kingdom to be a promise of ideal community among humanity with God. Marx's utopianism was rooted in his conviction that all elements in a society reflect the means of production. If the economic structure of a society were equitable and just (communism) all else would fall into place. The distortive parts of human communities (e.g., crime, violence, repressive ideologies, etc.) reflect and serve the interests of an exploitive economic system. Establish a just system and these distortions will fall away. In a communist society the truth will out because thought always follows economic structure.

Boff's option for the poor, and his insistence on the priority of orthopraxis, reflect Marx's understanding of the relationship between social systems and thought. The work (orthopraxis) of Christianity is to try to build the kingdom. Boff's orthopraxis amounts to work for ideal community, a community of equity and justice. If one enters into this kind of work, into a collective effort to build this kind of community, that praxis will open up the meaning of Jesus' message. A deeper understanding of what Jesus proclaimed (orthodoxy) will emerge from such praxis. Thought follows structure.

My suggestion is that Boff's "Marxist" anthropology is the glue which binds together and grounds the hermeneutical principles set out in the previous section. If one accepts the fundamental premise that the structure of social existence gives rise to theory (praxis gives rise to thought), then Boff's principles for interpretation are not mere preferences. Rather, they form a consistent pattern for doing theology from within an option for the poor. Moreover, this anthropology also unifies Boff's interpretation of Jesus. But, before we consider a few elements of that interpretation some last remarks on Boff's "Marxism" are in order.

Again, Boff is not a Marxist. He is not a materialist. He is not an atheist. He is certainly not a follower of Lenin or the discredited system that came out of the Russian revolution. Boff does not think we can build the kingdom on earth. He clearly holds the need for divine grace and intervention. He does not advocate violence or class warfare.

Why identify Boff with Marxism at all? As theologians have done since Christianity first entered the world of Hellenism, Boff makes use of philosophical insights from non-Christian thinkers. Augustine did not accept Plotinus whole and entire; Thomas did not accept Aristotle whole and entire. Theologians borrow elements from philosophy to enlighten Christian revelation. Thus Boff has borrowed elements of Marx's anthropology as a means of interpreting Jesus.

Critics of Boff, and of other liberation theologians, frequently point out that Jesus was no Marxist or political revolutionary. This is certainly true. But Jesus was not a Platonist, Aristotelian, or "Christian" for that matter. Interpretation always involves the horizon of the interpreter. Boff argues that the horizon of the interpreter reflects more than abstract theory. One's horizon is constituted by a social, economic and political context. The interests of that context influence interpretation. Boff calls this to attention and identifies what interests he chooses to serve. He identifies himself with the poor and the weak. He observes that this identification with the poor reflects the ministry of Jesus and, thus, has a privileged position within Christian theology. To disagree with Boff involves more than criticizing his exegesis. One must address his anthropology (epistemology) and its premises.

### III. SOME ASPECTS OF BOFF'S CHRISTOLOGY

Boff accepts the common view of historical critics that the core message of Jesus was: repent, the kingdom of God is near. How are we to understand this message? Boff suggests that the promised kingdom reflects the universal human hope for utopia, for an idyllic society. The kingdom promised by Jesus is an idyllic society of perfect community among humanity with God. The utopian principle mentioned above provides both the content of Jesus' message and the hermeneutical grounds for understanding that message.

Jesus identified God with humanity's universal hope for utopia. While he proclaimed a message of liberation, Jesus rejected political power and the use of violence. Rather, he called for a personal transformation which rejects the established order. He set himself against those elements of his society which suppress. For example, Jesus rejected interpretations of the law which inhibit the praxis of the kingdom, of love. He proclaimed a liberty for love by curing on the sabbath. He rejected social stratification by having in his company all elements of society. His message required that the pharisees de-establish themselves. The world in its present form is not open to God's promised community. The present order must be replaced.

One notes that Boff's interpretation of Jesus emphasizes structural issues. Salvation is not primarily a personal matter between God and the individual. Salvation is communal—the kingdom. While this neglected emphasis certainly finds warrants in New Testament texts and in the tradition, it also reflects Boff's anthropology. Personal existence is formed by societal structures. God's work in Jesus conforms to this given of human nature. If humanity is to be saved its distorted social structures must be transformed.

Jesus was killed because of this attack on the established order. His message was a blasphemy against the religious establishment. The Romans killed him for a political crime. He made himself king of the Jews. The cross seemed the end of Jesus, the death of his promise and hope. Jesus' resurrection is God's confirmation of Jesus' message, the establishment of the kingdom in Christ.

What do Christians mean when we proclaim Jesus rose from the dead? What are we asserting happened to him? Simple resuscitation, like Lazarus, is obviously not the answer. Contemporary theologians have sought a reference in our experience to offer meaning to the foundational Christian proclamation, "He is risen." For example, Karl Rahner identifies transcendental hope as the horizon for grasping the Easter message. Schillebeeckx sees resurrection as one way to interpret the experience of conversion to Jesus and his historical message.

Boff's anthropology, and the utopian principle, offer the grounds for his interpretation of Jesus' resurrection. In raising Jesus God establishes the kingdom, topia. Jesus attains perfect community with all people and with God. Jesus' earthly body, limited to one place and time, is transformed so that the risen Lord is with God and present to all humanity for all times. The eschatological kingdom occurs in Jesus as promise and guarantee of our own resurrection, our participation in that perfect community among humanity and with God (134–138).

Boff's interpretation of the resurrection flows directly from his understanding of Jesus' teaching about the kingdom. In raising Jesus from death God establishes the kingdom in him. Jesus is transformed from death to a state of perfect community with God and with all humanity. His notion of the kingdom as utopia, perfect community among humanity with God, allows Boff to offer an explanation of the scriptural and doctrinal teaching about the risen Lord. Easter faith proclaims that Jesus is alive, with the Father, and universally present to all humanity. In brief, Jesus is topia (utopia achieved), the kingdom.

Our understanding of Jesus' message and resurrection, like all knowledge, is determined by praxis. If we are to grasp the meaning of both Jesus' message about the kingdom and Jesus' risen state in that kingdom, we must work for utopia. The closer the community in which we live is to that idyllic community the more we will grasp the meaning of, "He is risen." Orthopraxis, the work of the kingdom, makes possible orthodoxy.

Boff's treatment of the divinity of Jesus follows a similar pattern. Boff offers an account of the dogma of Chalcedon, that Jesus is fully human and fully God, two natures united in one hypostasis (one person). In a way typical of much of modern thought, Boff describes human nature as not a fixed essence. Human existence is freedom. What we become is determined by how we relate to the world. Jesus opened himself, emptied himself for God and for others. He did not pursue his own being but was a man for others. "Jesus does not possess what the Council of Chalcedon taught: He was lacking a 'hypostasis,' a subsistence, enduring in himself and for himself. He was completely emptied of himself and completely full of the reality of the Other, of God the Father" (196).

In other words, Jesus determined his being through perfect relationship with God and with others. In this he fulfilled humanity's highest potential, divinization. By not being "for himself" but by "surrendering and communicating his 'I' to others and for others, especially for God, to the point of identifying with others and with God," he became the very incarnation of the divine. His resurrection was, thus, the completion of his life's task. In raising him from death God's transforming grace brings to completion Jesus' praxis of the kingdom.

How are we to understand the divinity of Jesus? What in our own experience offers us access to this dogma? The answer by now ought to be obvious. The more we work for that perfect community among humanity with God, the closer our community is to that utopia, the more we will grasp the meaning of incarnation. Orthodoxy, correct belief in the church's teaching on the divinity of Jesus, flows out of orthopraxis.

## BIBLIOGRAPHY

As suggested in the preceding text, chapters 2–4, 7 and 10 of Boff's *Jesus Christ Liberator* treat the material covered in this essay. For the elements of Karl Marx's thought mentioned in this chapter see his *A Contribution to the Critique of Political Economy* or *The German Ideology* written with Friedrich Engels. David McLellan's *Karl Marx* is a good secondary source. Alfred Hennelly has edited an excellent anthology, *Liberation Theology: A Documentary History*. This volume includes the Congregation for the Doctrine of the Faith's "Instruction on Certain Aspects of the 'Theology of Liberation'" (chapter 45), the congregation's critique of Boff's book *Church: Charism and Power* (chapter 48) and Boff's response (chapter 49).

# CHAPTER 15

# PHILOSOPHY AND THEOLOGY

We began with the teaching of Vatican I on the relationship between reason and faith. In this concluding chapter we consider again magisterial teaching on the place and character of philosophy within Catholic theology.

Recent magisterial teaching on philosophy has been occasioned, in no small part, by the emergence of historical consciousness within theology. Chapters 10 through 12 noted some of the questions history raises for the faith. A key question, mentioned at the end of chapter 12, has to do with the unity of Christian truth. If all human knowledge is historical, how is it possible to assert a common truth held by all? But this is a very abstract formulation of the question. An example can clarify the issue.

Since Nicea the church has promulgated dogmas, truths which must be held by all members of the church. Chalcedon teaches that Jesus is two natures, fully God and fully human, unmixed, united in one hypostasis, one prosopon. Chalcedon's dogmatic formula reflects philosophical categories characteristic of the fourth and fifth centuries. We no longer live within that philosophical context, in that world. But the dogma of Chalcedon remains. What precisely are we required to believe? Are we bound to the categories of nature and prosopon, and to the philosophical system which gave rise to them?

Recent magisterial teaching suggests a negative answer to this question. As the International Theological Commission stated in 1972: "Dogmatic definitions ordinarily use a common language; while they may make use of apparently philosophical terminology, they do not thereby bind the Church to a particular philosophy."[1]

Christianity is not bound to any one philosophical system. But, then, how are we to understand Chalcedon's teaching today? If we are not bound to its philosophical categories, how do we identify its lasting truth? How can there be a unity of faith when the language and categories which express the faith are historically conditioned and transitory? The magisterium's teaching about philosophy has much to do with this question.

## I. MEANING AND EXPRESSION

"The substance of the ancient doctrine of the deposit of faith is one thing, and the way in which it is presented is another." These words, spoken by Pope John at the opening of the Second Vatican Council, reflect what has become the common Roman Catholic understanding of the relationship between the permanence of dogmatic truth and the historically conditioned character of its expression.

The First Vatican Council, in chapter four of *Dei filius*, declared that the meaning of dogmas, once taught by the church, does not change (DS 3020). Commenting on this teaching, Bernard Lonergan states that "the meaning of the dogma is not apart from a verbal formulation, for it is a meaning declared by the church. However, the permanence attaches to the meaning and not to the formula."[2] This distinction, between truth (meaning) and its expression, seeks to preserve the permanent truth claim of dogmas in view of the historically conditioned character of their formulation.

Recent magisterial documents recognize the problematic character of the relationship between historically conditioned propositions and permanent meaning. *Mysterium Ecclesiae*, for example, distinguishes between "truths the Church intends to teach" and the "changeable conceptions of a given epoch" used in dogmatic formulas.[3] These truths can be expressed without such historically conditioned "traces." Dogmatic formulas were suitable for communicating revealed truth within their original context and, when correctly interpreted, that truth remains. Scholars are commended for helping the church grasp this lasting meaning.

But the distinction between meaning and expression raises serious epistemological questions. These documents of the magisterium posit a meaning that is separable from language, a common meaning that can be expressed within the multiple contexts of human history. *Mysterium Ecclesiae* interprets Pope John's remarks to mean that "we can know the true and unchanging meaning of dogmas" while allowing for changes in that meaning's expression. But how are we to understand this meaning which is separable from expression? On what basis can we assert a unity of meaning when expression is intrinsic to shared meaning? A philosophical foundation is required if the distinction between permanent meaning and variable expression is to be maintained. Does Christian revelation thus imply a philosophy? Is there an epistemology implicit in Christian revelation?

In 1950, Pius XII's encyclical *Humani generis* insisted on an intrinsic relationship between the categories of dogmatic expression and their content (.16). Does this mean that orthodoxy requires a specific philosophical perspective? Pius XII's positive answer reflects his conviction that the church must be able to identify lasting truths and this implies a philosophy which "safeguards the genuine validity of human knowledge, the unshakable meta-physical principles of sufficient reason, causality, and finality, and finally the mind's ability to attain certain and unchangeable truth" (.29).

The pope recognizes that there will be growth and change in philo-sophical expression, but the basic philosophical principles mentioned above cannot change. "For truth and its philosophic expression cannot change from day to day, least of all where there is question of self-evident principles of the human mind or of those propositions which are supported by the wisdom of the ages and by divine revelation" (.30). In light of this general principle the pope goes on to recommend the teaching of Aquinas (.31).

A little more than a decade later, when the Second Vatican Council briefly took up the subject, it manifested a more open attitude toward philo-sophical pluralism. In its Decree on Priestly Formation the council did not specify Aquinas but recommended that "the students should rely on that philosophical patrimony which is forever valid, but should also take account of modern philosophical studies" (.15). A similar openness to other philo-sophical traditions appears in the council's Decree on the Missions which states that "in philosophy and theology they (seminarians) should examine the relationship between the traditions and religion of their home land and Christianity" (.16).

In 1972 the Congregation for Catholic Education issued a letter "On the Study of Philosophy in Seminaries." While this letter has less authority than a conciliar decree or a papal encyclical, it reflects a consistent, magister-ial position. After arguing for the importance of philosophy, and recognizing contemporary philosophical pluralism, the letter takes up the question of what is philosophically essential to Christian revelation. The teaching of phi-losophy must lead to "a coherent vision of reality." This vision "cannot be in contrast to Christian revelation." There is a healthy philosophical pluralism, reflecting various cultures and historical periods, which seeks and expresses the same truth in various ways. "However, it is not possible to admit a philo-sophical pluralism which compromises the fundamental nucleus of affirma-tions connected with revelation, since a contradiction is not possible between the naturally knowable truths of philosophy and the supernatural truths of faith." The letter goes on to assert an incompatibility between revelation and "all relativism—epistemological, moral or metaphysical."

In sum, the church's response to the challenge of historical conscious-ness is to assert a unity of meaning which undergirds the pluralism of histori-cal expression. The unity of dogmatic truth is thereby attached to meaning rather than the categories of expression. Granted this premise, a philosophy can be judged compatible with the faith only if it can establish the epistemo-logical and metaphysical grounds for such a transhistorical meaning. We will now consider how some Catholic thinkers work out this magisterial teaching.

## II. PERSISTENT PLURALISM

This section briefly introduces four approaches to the church's teaching about the permanence of dogmatic meaning. My purpose is simply to suggest the variety of philosophical approaches employed by Catholic thinkers. What follows is determined by this limited goal. An adequate understanding of these thinkers would require a far more extensive treatment of their rich thought.

### A. Robert Sokolowski

Robert Sokolowski's book *The God of Faith and Reason* suggests a fascinating way to work out the church's teaching about the relationship between reason and faith, between philosophy and theology. He holds that the dogma of Chalcedon is decisive. Jesus is fully God and fully human, two natures unmixed. Thinking about this revealed truth discloses the distinction between creation and God. This distinction determines the relationship between reason and faith.

How is it possible that two natures, unmixed, are hypostatically united in Jesus? Nature is that which distinguishes a thing from everything else. To unite a nature with something else is to alter that nature. If, for example, a human being could be united with an angel, the human nature would be elevated. It would become more, while the angel would become less. Each nature would cease to be what it is.

Yet Chalcedon states that in the incarnation the humanity of Jesus retains its full integrity. It is not mixed with divinity to form some third kind of nature (35–40). Thinking about this doctrine discloses the unique distinction between God and creation.

One way to grasp Sokolowski's point is to appreciate that, when thinking about God and creation, imagination fails. We tend to picture God at the top of creation, as the first and highest Being from whom all else flows. In other words, we picture God as part of reality, part of the whole, of all that is. But this is precisely the kind of thinking excluded by Chalcedon. For the unity of the incarnation to occur, a unity of natures which leaves Jesus' humanity intact, God cannot be thought of as the highest of all natures or as part of the whole of reality.

The doctrine of Chalcedon requires a different way of thinking about divinity. The two great expositors of this way of thinking are Saints Anselm and Thomas Aquinas.

For Anselm, God is that, than which nothing greater can be thought. Anselm presents this notion of divinity in his *Proslogium*, his argument for God's existence. We need not enter into that argument here. One point is critical for Sokolowski's position. Anselm's notion of God means that creation adds nothing to divinity. God is, by definition, complete and perfect, already that to which nothing can be added. Thus creation adds nothing, changes nothing in God.

Thinking this notion of God suggests the possibility of creation, of our world, not existing. God remains the same. "Christian theology is differentiated from pagan religious and philosophical reflection primarily by the introduction of a new distinction, the distinction between the world understood as possibly not having existed and God understood as possibly being all that there is, with no diminution of goodness or greatness" (23).

St. Thomas Aquinas pursues this thinking, a thinking about God we considered in chapter 7. God is thought of over and against nonexistence. God is the sheer act of existing, *esse subsistens* (41–42). God is not one nature among many, but that being whose essence it is to be.

Thinking in this manner allows created nature its own integrity. What creation is stands on its own. Creation is not part of what God is, nor is God one more nature alongside the world. Thus, God's incarnation does not disturb the integrity of human nature since the incarnation is not a unity of two kinds of things within the whole. God's incarnation leaves nature intact.

Chalcedon's dogma thus manifests the distinction between God and creation. The distinction "is glimpsed on the margin of reason, and because of the importance it has for belief in the other Christian mysteries and for the Christian life generally, it may be said to be at the intersection of reason and faith. Because of it the Christian faith remains faith, but a reasoned faith" (39). The doctrine of the incarnation requires the distinction. Revelation thus guides thought toward what reason can glimpse though, unaided, might never achieve.

For our purposes, two significant consequences flow from the distinction. First, Sokolowski argues that the distinction, and its consequent notion of God and metaphysics, are transhistorical. They are not historically conditioned moments in the history of Christian thought. The history of religious thought and philosophy occur within the whole where God is conceived of as the highest of all natures. Such thinking clothes the divine in various culturally and historically conditioned categories. In contrast, the Christian distinction thinks of the divine in a manner which transcends the flux of history. "The Christian sense of God is, not simply a human or religious improvement on other senses of the divine, but a new kind of completion that does not appear as a possibility in simply natural religions and philosophy." While Christianity always takes historically and culturally conditioned form, its essential understanding of the divine, and consequent metaphysics, are perennial (48, 117).

Second, the distinction, and the integrity of nature it implies, establish for Sokolowski the fundamental relationship between reason and faith, nature and grace, philosophy and theology. Human reason knows the rational order. The incarnation does not interfere with that order, but leaves it intact. We have here something like the notion of pure nature mentioned in chapter 2. Sokolowski's account of the theological virtues exemplifies his perspective.

Since created nature retains its integrity, so does natural virtue. By natural virtue Sokolowski means Aristotle. Revelation does not alter or contradict the naturally virtuous. What then has Christianity to do with moral conduct? What do the theological virtues of faith, hope and charity add? Sokolowski answers through an interpretation of Aquinas' retrieval of Aristotle.

Faith, hope and charity "are not simply new virtues to be added to what Aristotle, Plato, or the Stoics described as the excellences of human beings." Rather, they are "dispositions for 'acting' in the setting disclosed by Christian faith." They are "reactions" to the God who has freely involved us in the divine life. The natural virtues are manifest in human actions. The supernatural virtues do not result in a new way of acting, they are not publicly visible. Rather, the theological virtues have to do with why a Christian acts according to the natural virtues. Grace builds on nature "and shares in the reasonableness associated with nature." The theological virtues, and all supernatural (infused) moral virtues "make us capable of acting in respect to our life with God, while the natural ones make us fit to act in human affairs" (72–83).

Sokolowski's account of the virtues privatizes Christian morality leaving the realm of public affairs untouched. One might want to compare this approach with the thought of Boff considered in chapter 14. The practical consequences of these two approaches can help in understanding the categories of conservative and progressive in contemporary theology. Sokolowski's approach bolsters the traditional order of society which he identifies with nature. The theological virtues are supernatural motives for conforming to that order. Boff, in contrast, interprets Christ as a critic of the established order. Christianity requires a constant transformation of society, never resting short of the ideal community promised by Christ's message about the kingdom and resurrection.

This summary hardly does justice to Sokolowski's subtle and substantial argument. I introduce it here to exemplify one way in which the church's teaching about philosophy can be carried out. Sokolowski contends that the thought of Aristotle and Aquinas captures the perennial and essential element within Christianity, the distinction between God and creation and the consequent integrity of the natural order. The careful reader may have already noticed that Sokolowski therein represents that school of Thomists, mentioned in chapter 6, who eschew modernity and argue that Christian orthodoxy is bound to the pre-modern realism of Aristotle and Aquinas.

## B. Karl Rahner

In contrast, Rahner turns to modernity to identify the common meaning which underlies all Christian doctrine. Chapter 9 offers enough information about Rahner's theology to understand his explication of the church's teaching that dogmas assert lasting meaning midst historical change. Rahner's transcendental retrieval of Aquinas locates an openness to divinity in transcendental consciousness. An openness to, and experience of infinite Being are the necessary condition for the activity of the agent intellect and for human freedom.

Rahner's transcendental argument is guided by Chalcedon. Jesus is the unity of humanity and divinity in one individual. Human nature must, therefore, have the potential for God's incarnation, even if that potential can only be actualized by God's unique action. Human openness to the divine occurs in transcendental consciousness. Jesus reveals that this is not mere openness to infinite Being, but God's very Self-offer. All humanity is the event of God's Self-communication. Jesus reveals this truth by being God's perfect Self-offer and human freedom's perfect response.

With this move Rahner has identified a universal experience of God which occurs in transcendental consciousness. This universal experience is always mediated by, and expressed through historically conditioned categories. But it remains the reference of all Christian doctrine. Christian doctrines are historically conditioned statements that refer to the transcendental truth of God's Self-gift. Rahner's theology amounts to an interpretation of Christian doctrines by correlating them with the transcendental experience of God and its implications.

For example, Jesus' message about the nearness of the kingdom does not bind us to the apocalyptic categories of first century Judaism. Rather, it expresses the nearness of God, the divine Self-offer. Or, the meaning of the proclamation that "Jesus is risen" is attained when one correlates that proclamation with the transcendental experience of hope consequent on God's Self-gift.

Thus, Rahner has identified the enduring meaning of doctrine which underlies the variety of historical expression. The formulation of Christian truth might vary with the flux of history, but the truth itself, what is ultimately intended by doctrine, remains the same.

Rahner's resolution of the problem of history is modern. He has identified the lasting meaning of Christian doctrine in transcendental consciousness. This resolution is achieved through Rahner's Kantian (transcendental) interpretation of St. Thomas. What endures across history is the structure of human consciousness or, more precisely, the divine Self-communication manifest as the necessary condition for knowledge and human freedom.

## C. Bernard Lonergan

We are examining how some theologians work out the church's teaching that dogmas assert permanent meaning midst historical change. The distinction between meaning and expression implicit in this teaching requires a philosophical foundation. Is there a philosophy implicit in the church's teaching about dogma?

Bernard Lonergan's epistemology and notion of being were briefly mentioned at the end of chapter 7. The late Carl Peter suggested that Lonergan's entire philosophical project was guided by Vatican I's doctrine about doctrine. *Dei filius* states that the permanent truth of dogmas is the meaning intended (understood) when they were proclaimed. Granting the historicity of dogmatic formulas, and the categories they employ, Lonergan's thought offers epistemological and metaphysical grounds for asserting such a permanence. Peter observes that "There is undeniably a sense in which he (Lonergan) finds in human subjectivity what one would expect to find in the subjectivity of a believer committed to the permanent truth of certain basic positions of Christianity."[4] "Human subjectivity" alerts one to the modern character of Lonergan's project.

Lonergan contends that his critical realism is implied by the fact that the church proclaims dogmas. The dogmatic tradition reflects the truth of God's revealed word. During its first centuries the church was faced with specific questions about revelation, about the relationship of the Son to the Father, about the relationship between divinity and humanity in Jesus. The councils of Nicea and Chalcedon gave dogmatic answers to these questions. The results were not only specific dogmas but an implicit notion of dogma, a notion which would become explicit with later reflection.[5] These dogmas are judgments about something which "is," "is not," and "is the same as."[6] Such judgments imply a realism. "The truth that is acknowledged in the mind corresponds to reality."[7]

Doctrinal debates and dogmas occurred within historically conditioned contexts but those contexts have no permanent claim on believers. Dogma deals with judgments about the real, not historical categories. What is true, the real (being) does not change.

"From the beginning the word of God contained within it an implicit epistemology and ontology, but what was there implicitly became known explicitly only through dialectic process that was spread over time."[8] That this process would take time is another example of the epistemology manifest. One must know, attain truth, before one can attend to the act of knowledge itself. An implicit epistemology and ontology were manifest in the church's capacity to assert the truth, to reach true answers to the questions raised by Arius, Apollinaris and Nestorius. It is the same epistemology implicit in all judgments of truth. In the modern period philosophers turned their attention to the act of knowing. Based on the performance of knowledge they attended to the subject who achieves truth, to the operations manifest in that achievement.

I shall not attempt a summary of Lonergan's critical realism here. Our interest is simply to indicate how Lonergan works out the church's teaching about the permanent meaning of its dogmas.

The distinction between conceptualization and judgment is key. Dogmas, like all knowledge, occur within cultural, historical contexts. Questions arise and answers are achieved within the categories of that context. Lonergan rejects what he calls classicist dogmatic theology which identifies truth with the historically conditioned categories of a dogmatic proposition.[9] This identification mistakenly locates truth in the categories of conceptualization rather than in judgment.

Concepts are the means by which mind renders sensation intelligible. When the intellect reaches judgment it reaches the intelligibility of the known. When I assert, "This is a car," I affirm the being (intelligibility) of the object, not the existence of a concept. Dogmas are judgments of truth. They affirm (or negate) an intelligible "object," i.e., revealed truth.

The *homoousios* of Nicea can serve as an example. The dogmatic assertion that the Son is *homoousios* (same substance, one in being) with the Father is a judgment of truth, what is. The dogma rose out of long theological debate. The categories, questions and answers of that debate reflect the middle Platonism of the third and fourth centuries. But the dogma does not tie the church to a specific philosophy. The term *homoousios* expresses the judgment that whatever is affirmed about the Father is affirmed of the Son, save the name Father. It is like the judgment "A equals B." One can grasp the intelligibility of this judgment without any concept (we do not know what A and B are). So Nicea asserts the Son is equal with the Father. But this judgment does not tie the church to a middle Platonic conception of divinity.

Similarly, Chalcedon's dogmatic assertion that Jesus is fully human implies no particular anthropology. Whatever it means to be human is true of Jesus. This is a revealed truth. It is a truth formulated within the context of Hellenist philosophy, but it idoes not absolutize that philosophy or its anthropology.

For our purposes only one point is at issue. The fact that truth occurs in judgment, rather than conceptualization, grounds the possibility of enduring meaning midst historical flux. Dogmas are propositions which employ historically conditioned language and categories. Scholars must study the period within which dogmas were proclaimed. Such study can introduce one into the context of the dogma's formulation and to the question addressed by the dogma. Having thus identified the church's response to that question the contemporary scholar can translate the meaning of that response into contemporary categories. In this way the truth, the meaning intended, perdures while the categories of expression change.

## D. Peter Chirico

Peter Chirico's work *Infallibility: The Crossroads of Doctrine* offers another approach to the magisterium's teaching about the permanence of meaning midst historical change. Rahner, Sokolowski and Lonergan take the dogmatic teaching of the early councils as their starting point. In contrast, Chirico begins with the foundational Christian belief in the resurrection of Jesus. His understanding of Jesus' resurrection provides the key for establishing the permanent character of dogmatic teaching.

How are we to understand the proclamation that Jesus is risen? What happened to him? Chirico suggests that in his risen state Christ has attained the perfection of human potentiality. Christ is in perfect communion with God, with humanity and with all of creation. The poles of potentiality and perfection undergird Chirico's position. If Christ is the perfection of human potentiality then we can grasp elements of his perfection by attending to that potentiality. More specifically, Chirico suggests an anthropological turn. If Christ is the perfection of human possibilities we can come to know him by identifying universal possibilities, those potentialities which constitute human existence in all its cultural and historical forms.

When Chirico speaks of human potentiality he means our capacity to relate with reality on a variety of levels. We can know the created world, love other people and be open to the divine Mystery. In our finite existence all these potential relationships are limited by time and place. For example, there is no limit to what human beings would like to know about nature. Whatever we know leads to more questions. We really would like to know everything, but cannot. Or, while we are capable of knowing and loving only a few persons during our lifetime, we are drawn to a universal love for everyone which, in our finite condition, we cannot actualize.

Chirico argues that we can identify such universal possibilities of human nature, potentialities that characterize human beings in every time and culture. Christ is the perfection of these possibilities, human existence come to full potential, a human being in perfect relationship with God, with all humanity and creation.

With this move Chirico has established the grounds for explaining the church's teaching about the enduring meaning of dogma. Christian belief is always clothed in historically conditioned categories. The first Christians understood Jesus' fate within the eschatological and apocalyptic categories of their time and religion. The dogma of Chalcedon about Jesus' full humanity was understood in the categories of fifth century, Hellenist anthropology. But apocalyptic images and a historically conditioned anthropology can have no universal claim. The universal character of dogma is rooted in the universal elements of human existence. Enduring meaning refers to the enduring, universal potentialities of human nature brought to perfection in the resurrection.

Lacking the perfection of the risen state, how can we assert such lasting meanings? "[B]y extrapolating from the basic conditions of present existence and its inner exigence towards universal relationship with creation and the Creator, we can gain an anticipatory notion of what the risen condition of Christ might be once the Faith postulates its existence."[10] In turn, different universal aspects of human existence, viewed in light of the Easter faith, are the hermeneutical key for identifying the universal meaning expressed in the historically conditioned dogmatic formulas.

The doctrine of the communion of saints is a good example of Chirico's hermeneutic. The human capacities to know the created world and to relate in a personal way depend on our living in a human community. What we can become as human beings depends on the possibilities offered by the community in which we live. This is the case for all human beings of every time and place. People born into the ancient world could not be nuclear physicists. The capacity for human relationships of children growing up in Nazi Germany was distorted by the hate they were taught. It is a universal fact of human existence that our possibilities depend on the community in which we find ourselves.

This is the universal meaning embodied in the doctrine of the communion of saints. As with all human potentiality, our ability to relate to God depends in no small part on the human community in which we live. The Christian relationship with God is made possible by the church, by the saints past and present. This is the permanent truth, the lasting meaning present in the doctrine of the communion of saints.

Or, the perfection of human potential must involve all aspects of human existence—biological, psychological, intellectual and volitional. The dogma of the assumption proclaims such a total perfection. Mary, the church's first member, a type of all the church, enjoys the perfection and completion of the whole human person. The lasting meaning of the dogma of the assumption is not a description of a spacial event that occurred centuries ago. Nor does the dogma bind us to the cosmology such a description implies. Dogmas deal with lasting meaning and lasting meaning is not found in the cultural categories of expression. Rather, what is lasting is the human condition which is open to "universal relationship with creation and the Creator," a potential brought to fulfillment in Mary, the first of the saints.[11]

These brief remarks do not do justice to Chirico's rich thought. Only one point is at issue. Chirico roots transhistorical meaning in the universal characteristics and potentialities of human existence. His hermeneutic of dogma is a kind of correlation between the Christ event and these universal elements of human nature. The transhistorical meaning of dogma is grounded in the human potentialities which are characteristic of people in every time and place, potentialities brought to perfection in the resurrection.

### III. A PROPOSAL

The first and, perhaps, most important conclusion we can draw from this chapter, and from this entire book, is that orthodoxy does not require a specific philosophy. Or, put positively, the theological enterprise involves a continuing conversation between faith and philosophies. In the four thinkers treated above, and in the topics considered in the preceding chapters, we have seen how different philosophical perspectives offer different accounts of the faith. While the magisterium clearly asserts a unity of meaning which unites history's pluralism, different philosophical perspectives suggest different understandings of that meaning.

In this concluding section I would like to offer an additional way to think about the unity of faith. Chapter 1 alerted the reader to the Gadamerian perspective which underlies this work. The relationship between philosophy and theology is likened to a conversation. Various philosophical perspectives have disclosed and enriched the Christian understanding of God's revelation in Jesus Christ. We, believers in the late twentieth century, are heirs of a rich tradition who, like Christians before us, must place the faith in conversation with the questions and knowledge of our own time.

Granting the obvious pluralism of philosophy and theology, this concluding chapter has raised an essential question. What unites the faith? Or, in view of this pluralism, how can we assert a common meaning to the faith?

The four thinkers considered above seek the unity of faith by identifying something unchanging beneath the explicit categories of scripture and doctrine. Sokolowski argues that the distinction between God and creation implicit in the incarnation, and clarified by Anselm and Aquinas, determines the Christian philosophical perspective and the relationship between faith and reason. Rahner, Lonergan and Chirico turn to anthropology, to transhistorical characteristics of human existence, to give unity to the tradition. I propose another approach.

It seems problematic to base the unity of faith on a previously unspoken meaning which underlies the tradition. For example, Karl Rahner holds that God's Self-offer is the fundamental revealed truth which underlies and gives meaning to history's many categorical expressions. Rahner's hermeneutic correlates specific doctrines with the experience of God's Self-offer and with the implications of that offer.

This method identifies a universal truth (God's Self-gift) underneath the pluralism of expression. This truth is what was always "meant," though the authors of scripture and doctrine were innocent of this meaning at an explicit level. The primary example is Rahner's interpretation of Jesus. Rahner interprets Jesus' proclamation, "The kingdom of God is near," to mean the nearness of God, i.e., God's Self-communication. The historical Jesus understood his message in apocalyptic categories. He thought the end of the world was near. The lasting meaning of his proclamation, however, is not located in Jesus' apocalyptic categories but in the transcendental experience of God's very Self identified in Rahner's anthropological turn. [12]

The assertion of an unspoken meaning underneath the tradition, and only recently identified, strikes this writer as an unsatisfactory way to explicate the unity of Christian truth. First, the assertion of an implicit meaning beneath the categories of expression (Jesus' message, scripture and doctrine) is epistemologically problematic. What is the character of this common meaning which transcends expression? On what basis can one assert such meaning when the only access we have to other Christians is through expression?

The identification of universal meaning through an anthropological turn, a turn made possible by modern philosophy, appears to be a kind of contemporary imperialism which absorbs the tradition into current categories. This observation suggests a second reason for questioning whether we should seek the unity of Christian truth in a transhistorical meaning beneath categorical expression.

As indicated in section II of this chapter, there exists a pluralism in contemporary ways to explain the common meaning that underlies historical expression. The few thinkers considered here hardly exhaust the approaches to fundamental theology today. The notion of universal meaning appears rather unsatisfactory when we recognize that there is no consensus as to what that meaning is. This universal meaning is quite illusive, like Hegel's dark night when all the cows are black.

My suggestion is that we not look to something below, behind or beneath the tradition to find its unity. The unity of the Christian tradition occurs precisely in its perennial elements. Specifically, in every age Catholic Christians proclaim and live the Christ presented in the scripture and ecclesial doctrine. We read the same gospels, celebrate the same eucharist, profess the same creed, struggle to put into practice the same command of Christ for perfect love, and so on.

In various times and places these perennial elements of church life take different forms. They are understood, appropriated, explained, enriched, and lived in different ways.

Magisterial teaching insists that a common meaning unites this pluralism of expression. But what is meaning and where does it reside?
Sokolowski argues that distinction between God and creation, achieved in
Aquinas' retrieval of Aristotle, establishes a permanent Christian view of the
world, a perennial philosophy, a lasting truth. In this he eschews the modern
project and absolutizes a moment in the history of Christian thought.

The other theologians we considered turn to modern thought in order
to offer an account of the unity of faith. In modern thought, especially after
Kant, meaning is viewed as the achievement of the subject, an act of the
knower uniting data. The notions of common meaning offered by Rahner,
Lonergan and Chirico reflect this kind of thinking. The meaning of dogmas
is achieved by reflection on human existence. One must attend to the recurring operations of the subject (Lonergan), or correlate dogmatic assertions
with experience (Rahner) or with human potentiality (Chirico).

However, if one accepts Heidegger's description of human existence as
"being-in-the-world," as Gadamer does, then meaning is not primordially an
achievement of the subject. Rather, meaning is a public reality deposited in
the world, in language and in the ways of being that constitute a time and
place. This approach to human existence suggests that a common meaning
occurs because of common elements within various worlds.

The public character of meaning was suggested in chapter 12.
Individuals are born into communities. Communities are constituted by public symbol systems. Communities share a common language. They have family systems, political structures and the like. What one becomes is determined by these public structures. One appropriates what one's world offers,
what is deposited in the public modes of being characteristic of a community. The commonality among citizens is constituted by their appropriation of
what is common. They share common meaning because they participate in a
common symbol system. Thus, meaning is first of all deposited in public
modes of being. An individual's grasp of meaning is derivative through
appropriation.

Common Christian meaning is deposited in those elements of church
life characteristic of Christians in every time and place. Christians in every
age and place have heard Jesus' words, "Repent, the kingdom of God is at
hand." The various interpretations of this proclamation that have been noted
throughout this book reflect the rich history of the Church. These interpretations reflect the continuing conversation between Christianity's classic texts
and the horizons within which those texts are appropriated. What unites this
history is not a common interpretation or an implicit meaning. The tradition
is unified precisely by what gets appropriated in every age, i.e., Jesus' words.

The unity of Christian truth occurs in the common elements constitutive of Christian existence in every time and place. Here resides that com-

mon meaning asserted by magisterial teaching. We need not turn to some implicit, or previously unrecognized characteristic of human subjectivity in order to locate common meaning. Nor need we absolutize one appropriation of the faith. The common meaning which unites the faith is deposited in scripture, doctrine, worship, and praxis common to every Christian age. The pluralism of philosophy, theology, doctrinal formulation and praxis reflects how these common elements are appropriated within the various contexts which constitute the history of the faith.

The pluralism of interpretations is, thereby, neither a threat to Christian unity nor a problem to overcome. God's Word is truly incarnate, a Word spoken into human history. The appropriation of the Word in various contexts, its effective history, unfolds that Absolute Mystery which forever eludes humanity's grasp.

Of course, this proposal requires further explication and testing. These tasks cannot be pursued here. But I suggest that this book's examples of the relationship between philosophy and theology point in the direction of my proposal. Revealed truth gives itself in the continuing conversation between classic Christian texts and the historical contexts of their appropriation.

## BIBLIOGRAPHY

Pope John's address, opening the Second Vatican Council, can be found in Walter Abbott's edition of *The Documents of Vatican II*. For *Mysterium Ecclesiae* see *Origins* 3 (July 19, 1973) and for the Congregation for Catholic Education's letter "On the Study of Philosophy in Seminaries" see *Origins* 1 (March 16, 1972). The material in this chapter about Robert Sokolowski is taken from his book *The God of Faith and Reason*. Chapter 9 of this book treats Rahner's position in detail and offers pertinent references to his works. Lonergan's explication of the nature of dogma and its lasting meaning can be found in his *Method in Theology* and *The Way to Nicea*. Chirico's notion of dogmatic meaning can be found in his *Infallibility: The Crossroads of Doctrine*. A number of the issues raised in this final chapter are treated by Avery Dulles in the essay "Theology and Philosophy" found in his book *The Craft of Theology*.

## NOTES

1. International Theological Commission, *Texts and Documents 1969–1985* (San Francisco: Ignatius, 1989), p. 91.
2. Bernard Lonergan, *Method in Theology* (New York: Herder and Herder, 1972), p. 323. Here Lonergan is commenting on chapter four of *Dei filius,* DS 3020, and its third canon, DS 3043.

3. *Origins* 3 (July 19, 1973), 110–111.
4. Carl Peter, "A Shift to the Human Subject in Roman Catholic Theology," *Communio* 6 (1979), 68–69.
5. Bernard Lonergan, *The Way to Nicea* (Philadelphia: The Westminster Press, 1976), pp. 8–13. See note six on page 11.
6. *The Way to Nicea*, note 5 on p. 11.
7. *The Way to Nicea*, p. 128.
8. *The Way to Nicea*, p. 133.
9. Bernard Lonergan, *Method in Theology*, p. 333.
10. Chirico, p. 79.
11. Chirico, p. 88.
12. Karl Rahner, *Foundations of Christian Faith,* trans. by William Dych (New York: The Seabury Press, 1978), p. 249.

# SELECTED BIBLIOGRAPHY

Abbot, Walter, ed. *The Documents of Vatican II.* New York: Guild Press, 1966.

Aristotle. *The Basic Works of Aristotle.* Edited by Richard McKeon. New York: Random House, 1941.

Augustine. "Lord's Sermon on the Mount with Seventeen Related Sermons," *The Fathers of the Church* Vol. 11. Translated by Denis J. Kavanagh. Washington D.C.: The Catholic University of America Press, 1951, Sermon 6.

_____. "Sermons on the Liturgical Seasons," *The Fathers of the Church,* Vol. 38. Translated by Mary Sarah Muldowney. New York: Fathers of the Church, Inc., 1959, sermons 225, 227, 231, 243, 261 263.

_____. *Tractates on the Gospel of John,* vol. 79 in *The Fathers of the Church,* translated by John W. Rettig. Washington D.C.: The Catholic University of America Press, 1988.

Boff, Leonardo. *Church: Charism and Power.* Translated by John Diercksmeier. New York: Crossroad, 1985.

_____. *Jesus Christ Liberator.* Translated by Patrick Hughes. Maryknoll: Orbis Books, 1984.

Bonsor, Jack. *Rahner, Heidegger and Truth.* Lanham: University Press of America, 1987.

Brown, Peter. *Augustine of Hippo.* Berkeley: University of California Press, 1967.

Brown, Raymond. "The Resurrection of Jesus," *The Jerome Biblical Commentary.* The first edition, 78:146–149, pp. 791–795; Second edition, 81:118–134, pp. 1373–1377.

Brown, Donfried, and Reumann, eds. *Peter in the New Testament.* Minneapolis: Augsburg Publishing House, 1973.

Brown, Raymond and Meier, John. *Antioch and Rome.* New York: Paulist Press, 1983.

Burrell, David. "Creation or Emanation: Two Paradigms of Reason." In *God and Creation: An Ecumenical Symposium*. Edited by David Burrell and Bernard McGinn. Notre Dame: University of Notre Dame Press, 1990, pp. 27–37.

_____. *Knowing the Unknowable God*. Notre Dame: University of Notre Dame Press, 1986.

Chenu, M. D. *Toward Understanding Saint Thomas*. Chicago: Henry Regnery, 1964.

Chirico, Peter. *Infallibility: The Crossroads of Doctrine*. Kansas City: Sheed Andrews and McMeel, Inc., 1977.

Clarkson, Edwards, Kelly, and Welch, eds. *The Church Teaches*. Rockford: Tan Books and Publishers, Inc., 1973.

Congregation for Catholic Education. "On the Study of Philosophy in Seminaries," *Origins* 1 (March 16, 1972).

Congregation for the Doctrine of the Faith. *Mysterium Ecclesiae. Origins* 3 (July, 1973).

Copleston, Frederick. *A History of Philosophy*. New York: Doubleday, 1985.

Cwiekowski, Frederick. *The Beginnings of the Church*. New York: Paulist Press, 1988.

Denzinger, H., ed. *Enchiridion symbolorum*. 32nd edition, edited by A. Schonmetzer. Freiburg, 1963.

Dulles, Avery. "Theology and Philosophy." In *The Craft of Theology*. New York: Crossroad, 1992, pp.119-134.

Dunn, Patrick. *Priesthood*. New York: Alba House, 1990.

Fiorenza, Francis Schüssler. *Foundational Theology,* New York: Crossroad, 1984.

_____. "Karl Rahner and the Kantian Problematic." Preface in Karl Rahner, *Spirit in the World,* pp. xix-xlv.

Flannery, Austin, ed. *Vatican Council II.* Northport: Costello Publishing Co., 1988.

Fuller, Reginald. *The Formation of the Resurrection Narratives.* New York: Macmillan Co., 1971.

Gadamer, Hans-Georg. *Truth and Method.* Translation and revision by Joel Weinsheimer and Donald G. Marshall. New York: Crossroad, 1991.

Galot, Jean. *Theology of the Priesthood.* San Francisco: Ignatius Press, 1985.

Gilson, Etienne. *Thomist Realism and the Critique of Knowledge.* Translated by Mark A. Wauck. San Francisco: Ignatius Press, 1986.

Grillmeier, Aloys. *Christ in Christian Tradition* I, *From the Apostolic Age to Chalcedon.* Translated by John Bowden. Atlanta: John Knox Press, 1975.

Hegel, G. W. F. *Phenomenology of Spirit.* Translated by A. V. Miller. Oxford: Oxford University Press, 1977.

Heidegger, Martin. *Being and Time.* Translated by John Macquarrie and Edward Robinson. New York and Evanston: Harper & Row, 1962.

Hennelly, Alfred, ed. *Liberation Theology: A Documentary History.* Maryknoll: Orbis Books, 1990.

Hines, Mary. *The Transformation of Dogma.* New York: Paulist Press, 1989.

International Theological Commission. *Texts and Documents 1969–1985.* San Francisco: Ignatius Press, 1989.

John Paul II. "Catholic Higher Education." *Origins* 17 (October 1, 1987).

Kant, Immanuel. *Critique of Pure Reason.* Translated by F. Max Muller. Garden City: Doubleday and Co., 1966.

Kelly, J.N.D. *Early Christian Doctrine,* San Francisco: Harper & Row, 1978.

Komonchak, Joseph. "Theology and Culture at Mid-Century: The Example of Henri de Lubac," *Theological Studies* 51 (Dec. 1990):579–602.

Kreeft, Peter, ed. *Summa of the Summa.* San Francisco: Ignatius Press, 1990.

Krentz, Edgar. *The Historical-Critical Method.* Philadelphia: Fortress Press, 1975.

Lane, Dermot. *The Reality of Jesus.* New York: Paulist Press, 1975.

Leo XIII. *Aeterni Patris* in *The Papal Encyclicals 1878–1903.* Edited by Claudia Carlen. Salem: McGrath Pub., 1981, pp. 17–28.

Linge, David. "Editor's Introduction." In *Philosophical Hermeneutics.* Edited and translated by David Linge. Berkeley: University of California Press, 1976, pp. xi–lviii.

Lonergan, Bernard. *Insight: A Study in Human Understanding.* New York: Philosophical Library, 1957.

_____. *Method in Theology.* New York: Herder and Herder, 1972.

_____. *Philosophy of God, and Theology.* Philadelphia: The Westminster Press, 1973.

_____. *The Way to Nicea.* Philadelphia: The Westminster Press, 1976.

Maréchal, Joseph. *A Maréchal Reader.* Translated and edited by Joseph Donceel. New York: Herder and Herder, 1970.

Marx, Karl. *The German Ideology,* Part I. C. Arthur, ed., New York: International Publishers, 1970. (Written with Friedrich Engles.)

_____. *The Essential Writings.* Edited by R. Bender. New York: Harper and Row, 1972.

McBrien, Richard. *Catholicism.* Minneapolis: The Winston Press, 1981.

McCool, Gerald. *Catholic Theology in the Nineteenth Century.* New York: The Seabury Press, 1977.

McLellan, David. *Karl Marx.* New York: Penguin Books, 1975.

Mueller-Vollmer, Kurt, ed. *The Hermeneutics Reader.* New York: Continuum, 1988.

Palmer, Richard. *Hermeneutics.* Evanston: Northwestern University Press, 1969.

Pannenberg, Wolfhart. "The Appropriation of the Philosophical Concept of God as a Dogmatic Problem of Early Christian Theology." *Basic Questions in Theology II.* Translated by George H. Kehm. The Fortress Press, 1971, pp. 119–183.

_____. *Jesus—God and Man.* Translated by Lewis Wilkins and Duane Priebe. Philadelphia: The Westminster Press, 1968.

_____. *Theology and the Kingdom of God.* Edited by Richard John Neuhaus. Philadelphia: The Westminster Press, 1969.

_____. "What is Truth?" *Basic Questions in Theology* II. Translated by George H. Kehm. The Fortress Press, 1971, pp. 1–27.

Pelikan, Jaroslav. *The Christian Tradition: A History of the Development of Doctrine* I, *The Emergence of the Catholic Tradition (100–600).* Chicago: The University of Chicago Press, 1971.

Pius X. *Pascendi Dominici Gregis* in *The Papal Encyclicals 1903–1939.* Edited by Claudia Carlen. McGrath Pub., 1981, pp. 71–98.

Pius XII. *Humani Generis* in *The Papal Encyclicals 1939–1958.* Edited by Claudia Carlen. McGrath Pub., 1981, pp. 175–184.

Plato. *The Collected Dialogues of Plato.* Edited by Edith Hamilton and Huntington Cairns. Princeton: Princeton University Press, 1961.

Rahner, Karl. *Foundations of Christian Faith.* Translated by William V. Dych. New York: The Seabury Press, 1978.

_____. *Hearers of the Word.* In *A Rahner Reader.* Edited by Gerald McCool. New York: The Seabury Press, 1975, pp. 1–65.

_____. *Spirit in the World.* Translated by William Dych. New York: Herder and Herder, 1968.

_____. "Theology of Freedom." *Theological Investigations* 6. Translated by Karl-H. and Boniface Kruger. Baltimore: Helicon Press, 1969, pp. 178–196.

Singer, Peter. *Hegel.* Oxford: Oxford University Press, 1983.

Sokolowski, Robert. *The God of Faith and Reason.* Notre Dame: University of Notre Dame Press, 1982.

Trigg, Joseph, ed. *Biblical Inspiration.* Wilmington: Glazier, 1988.

Tupper, Frank E. *The Theology of Wolfhart Pannenberg.* Philadelphia: The Westminster Press, 1973.

Tyrrell, Bernard. *Bernard Lonergan's Philosophy of God.* Notre Dame: University of Notre Dame Press, 1974.

# GLOSSARY

**Apocalyptic:** A literary genre which depicts the future through visions, signs and predictions. The biblical books of Daniel, Ezekiel and Revelation are written in this style. When used in this book *apocalyptic* refers to the end of the world, the end of history, when the dead rise and the Son of Man comes in the clouds to judge all humanity.

**A posteriori:** Refers to data that comes to the individual, data that does not belong to the native structure of the mind (see *a priori*). *A posteriori* also refers to that form of argument which moves inductively from data to generalization.

**A priori:** In this text *a priori* refers to the conditions of the subject which make the act of knowing possible. These conditions (native capacities) must exist logically prior to any act of knowing, though they are only manifest in that act. The term is also used more broadly. For example, supernatural revelation is excluded *a priori* from scientific debate. The scientific method excludes revelation as data. This exclusion is intrinsic to the scientific method and, thereby, occurs prior to (*a priori*) any particular investigation.

**Beatific Vision:** The supernatural goal of eternal participation in the divine life (heaven) which God freely offers humanity. Humanity's participation in God's Self-vision, in God's very being.

**Being:** This word has a variety of related uses. A *being* or *beings* refer to things which exist. Dogs, trees, angels and people are all *beings*. As an extension of this meaning, the word can also indicate everything that exists, all that is, all *being*. The word can sometimes mean the essence of something as, for example, when we speak about participating in God's very *being*. Finally, *being* refers to the act of existence as such and as distinguishable from any thing. In this last meaning the *ontological distinction* occurs, i.e., the distinction between *beings* (things, what exists) and *being* (existence as such).

**Cosmology:** A philosophy of the universe, a view about the structure and origin of all reality.

**Dasein:** The human existent, a term for the individual human being as representative of human nature. Literally, "there-being."

**Doctrine:** A very general term for the teaching of the church. The term covers everything from homilies and common opinion to the formal teaching of an ecumenical council.

**Dogma:** A doctrine taught by the highest authority of the church which Catholics must believe. An infallible teaching of a council and/or of the pope.

**Empirical:** That which is experienced by the senses. What is given in sensation, sense data.

**Epistemology:** A branch of philosophy which examines human knowing. It asks questions such as: What do we know? How did we come to knowledge? Can we be certain?

**Eschatological:** Dealing with the last things, i.e., death, judgment, heaven, hell, resurrection and Christ's return.

**Essence:** What a thing is. The answer to the question, "What is it?"

**Faith:** Trust in God and in divine revelation. The act of belief in divine revelation and the knowledge which flows from it. Faith is God's gift (grace). It is also a free and reasonable human action, an act which is salvific.

**Fideism:** The view that the Christian faith is *solely* a gift from God. There are no rational grounds for the act and content of belief.

**Freedom:** In this book, *freedom* is generally used to indicate the unique character of human existence as open to possibilities. To be human is not to be a fixed essence or nature. Rather, human existence is a becoming. One becomes who one is by appropriating the possibilities offered by the given time and place in which one finds oneself. The capacity to make specific choices is rooted in humanity's fundamental mode of being as *freedom*.

**Grace:** God's presence with us. *Uncreated grace* is God's gift of God's Self. This gift affects human existence (*created grace*) and guides us in our choices and actions (*actual grace*).

**Hermeneutics:** The philosophy or study of interpretation. *Hermeneutics* seeks the grounds for the possibility of interpreting texts and the conditions for a valid interpretation. It is especially concerned with the problem of bridging the historical distance between a text from the past and the contemporary interpreter. The term *hermeneutical* is also used to identify philosophers and theologians who view interpretative theory as the key for understanding human existence and the Christian tradition.

**Hypostasis:** An individual existing entity. The concrete occurrence of a nature. For example, the nature dog does not exist as such. There are only individual dogs, i.e., hypostases of this nature. The Council of Chalcedon used this term to assert unity of two natures in Jesus. When speaking of Jesus one must assert that he is two, full and unmixed natures (human and divine) united in one individual (one *hypostasis*). Sometimes Aquinas uses *suppositum* which is a Latin synonym for the Greek word *hypostasis*. See also *Prosopon (person)*.

**Idealism:** The philosophical perspective which takes ideas or mind to be the ultimate reality. Epistemologically this means that the goal of knowledge is to grasp an idea. Plato, for example, holds that the object of knowledge is the form rather than the ever-changing physical thing. See and contrast to *Realism*.

**Ideology:** A system of ideas. In this book the word is used in its Marxist and pejorative sense. Ideology refers to a theoretical system which covers over and disguises an oppressive and unjust social structure.

**Magisterium:** The teaching authority of pope and bishops within the church. The modes of magisterial teaching are many, ranging from homilies to the decrees of ecumenical councils. The authority of such teachings, and the appropriate response of Catholics, likewise varies.

**Metaphysics:** The study of being as such. The word was first used to indicate what one studies after physics, i.e., after the study of physical reality. Thus, for example, metaphysics considers the first cause of all that is—God. This philosophical use of the word *metaphysics* should be distinguished from the kind of strange topics which appear under this word in today's bookstores.

**Nature:** What a thing is. The answer to the question, "What is it?"

**Neoscholasticism:** Refers to the renewal of scholastic theology, especially the revival of the study of St. Thomas which followed Leo XIII's *Aeterni Patris*. See *Scholasticism*.

**Obediential Potency:** A passive capacity. Specifically, the fact that human nature is capable of unity with God in an incarnation. This capacity is passive in that human beings cannot achieve such a unity. The capacity can only be actualized through a divine initiative.

**Ontological:** An adjective describing something as real and existing. That which exists as it is whether known or not.

**Ontological Distinction:** The distinction between things that exist (beings) and the act of existence as such. See *Being*.

**Ontology:** The science or the philosophy of being as such.

**Orthodoxy:** Correct belief, consistency with the church's teaching. An individual or a point of view are orthodox if they are in agreement with the teaching of the church.

**Person:** See *Prosopon*.

**Prosopon:** The *hypostasis* of an intelligent nature (see *Hypostasis*). The occurrence of a rational nature. For example, human nature does not exist in the abstract. There are only individual human beings. Each individual is a *hypostasis* of human nature. Since human nature is intellectual—has the use of reason—one may call this *hypostasis* a *prosopon*. One may *not* call the *hypostasis* of the nature dog a *prosopon* because dogs are not rational. Note the difference between this technical meaning and the common use of the word *person*. In contemporary parlance *person* means the self, the psychological center of human consciousness.

**Rationalism:** A philosophical point of view which limits human knowledge to what can be demonstrated by reason alone.

**Realism:** The philosophical perspective that things exist in themselves and apart from knowledge of them. Epistemologically this means that the known is a real object, not an idea. See and contrast to *Idealism*.

**Retrieval:** A method of interpretation associated with Martin Heidegger. Its goal is not the original meaning of the text. Rather, the interpreter seeks new possibilities from a text by asking new questions of it and by appropriating it within a new historical context. In this way the interpreter may *retrieve* insights into the subject matter forgotten or neglected by the original author.

**Scholasticism:** From the word "school," and refers to the philosophy and theology which came out of the medieval universities.

**Solipsism:** An epistemological perspective which begins with self-consciousness and doubts all else. "I know I exist but I am uncertain of anything else."

**Substance:** What a thing is. When an object is known the intellect has grasped that object's substance.

**Supernatural:** Pertaining to the divine Self-gift, to God's *grace* which transcends human nature. The theological use of the term must be distinguished from its meaning in common parlance where it refers to ghosts, etc.

**Transcendental:** The term suggests two related notions: 1) a way of doing philosophy and theology (identified with Kant) which asks about the conditions of subjectivity which make knowing possible; 2) having to do with transcendence, with transcending the world of the ordinary and concrete. In this book the first meaning is generally intended.